EVERETT RUESS

A VAGABOND FOR BEAUTY

Frontispiece. Everett and his two horses in Canyon de Chelly, 1932.

EVERETT RUESS
A VAGABOND FOR BEAUTY

W.L. RUSHO

Introduction By
JOHN NICHOLS

Afterword by
EDWARD ABBEY

PEREGRINE SMITH BOOKS

SALT LAKE CITY

© Gibbs Smith, Publisher (2007)

Published by Gibbs Smith, Publisher
P.O. Box 667, Layton, UT 84041

Printed in the U.S.A.

Library of Congress Cataloging in
Publication Data

Rusho, W. L., 1928-
    Everett Ruess, a vagabond for beauty.

    1. Ruess, Everett, b. 1914 – Biography.
2. Ruess, Everett, b. 1914 – Correspon-
dence. 3. Poets, American – 20th Century –
Biography. 4. Explorers – Southwest,
New – Biography. 5. Southwest, New –
Biography. 6. Southwest, New – Description
and travel. I. Ruess, Everett, b. 1914.
II. Title
PS3535.U26Z85   1983   811'.52 [B]
83-643 ISBN 0-87905-210-4 — ISBN 13:978-0-87905-210-2

CONTENTS

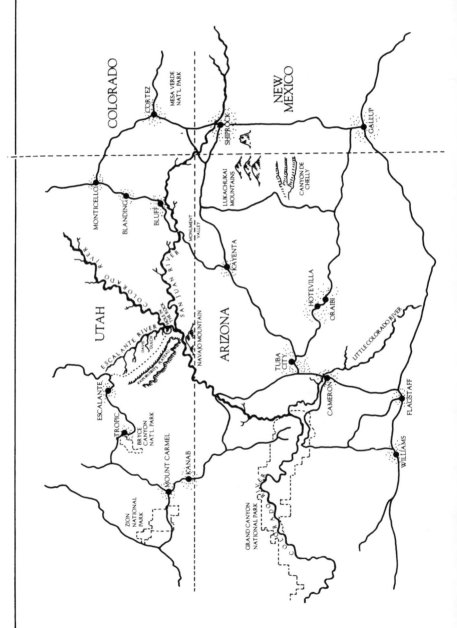

EVERETT RUESS
COUNTRY

Everett Ruess's story is a half-century old and time has almost obscured it. It is usually a campfire legend or an item of canyon country trivia. A person relating the account can almost always count on his listeners' never having heard Everett's name. The book *On Desert Trails with Everett Ruess*, first published in 1940, included some of his letters and a few poems. But the book has long been out of print and is rarely seen.

Coincidentally, Gibbs Smith, president and publisher of Peregrine Smith Books, and I had both separately read *On Desert Trails*. With some detective work, editor Buckley Jeppson located Everett's brother, Waldo, in Santa Barbara, California.

Waldo, the only remaining member of the Ruess family, not only had most of the known letters, photographs, and paintings of Everett in his possession, he agreed to make them available for publication. The next two years were full of hard work and discovery. Every one of the hundreds of items either authored by, or written about, Everett Ruess had to be read. All documents were sorted and classified according to their dates, importance, and interest.

Then I entered the picture. I had spent considerable time visiting, writing about, and photographing the northern Arizona/ southern Utah area where Everett did his vagabonding in the early 1930s, so I welcomed the opportunity.

My knowledge of Everett himself was, however, still sketchy when the three of us drove to Escalante, Utah, in September of 1982 to make inquiries. Surprisingly, many people in the village still remembered Everett from his two-week stay there in November of 1934. We then drove southward into the spectacular canyon and cliff country near Hole-in-the-Rock. After a night in a range cabin tucked between towering domes of red sandstone, we rode horseback into the depths of Davis Gulch, where Everett's last camp and his inscriptions were found.

There were other trips to other cities in Utah, Arizona, and Mexico to interview witnesses like Clayborn Lockett, Tad Nichols, Randolph "Pat" Jenks, who had all known Everett. I spent a great deal of time discussing Everett and the country in which he disappeared with Ken Sleight, noted river and canyon country guide, who has investigated Ruess over a period of many years. I took notes, recorded conversations, took photographs, and listened to the lore of the canyon country.

Thus the book grew in scope, depth, and significance. I cannot state that nothing more remains to be learned about Everett. Some of his friends from his early years in Los Angeles are undoubtedly still alive, as are people he met in San Francisco in 1933-34. Many of them have not yet been located. Maybe the publication of this book will cause some to come forward with new information which sheds further light. Perhaps Ruess's missing writings, such as his 1934 journals, will surface because of the publication of this book. The publisher and the Ruess family would appreciate the extra information and the study can go on.

Everett Ruess was a highly complex young man with multiple consuming motivations we can only begin to understand. We have hints in his correspondence that he was poorly understood even in his lifetime. That he may have concealed part of his nature even to his close friends and relatives is a possibility subject only to educated guesses. Fortunately, his letters and other writings are so replete with descriptive, introspective detail that from them alone Everett's basic personality and character begin to emerge. To have been able to add color and dimension to this image of the young man who could write so well has itself been a fascinating mission of discovery.

W.L. Rusho
Salt Lake City
April 1983

INTRODUCTION

JOHN NICHOLS

By the time Everett Ruess disappeared, he had fashioned a magnificent obsession that probably killed him.

His determination to plod alone through the southwestern wilderness was so fierce and arrogant that at times he seemed to be utterly consumed. Eventually, it is probable he lost all understanding of natural scale or human endurance. And along the way that ordinary awareness of danger we human beings carry must also have dissolved from his consciousness.

It is not that the man took leave of his senses, but rather that he was totally enflamed by a wonderful awareness of them. The documentation of his pursuit of enlightenment, as contained in his letters and journals, is the valuable gift of Everett. And it is not necessarily a tragedy that in the end the deserts and canyonlands of Arizona, Utah, and New Mexico proved larger, and more powerful, than his solitary existence could incorporate.

Repeatedly, as this erudite, sometimes penniless romantic wandered behind his burros through impressive and almost uncharted regions during the 1930s, he protested in letters to the outside world: "I have seen almost more beauty than I can bear."

And, repeatedly, he acknowledged, as have so many others, that places like Keet Seel and Kayenta, Escalante and Monument Valley, Navajo Mountain and Skeleton Mesa had "such utter and overpowering beauty as nearly kills a sensitive person by its piercing glory."

At the beginning of his multiple treks into the desert, Ruess had no real idea of exactly what he hoped to accomplish. Toward the end of his recorded wanderings a few years later, that lack of focus no longer mattered. Outsiders probably had no difficulty viewing this out-of-kilter sojourner as a self-indulgent and extravagant oddling overcome by awkward and self-conscious sensibilities. Often his prose—and his actions—seem, variously, childish, purple, ludicrous, pretentious, and precious. And yet to Ruess, his life must have come to seem incredibly whole as he wandered over the land, his only purpose to experience weather, distant buttes, rivers . . . and the mysterious halos that float across desert horizons like the inner fires of unbridled imaginations.

So the landscape, and his simple, painful act of traversing its cruel and beautiful skin, forged in Ruess an extraordinary passion. Ultimately, it was his life that was his greatest work of art, and we experience it though his letters. At times his writing seems pompous; often it is truly beautiful. Thinking about this eccentric loner confronting the Southwest, one is reminded of F. Scott Fitzgerald's moving words toward the end of *The Great Gatsby,* that famous eulogy for early explorers when first they arrived at the green uncharted realm of America—humanity, for the last time in history, face to face with a geography, a continent, an "aesthetic contemplation" commensurate with its capacity for wonder.

Today, for the most part, we have lost the capacity for wonder which so moved Fitzgerald, and which drove Everett Ruess toward the fascinating doom he yearned to embrace. It is also quite clear that if we do not soon rediscover how to stand in awe of this planet we are so greedily dismantling, human history will soon be over. Hence, a most basic problem currently facing civilization is: How can we relearn to love our natural world, whose magnificence, in this day and age, is superseded only by its no longer mystifying fragility?

Albert Einstein once wrote, "The most beautiful experience we can have is the mysterious. It is the fundamental emotion which stands at the cradle of true art and true science." The more he meandered around the Southwest, the more Everett Ruess must have understood something approximating that axiom. It guided his life for a while. He controlled it momentarily. Then ultimately the quest for that mystery took over, became his destiny, and finished him off—no doubt in exaltation.

"I am always being overwhelmed," he once bragged. "I require it to sustain life." At times, the impact of the natural world was "so far beyond my powers to convey that it almost made me despair."

After a trip into the California mountains about a year before vanishing into the southern Utah wilderness, he wrote:

"Much of the time I feel so exuberant I can hardly contain myself. The colors are so glorious, the forests so magnificent, the mountains so splendid, and the streams so utterly, wildly, tumultuously, effervescently joyful that to me, at least, the world is a riot of sensual delight."

It would be easy to make fun of Ruess, conjecturing that in the end he must have literally exploded, his slight body incapable of containing all the melodramatic sensations he tirelessly ladled into it. But I picture him simply expiring on the edge of a sandstone cliff, in the shadow of some high circling buzzard, convinced that he could never again return to civilization.

These words he penned a few months before his disappearance: "I am roaring drunk with the lust of life and adventure and unbearable beauty." And, overcome with a "restlessness and wild longing," he steadfastly journeyed ever deeper into the wilderness, and into his bizarre and solitary fervor. The danger of those dry and hostile territories claiming him was not a worry:

"Finality does not appall me, and I seem always to enjoy things more intensely because of the certainty that they will not last." He admitted that a reason for becoming so unrestrained was that "Always I sense the brink of things."

Although he became an increasingly anti-social being, it tortured Ruess to know that he might not make other people understand the passions building in himself. "I cannot bear to contain these rending flames, and I am helpless to let them out. So I wonder how I can go on living and being casual as one must."

Finally, his mergence with the landscape bred ". . . a reckless self-confidence" that enabled him to face the wilderness with an utter disregard for his personal safety. And in his last letter to reach the world, he admitted: "I have known too much of the depths of life already, and I would prefer anything to an anticlimax."

Whereupon, still shy of his twenty-first birthday, this tormented and eloquent pilgrim was engulfed and erased by the territory whose mysteries had absolutely conquered his entire being.

The message every poet and vagabond seeker like Ruess leaves behind is simple: Life on this earth is very precious and very beautiful.

We must learn to heed the pure and delicate voices of those who cherish it.

John Nichols
Taos, New Mexico
February 1983

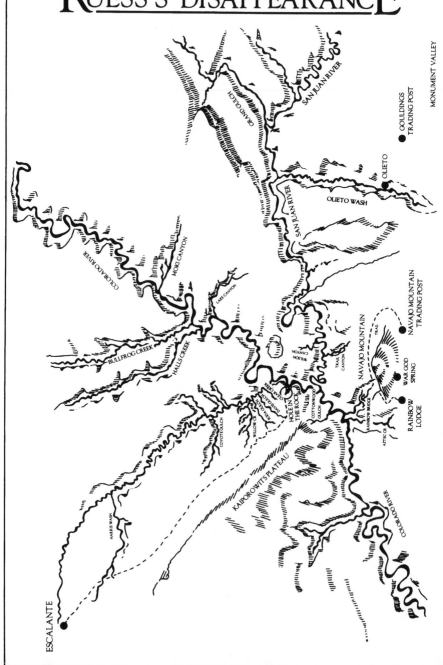

GENERAL AREA OF RUESS'S DISAPPEARANCE

CHAPTER
◆ 1

THE BEAUTY AND
THE TRAGEDY OF
EVERETT RUESS

Portrait of Everett Ruess by Dorothea Lange, 1933.

In the mid-Depression year of 1934, Everett Ruess disappeared. His last known camp was in the Escalante River region of southern Utah, a place of bare rock, vertical cliffs, plunging canyons, and soaring mesas. Ironically, water has carved the land during rare, but violent cloudbursts, but water itself is scarce. It is a land where earth tones are daily enflamed by the rising sun, change constantly as shadows creep about, diminish, and lengthen throughout the hours, ever contrasting with patterns of colored light. It is canyon country at its finest. As a young artist, Everett Ruess was irresistibly drawn to the Escalante River, not so much to paint and draw as to experience and to draw upon that

1

experience to write, to articulate impressions and reactions, as he had done so often in northern Arizona and California. Everett disappeared before any of his written descriptions, in the form of letters, could be sent from the Escalante. His 1934 diary was never found.

From an abundance of letters written from other areas in previous months and years, however, we can learn much about Everett, as well as much about the regions he visited. In many ways he was just an ordinary American youth with a yen for wandering about in remote parts of the West. He was clean-shaven, of medium height and build, open in countenance, ready to smile, and did not appear at all unusual. He was young, only twenty years old when he disappeared, and he was still suffering—or alternately enjoying—the slow onset of maturity. As a family friend once wrote, "He was an old friend one moment and a young friend the next." He could be logical, then illogical. He could laugh and sing, could play-act, could assume roles, or could brood in sadness, silence, and isolation.

But above all, Everett Ruess could see, in a way that far transcended the mere act of vision. His reactions to the wonders of Nature went beyond what we would assume to be normal experience, to the point where he could almost resonate to the light waves that struck him from all points in the landscape. His was a strange gift that set him apart from acquaintances, friends, and relatives. Many people can feel emotion as they gaze upon some of the more sublime vistas of canyon, desert, or mountains. But rare indeed is an Everett Ruess, who could sense beauty so acutely that it bordered on pain. And he could write exceptionally well as he described his own reactions to the panoramas seen along his way.

It is lucky for us that Everett wrote so well. From his descriptions of what he saw and felt, a reader today can catch a glimpse of what it is like to be so passionately free. Like Everett, we all yearn to cut ourselves off from the comforts and securities of a drab existence at some point in our lives. We too feel a need to enter our own small wilderness in that difficult search for a unique destiny. Everett's story is the universal story of discovery of self.

Everett's letters contain statements such as, "I have seen almost more beauty than I can bear," or ". . . such utter and overpowering beauty as nearly kills a sensitive person by its piercing glory." He continued his travels, drawn as by a magnet away from the cities of California, across mountain, desert, and canyon, to his ultimate destiny. Traveling virtually without money, he spent his days with little food, almost no comfort, and little encouragement from others, for almost no one he met could understand his motivations or appreciate his sensitivity.

We in the 1980s, living half a century after Everett's disappearance, do not fully understand him either. There are only faint traces left behind, but what we have is intriguing. We have diaries of his 1932 and 1933 trips, as well as a few poems and essays, some snapshots, and some letters about him written by people he had known. Above all, and most important, we have letters he wrote to his parents, his brother, and to a few of his friends. These materials are valuable in that they tell much about Everett's character and personality, but they don't tell the whole story. No young man writes to his mother with a high degree of candor on *all* subjects. Even to his father, brother, and friends, a man will play roles calculated to conceal many of his innermost thoughts. Everett was probably better than most young people in expressing his true feelings, but no one can know how much of the essential Everett remains hidden in these writings. Thus to every statement about him by others must be attached an element of the unknown.

We can't even begin to understand Everett without becoming acquainted with his mother, Stella. A devotee of the arts and an artist herself, Stella Knight Ruess, daughter of noted California pioneer William Henry Knight, took courses in art at the University of Southern California and taught drawing in a school in Alhambra. She studied blockprinting at Columbia University. She was fond of composing poems, many of which were published. She was an active member of art and writing clubs, such as the National League of American Penwomen, the Ruskin Art Club, and the Poetry and Music Club in Los Angeles.

Everett, born 28 March 1914, the younger of two boys, probably received the bulk of Stella's attention, directed first toward motherly care, then later toward teaching him to write, to sketch, and to paint, eventually toward convincing him that he should make a career of art. It is hardly coincidental that the areas in which Everett was most proficient—lyric prose, poetry, blockprinting, and sketching—were identical to Stella's. They even worked together on some art projects—he would provide sketches and she would transfer them into blocks for printing. Everett later displayed, at least in his writing, a high degree of intelligence and natural ability, but it was in his capacity to see and to appreciate that Stella's training gave him such a solid foundation.

Although we have none of Stella's letters to Everett, it appears that her influence over him was profound. Like Everett, she was a true romantic who scarcely paused to count the cost. She was a follower of a philosophy typified by the great dancer Isadora Duncan, that women should freely express their idealistic and romantic inclinations and, above all, should determine their own destinies. As an art activist, she believed firmly in participation, if not creating art herself then working in study clubs where she could experience the art of others. To her, one must participate in art to be totally alive.

Stella thought of her family as an artistic institution, and she had her stationery imprinted "The House of Ruess." When she felt that the family needed an outlet for their creative writings, she printed the *Ruess Quartette*, a small format booklet containing poetry and articles by herself, her husband Christopher, and their sons Everett and Waldo. The family seal printed on the booklet showed a sun dial with the words "Glorify The Hour."

Stella's sense of urgency in matters of art must surely have been a fundamental factor in Everett's impatience to escape from school and to fling himself into the wilderness while still in his teens.

Everett's father, Christopher, earned his way through Harvard, graduating *summa cum laude* in only three years. He served as the first chief probation officer of Alameda County, California, and later as director of education and research in the Los Angeles County Probation Department. A graduate of Harvard Divinity School, he had worked as a Unitarian minister and in sales management. Active even after his retirement in 1949, he spent the last five years of his life with the American Institute of Family Relations helping older people find worthwhile and constructive objectives.

Christopher also wrote limited amounts of poetry. He was deeply interested in the philosophical questions of life, existence, and morality, and he communicated with his son on these subjects during the last few years before Everett disappeared. (See Christopher's letter to Everett of 10 December 1933.) Christopher also represented the practical side of the family, and to the extent that he was able, tried to guide his sons into good education and rewarding careers. The fact that Everett quit college after only one semester was a long-standing source of pain to Christopher.

Everett's brother, Waldo, was also one of the anchors in Everett's life at home. Waldo, 4½ years older, was already active by the early 1930s in his chosen career as a government diplomatic aide and later as an international businessman. Altogether, Waldo worked and lived in ten foreign countries, including China, Japan, Algeria, U.S.S.R., Iceland, El Salvador, Mexico, and Spain, and traveled in 100 others. Everett wrote frequently to Waldo, however, and his high regard for his older brother shows clearly in his letters.

It should be noted that the whole Ruess family formed a cohesive unit that gave each individual member much strength. Everett was repeatedly able to step forth into the unforgiving wilderness with neither adequate funds nor modern equipment, partly because of the moral and financial support he received from his parents and brother. His family also gave him a receptive audience for his paintings, sketches, poetry, and letters. Everett's letters, for example, for which he had assured readers, are much more interesting and beautifully crafted than his diary entries, which tend to be more documentary than lyrical.

Everett's greatest talent was his ability to see, and then articulate, the magnitude, color, and changing moods of nature. If he was good at describing the high Sierras (and he was), he was superlative in his descriptions of the red rock deserts of northern Arizona and southern Utah. His astonishing ability to awake in a reader those feelings one has when confronting the land, coupled with the mystery of his vanishing, have prompted the suggestion that he might have been a mystic. Of course, he was not a religious mystic, since he called himself an agnostic, but he certainly possessed unusual ability to see beyond the concrete world of his training and experience. Randolph "Pat" Jenks, who knew Everett in 1931, states, "Ruess was the most sensitive, the most intuitive person I have ever known. He could certainly see intrinsic and unspeakable beauty to a degree that could not always be put into words. But I can't say whether or not he was a mystic."[1] Whether or not Everett was a mystic is apparently a matter of opinion, or perhaps of semantics. The fact that the subject arises so often testifies to the strength of his personality and the evocative character of his writing.

It should be noted, however, that Everett's writing had one important limitation: he was apparently unable to fully appreciate or describe the human events and interactions with the landscape he understood so well. His writings contain very little information about the people who shaped, and were shaped by, the land. He saw the Indians as a noble race who had learned to live off the land. He saw non-Indians simply as intruders. Although the same zeal and pioneering spirit that possessed him could have—and probably did—inspire the early settlers, he could sense that most non-Indian philosophies seemed to emphasize alienation rather than communion with the land. Therefore, non-Indian history was irrelevant to the important matter—his own reaction to natural beauty.

Everett's real search was for his own identity and fulfillment. Undoubtedly he had experienced his need for purpose and direction from the time he first set off on his wanderings in 1930. His many months in the mountains and desert during the next four years gave him many marvelous experiences but still left him with the ache of isolation, even occasionally on the edge between reality and fantasy, sanity and incoherence. His winter in San Francisco, though it gave him the friendship of other artists, sharpened his consciousness and made him more aware of his very special vision. Yet he remained insecure as a painter, and as a writer, trying desperately, and passionately, to find and establish his niche as an artist.

As a visual artist, the young Ruess still needed considerable training. Everett's existing paintings, sketches, and water-colors, now in the family collection, show a naive lack of understanding of color relationships and an unsure drawing hand. His blockprints, however, some of which are reproduced in this volume, show a good eye for balance and composition, as well as for dramatic impact.

Probably the most intriguing paradox in Everett's personality was the balance between the inwardly-directed, intensely-sensitive visionary and the outgoing, courageous adventurer.

Everett's nerve—his absolutely fearless, ingenuous, childlike ability to face any situation as if it were simply routine made him unique. He hitchhiked to remote Monument Valley where he was dropped off with almost no money. But he made his way and reported that he was happy. It has been said that he often, and without invitation, simply entered a Navajo's hogan and made himself at home. His letters indicate an amazing lack of reticence around famous artists. If he wanted to meet someone he just knocked on the door and introduced himself. When those who encountered Everett remarked later that he was strange, they did not refer to his visionary experiences, but to his fearless, unhesitating manner. Some people liked it; some people thought he was crazy. Some Navajos thought he was a witch. But nobody thought he was anything less than highly unusual.

His self-confidence was massive, at least until late 1933, when, under the influence of many intelligent and gifted friends, he began to question some of his personal precepts. Even then, he only asked questions until it became too uncomfortable. Then he headed back to the desert where he could think and write about natural beauty, where he could dismiss his doubts about himself, and where he could resume his old, sure manner.

His extreme self-assurance, implanted and solidly backed by his mother, was the underpinning for almost everything Everett did from his high school graduation until his disappearance. The only exceptions were his five-month enrollment at UCLA in 1932-33, done at his father's insistence, and Everett's voluntary interlude in San Francisco in 1933-34. He was uncomfortable at UCLA, and he tired of the frantic pace and congestion of San Francisco.

If Stella communicated any of the harsh realities of the world to Everett before he left home, it was not reflected in his attitudes, as shown by his actions and by his writing. It appears that Stella not only did nothing to discourage Everett from leaving home as a teenager, but that she condoned—even encouraged—what she saw as his artistic independence.

A few words should be said about Everett's experiences in San Francisco during late 1933 and early 1934. After spending parts of three years journeying through mountains and deserts, he embarked upon a fast-paced, high-intensity learning experience with painters, photographers, musicians, writers, and political agitators in a Bohemian atmosphere. Many of the artists he met were established, well-known, and highly qualified in their media. But Everett's self-confidence, his ingenuous innocence, his eagerness to learn, and his apparent sensitivity, opened many doors. From his surviving letters to parents, we know only of a few major contacts with San Francisco artists during this period. Without doubt there were more. Considering that Everett still had a long way to go on the road to becoming a mature visual artist, the results of these contacts with established artists can be guessed. Undoubtedly many of them were frank, perhaps even blunt, about Everett's need for training and experience. He probably learned that he was not nearly as good as he thought, which could have been a severe blow to his self-esteem. Furthermore, he seems to have made the fateful decision at that point that no matter how much he needed further training and experience in the visual arts, he refused to remain any longer in large cities, cut off from his beloved wilderness. His letters from Arizona and Utah in 1934, while some of his most beautifully written, reflect an air of futility and a realization that he was now trapped by his love of the wilderness, his aversion to cities, and his need for further training. It was sobering as well as frustrating.

It appears that Everett may have been able with time and training to develop into a capable visual artist and successfully interpret the country he loved, like his friend Maynard Dixon. We are fortunate that he was able to develop remarkable discipline and skills in descriptive writing. Indeed, the focused energies make Everett's letters unique in American literature. Author Wallace Stegner, in his book *Mormon Country*, pays this tribute to Everett:

> What Everett was after was beauty, and he conceived beauty in pretty romantic terms. We might be inclined to laugh at the extravagance of his beauty-worship if there were not something almost magnificent in his single-minded dedication to it. Esthetics as a parlor affectation is ludicrous and sometimes a little obscene; as a way of life it sometimes attains dignity. If we laugh at Everett Ruess we shall have to laugh at John Muir, because there was little difference between them except age.

In his last known letter, sent to his brother, he pointed out, "I don't think I could ever settle down. I have known too much of the depths of life already, and I would prefer anything to an anticlimax."

It seems that Everett's basic difficulty was that as his extreme sensitivity developed he felt pulled outward faster than he matured or could be educated. Like a fine, but uncontrolled, thoroughbred colt, he rushed pell-mell into the race, without adequate pacing or training. His mother, so anxious to have Everett develop into a fine artist, failed to realize his need to be held back, and not only let him go, but apparently urged him on.

We must conclude that Everett's life was a partial tragedy because he hungered after the unattainable in visual art, while probably not realizing how unusually perceptive his writings had become. Nowhere else in the literature of the canyon country can one find the sensitive, thoughtful, sincere, emotional imagery found in Everett's letters. We must also appreciate, even marvel at, his gift of vision, which enabled him to respond to natural beauty with such depth of feeling that it often exceeded the power of mere words to communicate and seemed to consume his very being.

THE LETTERS

1930

Cypress Grove, Carmel. *Blockprint by Everett Ruess.*

When Everett Ruess headed into the mountains or out onto the desert, he did so with two overall objectives. First, he wanted to absorb impressions; to experience, even to revel in natural scenes. Second, he wished to record the scenes, either visually, in sketches or watercolors, or in writing. His aptitude, however, proved to be stronger in writing, which he turned into his principal vehicle of expression. He could have written a book, or essays, or magazine articles, but he chose letters, probably because they kept him in touch with his family and because they offered an assured, sympathetic audience.

Traveling slowly through the wilderness, Everett had leisure time in abundance, and he could compose dramatic word descriptions almost simultaneously as he received impressions from the scenery. On occasion he used the same phrases in letters written days apart to different people, as if he had either memorized the words or had used rough drafts. And the letters show careful and deliberate drafting and polishing.

Here are most of the extant letters written by Everett from June 1930 until his disappearance in November 1934. They were addressed to his parents or brother or to a small circle of friends. A few of these friends are poorly identified, some only by a first name. An occasional letter lacks even a salutation. The bulk of the collection, however, has been carefully preserved by the Ruess family for fifty years and is in very good condition.

Editing has been kept to a minimum so as to retain the flavor and the continuity of the narrative.

None of the replies, the letters sent to Everett, are included for the simple reason that none exist. The single exception is his father's reply to some philosophical questions, 10 December 1933. Apparently he destroyed the others in preference to carrying them around in his pack outfit. In his own writing, however, Everett rarely referred to letter comments from others; his focus remained on nature and on his reaction to it. All of this is, of course, our gain in that his letters speak not just to one person, but to us all—now as well as then.

Why did he work so hard on his letters? Obviously he wished to make an impression on his correspondents. More important is that he sought to capture in writing his intense, highly subjective impressions from the landscape. He sometimes complained of the inadequacy of words, but he succeeded with "mere words" far better than he could have realized.

Pledge to the Wind

Onward from vast uncharted spaces,
    Forward through timeless voids,
Into all of us surges and races
    The measureless might of the wind.

Strongly sweeping from open plains,
    Keen and pure from mountain heights,
Freshly blowing after rains,
    It welds itself into our souls.

In the steep silence of thin blue air,
    High on a lonely cliff-ledge,
Where the air has a clear, clean rarity,
    I give to the wind . . . my pledge:

"By the strength of my arm, by the sight of my eye,
    By the skill of my fingers, I swear,

As long as life dwells in me, never will I
Follow any way but the sweeping way of the wind.

I will feel the wind's buoyancy until I die;
I will work with the wind's exhilaration;
I will search for its purity; and never will I
Follow any way but the sweeping way of the wind."

Here in the utter stillness,
High on a lonely cliff-ledge,
Where the air is trembling with lightning,
I have given the wind my pledge.

—Poem by Everett Ruess

At the early age of sixteen, in the summer of 1930, Everett ventured away from his Los Angeles home on his first extended solo trip. Draped with a bedroll and a huge backpack, he hitchhiked up the coast to Carmel and camped out by the Pacific Ocean.

June 28

Dear Mother and Father,

Arrived safely at Morro Bay last night after riding with nine people, including a sailor's wife, a druggist, a salesman, and a dishwasher. I slept in the middle of a pocket in the sand dunes, building my fire just at dusk. I found that we had eliminated so many things that there wasn't much to eat. In the morning my blankets were very wet with fog and dew. I rode back to San Luis Obispo with the druggist's employer, and I am writing this in one of his stores. I am about to leave for Carmel now.

Love from Everett

Within two days of his arrival, Everett wrote in the next letter, "I went to Edward Weston's studio and made friends with him." Edward Weston was one of America's most famous and successful photographers. From Everett's unhesitating approach to Weston, and from similar events later, it seems that Everett had little natural reticence toward photographers, painters, musicians, writers, Indian traders, cowboys, or Navajos. It has been said that this boldness was a Ruess family trait, but more likely it was but a component of Stella's aggressive, positive attitude toward anything artistic, which Everett simply copied.

11

June 30
Carmel

Dear Mother,

I had a jolly time yesterday, tramping up and down the beach. Then I sat in a throne-like place on a rock that was out in the ocean. I didn't leave until a huge breaker came and splashed over me.

In the afternoon I hiked around the town until now I know it pretty well. I walked a mile or so to the San Carlos Mission and the Carmel River. When I got back in town I went to Edward Weston's studio and made friends with him. A man who gave me a ride near Morro Bay had told me about him. I saw a large number of his photographs. He is a very broad-minded man.[2]

Love from Everett

I slept among the pines last night. Write to General Delivery, Carmel.

July 1

Dear Father,

Yesterday I went for a walk and found that I was on the Seventeen-Mile Drive. So I kept on hiking for about fifteen miles, stopping to sketch at some picturesque place. At about two o'clock it was so dark and foggy that I thought it was five o'clock. I tramped over the sand dunes and saw six deer, two does and four fawns, going along in a curious procession. They were quite tame.

I also saw two huge gray squirrels. Not following any particular route, I took one road and another and saw an interesting part of the country.

Mr. Weston invited me to supper, and I met his two sons, very nice boys. I slept in his garage, which is empty. This morning I swept it and cleaned it out.

Love from Everett

July 2

Dear Waldo [Ruess],

Yesterday I had great fun with Mr. Weston's two sons, Neil and Cole. They are both younger than I. There are two other sons who are married. Mr. Weston has a house in Los Angeles, another in Topanga Canyon, and he rents the three houses here. They are all on the same lot. One is his studio, another is where Neil and Cole sleep, and the other

12

is where the cooking is done and Mr. Weston sleeps. There is also a girl named Sonia who does the housekeeping.

Yesterday evening Cole and I went down on his bicycle to the Carmel River and met Neil and a fat boy called Sam, who had caught the limit of trout in the river. I cooked some pancakes for everybody; then we all had bacon and trout. A short time later, we all went swimming in the river, which is quite wide at the mouth, where it goes into the ocean.

Love from Everett

July 4

Dear Mother,

Yesterday I phoned Harry and we met at Point Lobos to do some painting. We each did a marine in watercolor. Then we put our things down and hiked over the rocks. We found three starfish and a huge anemone. Then we watched all the sea lions on the rocks and listened to them barking. We threw stones at rocks down below.[3]

Later we each did another sketch. We saw a six-inch baby garter snake with a brilliant blue tail. Then we started home again. I got a ride home from a lady whose family owns Point Lobos.

That evening I had supper with the Westons and we sat around the fire while Mr. Weston read *Moby Dick* aloud. When Cole fell asleep we all went to bed.

I'm going out painting with Harry today.

Love from Everett

The Crash of Breakers and the Roll of Stones

I awoke with a quiver, nerves tautly on edge. It came again, what had wakened me—the harsh, weird scream of a grey gull swooping low above me in the darkness. A heavy, clinging fog had set in, making the place indescribably desolate. Nothing was visible. I was alone, on the tip of a solitary, knife-edged point of land, which, through some queer whim, I had selected for my resting place that night. My sleeping bag was wedged into a shallow crevice. On one side, the bare granite fell sheer away into the foaming sea. On the other, the rock was joined to the main promontory, but beneath, a narrow, high-vaulted tunnel had been eaten out by the ocean. A slender crevice pierced the roof through to the sky at one point. Each wave that came crashed far into the narrow mouth of the cavern, and a swift rush of cold air and spray was shot out of the vent at the top, as if from a bellows.

Wild Coastline. *Blockprint by Everett Ruess.*

Behind me, I could hear the low moaning and the mournful crash of breakers, and the roll of stones as the waves turned back from the beach. Once more I heard the sea gull's scream, fainter, and queerly remote. Then a shrill, high wind sprang up, shearing through the fog like an unseen knife. In a moment, all was glassy clear. The full moon illumined far-off whitecaps and the thundering cresters that shattered to spray in the tunnel, sending the expelled air whistling past my face.

Again I heard the sea gull's spectral shriek, almost inaudible. I closed my eyes and slept.

—From an Everett Ruess essay

Under the Sea

Flashing between curved sea plants in the sand
*   There darts a shining company of fish.*
Swirling through the sea's green depths they go,
*   Gleaming like silver ripples in a pool*
That dance and sparkle in the moon's cold light.
*   Then they are gone, as quickly as they came,*
And the wildly waving seaweeds move
*   More slowly and at last are still once more.*
Now through the silent forests of the sea
*   There slowly drifts in shimmering radiance*
A lustrous jellyfish. Suddenly,
*   From pale pink opalescence swiftly changed,*
It turns translucent and is almost gone,
*   Only to gleam once more, far off, against*
Black rocks where shadowy forms move hazily.
*   There at last it melts into the distance—*
Ghostlike, drifting slowly out of sight.
*   —Everett Ruess*

July 14

Dear Father,

I have just received your letter of the sixteenth, including the check, for which I thank you. I have received a dollar for the blockprints so far. One of them will be published next week. I have made two dollars caddying and fifty cents gardening. I am going to saw some wood tonight.

I have just finished doing my wash this morning. Now I am going in to Monterey to save some money on shoe leather. I've tried to reach Miss Graham, but the telephone was silent. I shall see her as soon as I get back from Big Sur next week.

As to food, I have consumed four loaves of bread, three jars of peanut butter, and about twelve pints of milk since I have been here. I also have eaten several cans of corn and peas, and about five boxes of breakfast food.

That is fine about Mother's blockprints and the poetry magazine cover. There is money in Art if you know how to find it.

Watchers of the Sea. *Blockprint by Everett and Stella Ruess. Mother and son jointly won a $25 first prize for this blockprint at the 1931 convention of the American Society of Penwomen.*

Yesterday, Leon Wilson [Harry Leon Wilson, Jr.] and I went out sketching on the rocks near Point Lobos. We went swimming in the icy waters of the Pacific, and explored several caves, swimming completely through the peninsula. Some of the caves were quite large, with high, arched roofs. Others were so low that you had to choose your time to swim them. One moment a wave would surge against me, and I would be stationary while I swam. Then a swell would roll up behind me and carry me about twenty feet. We were almost numb when we got out. When we got back to a small sandy beach from which we had started, I lit a fire and we dried ourselves.

Wishing you financial luck,

Love from Everett

July 24

Dear Father, Mother, and Waldo,

Last Sunday I went over to Harry's house, and we went fishing together. However, we caught nothing but a couple of sea urchins. I read part of a book, *The Legend of the Glorious Adventures of Tyll Ulenspiegel.*

16

The Sky-Seekers. *Blockprint by Everett Ruess.*

On Saturday night I was invited by Mrs. Greene to the play at the Forest Theatre, *Over the Fairy Line.* It was a pretty good children's play. Mrs. Greene had been given several tickets, but her family didn't feel like going.

On Monday morning I left for Big Sur, with a pack weighing about fifty pounds, with the blankets. I got a ride from the bridge over the Carmel River to Highlands Inn, four miles away. Then I walked a couple of miles, and got a ride in a lumber truck for ten miles, as far as Glen Deven. It was very cold and windy. The road is extremely mountainous. On most of it, there is not room for two cars to pass.

After the truck ride, I walked a couple of miles until I came to where the road made a long loop inland, to avoid a canyon. Across from me, I could see where the mountain was carved out, and I thought it was the road. Down below, at the oceanside, was a small beach. I decided to eat my lunch there.

So I slid and slipped and tumbled down the mountain 'till I came to a valley at the bottom, through which a small stream meandered. At the beach there were large quantities of driftwood, probably from some wreck. I ate my lunch perched on the arch of a small cave, under which the sea came splashing in. Below me were many brown seaweeds, waving their strands with every motion of the sea, and writhing like octopi.

I started up the mountainside. The angle was about 110 degrees. If I had stood up straight, I would have fallen backwards, overbalanced by my pack. It was a very tortuous climb, but I finally got up, only to find that what I had mistaken for the road was only a path. As I walked along it, I noticed a very large hummingbird moth, with a gray body and orange stripes.

After regaining the road, I hiked on for some distance, until I came to a valley, at the bottom of the Little Sur grade. After a pause, I started up, and entered the redwood forest. I passed a derrick and some men working on the road. A few of them were convicts.

At about four o'clock I was just entering the densest part of the redwood forest. I got a ride from a man who lived in Monterey and was visiting his grandchildren at Big Sur. He knew all the history of the place, so it was interesting to know him. The first inhabitants here were the Spanish 100 years ago. A huge territory was given as a grant to one man. Others soon followed, but now almost all the descendants are abandoning the ranches and farms, or else they are dying out.

The road was very difficult indeed to make. The first settlers had to do it all with pick and shovel, and lay it out without surveying instruments. The country is almost inaccessible by water, as the shores are too rocky. Out on the ocean, I could see a wreck of a Japanese boat which had been there for three months.

Finally arriving at Big Sur (the post office, that is) I made my camp beside the river (also Big Sur) and prepared my supper. I picked up a stone for my fireplace, and there was a large snake under it. I cooked a can of peas, but in removing them from the fire, I burned my fingers and spilled most of the peas. Soon after, I started to crawl into my blankets and wind them around me. Just at that moment, a man with four small boys and girls arrived.

It turned out that I had camped on the wrong side of the river, as one side was semi-public while the other was private. But, since I had already camped, the man said it would be alright for me to spend the night there. Soon after, I was asleep beneath the sycamores and alders.

Tuesday morning, I hid my pack under an oak tree, and hiked to the ocean. For a long distance, along the beach, there were inner tubes scattered here and there, washed up from the wreck. All were broken across or punctured by the seawater, but the rubber was unharmed.

I made a watercolor under the most difficult conditions I have yet endured. The wind blew sand into my paint and on my picture all the time I was painting. The sand is still stuck to the picture, and produced an interesting effect, but I don't think there will be much color left on the picture when the sand comes off.

Later in the day, I climbed up in the mountains, following little canyons filled with very picturesque oak trees. I sketched a few of them. There were also clumps of redwoods and sycamores. In many places, the ground was covered with thistles.

One time when I stopped to contemplate some oak trees, a curious little hummingbird flew by within an inch of my face, and perched on a twig a foot away. At night I camped above the highway in a little hollow.

I got back to Carmel by noon. Then I went to the Weston's house, and Neil and Cole and I went down to the beach to meet Mr. Weston, who was photographing kelp. Then we continued up the coast. We finished up by having sixty starfish in one small pool. They were of all sizes, and colored red, brown, purple, blue, yellow, and vermilion.

Love from Everett

August 1

Dear Father, Mother, and Waldo,

I am leaving for Yosemite this Sunday, and thence I will go to Mono Lake. I have earned $14 this week, $12 of it in three days. I don't intend to waste any more time on money, this summer, but will spend the rest of it painting and traveling.

Another of my blockprints was used by the *Carmelite*, and I am going to cut one for it today.

At the Criley place there were large coveys of baby quail. Every few minutes, I would see a shadow pass by on the ground below me (I was up working in the pine trees), and the mother quail would cluck in alarm. She would tell her chicks to stay still until the hawk passed by. No doubt the hawks got several of them.

Love from Everett

Sierra Juniper. *Blockprint by Everett Ruess.*

August 5

Dear Family,

Yesterday night, at sunset, I arrived in Yosemite. The valley hardly seemed real at first.

I forgot to tell you that some tramp found my pack in Carmel and ate a pound jar of peanut butter on the spot, as well as half a box of Pep. He did not molest anything else.

I found a camping place in Camp Seven, made my bed and had supper. Then I went over to another camp where the rangers and some of the campers were giving an entertainment. There was a large crowd. We sang some amusing songs and listened to some harmonica selections. Then a Scotchman played the bagpipes while a girl danced. He announced some different tunes, but they all sounded the same to me. I never have known such a deadly monotonous sound as the bagpipes. He wouldn't stop playing them, it seemed.

After the firefall, I went back to my camp, but I had a very difficult time finding it in the dark.

This morning I have just bought some groceries, paying a pretty good price for them. I don't expect to do much hiking today, but will walk around the valley and take it easy. What a relief it is to be here at last! Although the falls are mostly dry, everything is cool and green. The deer are as tame as dogs, almost. I shall have to be careful that the bears don't find my bacon.

Love from Everett

The Sound of Rushing Water

Then there will be no music but the sound of rushing water that breaks on pointed rocks far below, and the sighing of the wind in the pinyons—a warm wind that gently caresses my cheeks, ruffles my hair tenderly, and wanders downwards. Alone I will follow the dark trail, black void on one side and unattainable heights on the other, darkness before and behind me, darkness that pulses and flows and is felt. Then suddenly, an unreal breath of wind coming from infinite depths will bring to my ears again the strange, dimly-remembered sound of the rushing water. When that sound dies, all dies.

—From an essay by Everett Ruess

August 22

Dear Father, Mother, and Waldo,

After breakfasting on pancakes Monday morning I left Glen Aulin, taking the McGee Lake trail to Tenaya Lake. The granite boulders and slabs were polished like mirrors, by the glacier.

All along the Yosemite trails are dead trees which often fall across the path. They are never moved, and the trail is changed, to go around them. I was told that in Rainier Park, as soon as a tree falls the rangers dash out in a group and cut it up, clearing the path.

It seemed that I would never reach the end of the trail, but I finally arrived at Tenaya Lake in the early afternoon. Just as I walked into the campground, ready to throw down my pack, a man walked up and wanted to know if I were hungry. He wanted to know all about me. It turned out that he and his family were about to drive on farther, and they gave me a good lunch before leaving.

Then I hiked around the lake to the Tenaya Lake camp. It seems that all the people in charge of the High Sierra camps are likeable and friendly.

Sentinels of the Wild. *Blockprint by Everett Ruess.*

After sleeping between some young firs by the lakeside, I rolled up my blankets once more and began the hardest part of my trip— from Tenaya Lake to Little Yosemite, by way of Cloud's Rest.

I climbed up the steep slope of the Forsyth trail to Forsyth Pass. Then I seemed to hike more easily, and the trail slid away under my feet until I came to the foot of Cloud's Rest. I hiked over a sort of hump in the ground, then down a hollow, and up the shoulder of the mountain. On the smooth granite summit, I perched precariously as I ate my lunch, and surveyed the lowered skyline. Patches of snow were visible on some of the distant peaks. In back was Tenaya Lake, glistening turquoise in the sunlight. Half Dome, rounded and worn, was below me, and below me also was the narrow cleft of Yosemite Valley. A corner of Mirror Lake was in view.

Then I clambered down the mountainside over an abrupt trail. My eyes were soon full of dirt and gravel, but I continued for two or three hours until quite unexpectedly I saw Little Yosemite Camp a short distance below me. I finally arrived at the door of the mess shack, where I flung down my pack and blanket roll. It was good to be back again.

That evening, Mr. Cuesta, a visitor, and I climbed up the cliff behind the camp until we reached the top of a tremendous granite boulder. He showed us the Indian mortars and relics of an Indian camp, which had been there long ago. The three of us then took a log and industriously pried away at a large boulder at the edge. It finally slid off, and with a great flurry of sparks from the friction, it crashed down. There was a short silence, and it struck the ground far below, crashing through the brush and over some trees.

It was growing dark, so we started back, going down the face of the cliff this time. It was quite steep, but we all had rubber-soled shoes, and we successfully reached the bottom.

The next day I read three books: *Oh, Ranger!*, a book about the national parks, *The Lore and the Lure of Yosemite*, by Herbert Wilson, and *Yosemite Trails*, by J. Smeaton Chase.

Mr. Cuesta told me of his travels in Brazil, Cuba, and Jamaica, and then I made some arrowheads with a bone as the means of pressure. It is not as difficult as one might think, but the arrowheads usually break when you are half way through. It is also very dangerous to get one of the tiny obsidian flakes in your eye.

The next morning, I shouldered my pack once more, and started down to the valley. The whole atmosphere was one of anticlimax. I was returning from the mountains and the solitude to the valley, the noisy, uninitiated tourists, and eventually to the city and its sordid buildings and business places.

I was becoming extremely weary of being told by everyone that I had a load, or, "Say, isn't that heavy," or "What a load that boy has," etc. *ad nauseum*. So I went to the Camp Curry scales and weighed it. What was my surprise to learn that, with but a pound of food left, it weighed forty-eight pounds! Evidently I am not as weak as I thought I was.

However, I have thought for some time that I would like to have a burro next time I start a hike of this kind. They cost $1.50 a day, and you can buy them for $15 or less.

I read *The American* in the library for a while, and then had my shoes heeled. The last pair lasted for more than 200 miles.

23

Near my camp is an interesting college girl who majored in sociology.

I made an unsuccessful experiment with rice pudding for supper. Tonight, believe it or not, I am going to try the Indian dish of fried grasshoppers. There must be something to it if both Chinese and Indians liked it.

Love from Everett

Everett takes a daredevil pose.

THE LETTERS

◆3

1931

Everett and burros in the Sierras.

Upon his return to Los Angeles from the Sierras, Everett completed his high school education, graduating in January 1931 from Hollywood High School. He immediately began making preparations to spend several months traveling in northern Arizona, where he planned to "buy myself a little burro, change my name, and call him Everett." When he departed he headed specifically for Monument Valley. In his letters he gives no clue as to how he happened to know about this scenic red rock desert, since in those days general public knowledge about Monument Valley was limited. It was not yet a favorite location for Western movies, and references to the place that had appeared in books, newspapers, and magazines were brief and sparse. Possibly his mother, through her interests in art, had talked to an artist who had been there. At least when Everett arrived in Monument Valley he did seem to know just what to expect. It was a tough thing for him to do. Alone and friendless he wandered into this desert land of the Navajos in late winter, virtually penniless, paying his small expenses by doing odd jobs and occasionally selling one of his watercolors or blockprints. In the 1930s, even more than today, such an act was almost unheard of and thought of as genuinely foolhardy.

The Indian Council Cave

Wand'ring among the painted
rocks one day
I saw some ancient, moss-grown
boulders there
That leaned together in a friendly
way
And formed a cave that might
have housed a bear.
But on the high arched ceiling
were designs
And symbols that some Indian had
drawn;
A rising sun, marked out in faint
red lines,
A row of running wolves, a deer
and fawn.
Bones from forgotten feasts were
on the floor,
Picked clean by men who sat
around a fire
Discussing and deciding peace or
war
Or chanting solemn prayers, in gay
attire.
The cave is empty now, the paint-
ings fade . . .
And here the silent centuries invade.

—Everett Ruess, published in *The American Indian*, April 1929.

February 13
General Delivery
Kayenta, Arizona

Dear Bill,

Here I am at last on what was, ten years ago, the final frontier. An Indian mailcarrier brought me from Flagstaff. I haven't met a single person on the way who I thought ought to be shot.

I've been bargaining with some Navajos about a burro, and I'll have to put out eight dollars for one. Most of the Navajos don't speak English, and an interpreter is necessary. Practically all of the burros are down with the sheep now. In the summer it is much easier to buy them.

When I was going to Needles in a Buick Eight with an old gentleman and his dog Jerry, traveling seventy-five miles per hour, the famous miner's hat blew off. I have worn the wool cap most of the time, since there has been no sun to keep off.

I drove to Oatman with a potato truck. After I had unloaded a ton of potatoes to earn my lunch, a friend of the driver took me on to Kingman, before I could eat the lunch.

Beyond Kingman, I was picked up by a couple of Long Beach toughs who were driving to New York in a Dodge. Having no money, they had siphoned their gasoline from other people's cars. It got dark that night (!) and as they had no lights driving was difficult. For about ten miles we kept just ahead of another car, driving by its lights. Then it dropped behind and we nearly went into the ditch. Tearing up a few fence posts, we started a fire and waited for the moon to rise and show us the way. The moon became the standing joke. It didn't come up till four o'clock in the morning. In the meantime we all crouched around the fire. One of the men slept on a slope right next to the fire, with his arms across his breast. Gravity kept working, and every few minutes his arm would steal down to the ground and the fire. It would get hot and slowly return to his breast. Finally it got burnt and the sleeper awakened.

At moonrise, we rolled onward, through Seligman to Ash Fork, where we arrived on an empty tank. I gave them half a dollar, and they begged a few dimes from sympathetic strangers. Twenty-five miles from Flagstaff all the gas was gone. They picked up a tramp who gave them his only quarter. They walked a mile to a gas station and we drove on again till the gas gave out, eight miles from Flagstaff. I got out and walked.

I slept on pine needles in the Coconino Forest that night. I tried melting snow to drink, but it tasted smoky and utterly unpalatable. Next day no burros were to be purchased in Flagstaff, so I went on, and camped near Mount San Francisco.

In the morning it was snowing, but an Indian took me to Kayenta. We stopped at several trading posts along the way. We drove through the Painted Desert, over a very wild road. Passed the place where *The Vanishing American* was filmed. All the mountains are pink and red. No trees but pinyons.

As soon as I get the burro and it stops snowing I'm going to visit some ruins. I sleep in a hogan now. The only thing lacking is you to throw a snowball at.

Your Comrade,
Lan Rameau[4]

By no means was Everett a recluse, for he would, and did, talk to anyone he met. At Kayenta, the little village just south of Monument Valley, Everett lost no time looking up John Wetherill and his wife, Louisa, the leading Indian traders of the area.[5] John, one of the four famous Wetherill brothers who discovered so many major ruins at Mesa Verde in the late 1880s and early 1890s, had lived in the Navajo country since 1906, and had since earned fame as a guide and explorer. The Wetherills undoubtedly told Everett much about the red rock desert, its people, and about how to survive a trip across it. Wetherill also told a fascinated Ruess about some of the closer Anasazi Indian ruins. Later comments, however, by both Wetherill and Everett, show that the two were highly dissimilar, and that they held little respect for each other. (See letter of 17 June 1934.)

February 13
General Delivery
Kayenta, Arizona

Dear Waldo,

The Indians around here are very poor, having no income except from their sheep and the blankets they sell. A statistician here figured that the per capita income from sheep, including wool and hides, is $13.40 a year. The Navajos live in filth.

This town consists of the trading post, the missionary's house, the tuberculosis sanatorium, and John Wetherill's house, with a few

28

hogans scattered around. Wetherill is the man who discovered Mesa Verde and was in the party which discovered Rainbow Bridge. He is the best guide in the Southwest.

The snow is practically all melted now, so tomorrow I shall probably start out for some ruins. I have already written one letter and don't feel like reiterating. The territory, however, is all that I hoped it would be.

Sincerely,
Lan Rameau

March 1
Kayenta, Arizona

Dear Family,

It was quite a shock to receive the news about the poster.[6] I had no thought of the prize when I made it, and I slapped the paint on in a great hurry, during the last few days of school. The only reason I made it was so the art teacher wouldn't think I was letting him down.

The money will, of course, be very useful. I have spent $6 for a burro, $1 for a seamless sack, $2.50 for a Dutch oven, $2.00 for a Navajo woven cinch and some rope, $8 for a tarpaulin to keep out wind, rain, and snow. I've spent as much again on food, but I have enough to last several weeks now. Bread is not sold in this country, so I have learned to bake squaw bread, cornbread, and biscuits in my Dutch oven. Yesterday the biscuits were perfect.

I would appreciate it if you sent some Swedish bread, peanut butter, pop, and Grape Nuts. They are unobtainable luxuries in this country. Canned milk costs fifteen and twenty cents, raisins are sometimes thirty cents a pound, and lard costs the Indians seventy-five cents for two pounds.

Although my postal address is Kayenta, I am actually at Say-kiz-y Pass near Monument Valley, Utah. Tomorrow I am starting on a trip to discover some cliff dwellings and do some painting and camping. I don't know how long I'll be gone, but write to Kayenta, and I'll answer your mail as soon as I get it.

Please respect my brush name. It is hard to lead a dual existence. The first name begins with "L," not "S." How do you say it in French? *Nomme de broushe*, or what? I would like to know. If you use my new name in addressing letters it will save confusion. It's not the perfect cognomen but I intend to stick by it.

A chilly wind is whistling and I am in the shadow of a cliff, but the Monuments are glowing in the afternoon sunlight. There are no clouds, but it may snow or rain in a few days. There is usually a March snowstorm here. A week ago there were four inches of snow, and every night ice forms.

As to the Navajo rug, if and when I get it, I intend to use it, but if I get another, I shall send it home to you.

Love to all,
Lan Rameau

March 9
Say-kiz-y Pass
Kayenta, Arizona

Dear Bill,

Just received your letter, and another from my family which held heart-breaking news. Imagine the salt tears rolling down as I read a clipping from the *Times* stating that I won 1st prize for my Foreign Trades Week poster, in the Los Angeles Day School division. $25!! The worm must be turning.

I had to look at the clipping several times before I could believe it. And to think with what difficulty my art teacher persuaded me to make the poster at all! I made it with breakneck haste because Art was an afternoon class, and Seniors did not have to go to their afternoon classes.

As to my pen name, although it is really a brush name, I am still in turmoil, but I think that I will heroically stand firm in the face of all misunderstandings and mispronunciations. I'll simply have to lead a dual existence. If you have any brilliant suggestions, I won't consider myself too far gone to reconsider. Comment regardless. The name is LAN RAMEAU, and the friend who helped me select it thought it was quite euphonic and distinctive. Personally, I felt that anything was better than Ruess, but I may have been mistaken. I can't tell whether you made it Lan or San in your letter. It's an "L."

I am going to pack up my burro and take a jaunt through Monument Valley to a row of cliffs I know of, explore every box canyon, and discover some prehistoric cliff dwellings. Don't laugh. Maybe you thought they were all discovered, but such is not the case. In the territory I shall cover, a few cliff dwellings have been found but not investigated. Most of the country is untouched. Only the Navajos have been there, and they are superstitious. In the event that I find nothing, I shall do some painting and have some interesting camps.

I have been in several snowstorms and rainstorms, but water is not plentiful, and is only found in potholes.

I'm glad someone shares your sentiments about my art, but a man can't live on promises. Nevertheless, I have a couple of promises of Navajo rugs in case I make two paintings that please two Indian traders. I have already traded one blockprint for an old Indian bowl but I'm not carrying it with me.

As to the rides I accept, I am now an independent man (though not financially) and I have two legs of my own and four on my mildly recalcitrant burro. The burro is quite a joke, with a black coat, white nose and eyebrows, and the ear tips missing. The Indian began at $12 but I purchased it for $6.

As to when I start painting, I have already made half a dozen attempts, but I anticipate better work in the future. It would be great if you sold the painting, but don't let such a masterpiece (?) go for a song.

I didn't make a moneybelt, and when the printing started to wear off (in my shoes) I put the money in my pocket, but day by day the questionable virtue of poverty has approached me. However, I have enough grub for a month and enough equipment to last indefinitely, so while I am alive, I intend to live. I hope you are doing the same thing, as nearly as possible.

You misunderstood about the hat. It blew away, but was recovered. I have since worn the wool cap which you considered unmanly because it kept my ears warm. Question: "Has my equipment proven inadequate?" Answer: "Yes." That's where all my money went.

Believe it or not, I have learned how to cook. I have produced biscuits in which no flour could be found, and my other dishes, though less complicated, are satisfactory. My little oven and I are prepared to cook anything.

In the way of game, I have only seen jackrabbits, cottontails, and prairie dogs, but I intend to sample them all. As yet, I haven't fired a shot. From all I can gather, hunting is a passe sport which it is impossible to revive. A long time ago the white men started trading guns to the Indians for pelts, and now there are no deer, antelope, or buffalo, and the sheep eat all the grass, so there are few jackrabbits. Crows and desert sparrows are the only birds.

I have exciting times tracking my burro. Once the hobbles got unfastened, and I had to pay an Indian on horse four bits to bring it back. The burro was going back to Kayenta and home. At present I am in Utah, at Say-kiz-y Pass near Monument Valley.

The traders around here deride the "Indian-lovers" who drive through in cars and write articles about their picturesqueness and their wrongs. These Indians are not mistreated, but they are scrupulously dishonest, and they live in filth. The tuberculosis sanatorium is always full. It is 100 miles in either direction to a school, so the Indians in the vicinity do not speak English.

It is too bad that you sleep under a roof where you cannot see the falling stars at night. In a couple of days the moon will be full, too. I slept very coolly until I got the tarpaulin. Ice forms almost every night. In one camp next to a cliff, you could hear the echo of a bean dropped four inches above a plate. It sounded like a firecracker. (No hyperbole.)

Atmospheric effects are magnificent here. Among other storms, I saw a dust storm, which obscured everything beyond a quarter mile.

Enclosed are a few pottery chips.

You may think I've said a lot, but I haven't told you half of it. This country suits me nearly to perfection. The only things I miss are a loyal friend to share my delights and miseries, and good music, of which I would not hear much in the city, anyway.

Write lengthily, and criticize my name to your heart's content.

Your comrade,
Lan

March 21
San Juan River, Utah

Dear Family,

It is now the twenty-first, but I have just received your letters of the ninth and tenth, which you evidently wrote before receiving my third. You are right that mailboxes are distant. I am in practically the most remote place in America. The nearest mailbox is forty-five miles away at Kayenta. This is about 250 miles from Flagstaff, the nearest city. There are only trading posts in between. There is a town in Utah, about 100 miles distant. Mail only leaves Kayenta once a week.

As for hunting for me with Dorinda [the family automobile], I don't believe you could get the car here. It would sink in the sand, rattle to pieces on the rocks, get stuck in a river bottom, slide off a cliff, or run out of gas miles from a service station. There is, however, a road to the camp where I am staying now. I have helped to put it through, but personally I prefer a burro and a trail.

Everett, the burro, has been fattening out and becoming more lively and tractable. The first time I put a real pack on him, he ambled

Dramatic Monument Valley at sunrise. Photo by W.L. Rusho.

along for a mile and then lay down in the center of the path, but I think he is over that habit. When well treated he is a very droll creature, with his white nose and stubby ears. Every once in a while he snorts and shakes his head from side to side, ears flapping. He keeps turning his ears, individually too. At first I didn't know how to get the most out of him, but now I think he will do twenty miles a day.

Waldo is not the only one who went swimming Sunday afternoon. I had a great frolic splashing about in the San Juan with some of the younger people at camp.

Now I think I shall lead you up to where I am, and have been for a week. The day after I wrote the last letter, I left for Monument Valley, where I spent two days, sketching, reading, cooking, and camping. The coyotes howled close by at night, and the burro wandered far.

The next day, I started for some box canyons where there were cliff dwellings, but I did not go far before the pack began to shift. After lashing it on more securely, I plodded on until late afternoon, when I reached the mouth of a large canyon. A windstorm sprang up, and the burro sat down. A waterhole which I had expected to be full was completely empty. I kept going back and back into the canyon until I was nearly to the end, in a gloomy, sunless place. Unwilling to go any farther, I unloaded the burro and went on over some small hills to the end of the narrow cleft, with a high rock wall on each side. At the very end was a V-shaped pool of muddy water with a green scum on it. That night, four inches of snow fell. Two mornings later, I hit the trail once more, very glad to get out of Gloom Canyon. I had not gone many miles before I came to some very neatly constructed cliff dwellings, near which I made camp. I found many interesting pottery chips with various designs. A new difficulty in painting presented itself when the watercolor turned to thin ice while I painted. The next day, after viewing a few more ruins, I left the vicinity of Monument Valley and headed for the trading post of Oljeto, which means "moonlight on water." All of the ruins I saw had been investigated before.

After sunset I kept going, trying to reach an old Navajo hogan of which I knew. Finally I tied the burro to a tree and floundered around in the darkness and sandhills until I found the hogan. Then I couldn't find the burro. Then I couldn't find the hogan, after locating Everett. After two more searches for each, I made camp with the burro. A flying spark burnt a hole in my packsack. My knife got lost, somehow.

Next day I reached Oljato and went on for two days till I found the camp at the San Juan, where I hoped to get a temporary job. There were five white men and a couple of Navajos working on a road. Some mining men are trying to get things ready for production, but the whole proposition is being kept quiet. I doubt if I shall get a job, but meanwhile I have been earning my board and learning to cook, as well as having much valuable experience. I have been building stone walls, sawing and chopping wood, shoveling on the road, carrying pipes across the river, washing and wiping dishes, carrying water, riding mules, sketching, hiking, and taking advice from the old-timers. [John] Wetherill is a famous camper, and discovered Rainbow Bridge and Mesa Verde. There are two fat men, recently from Hollywood, who are getting toughened up. There is another young fellow named Shelby MacKauley but we call him Mack. The fat ones are Johnny and Austin. Altogether, they are a very likeable and interesting bunch. Three of them are not so much older than I.

I have to hurry and try to get this letter to a car before it leaves, unless it is already gone.

The candle burning is a beautiful thought.

More later,
Love from Lan

April 2
Kayenta, Arizona

Dear Family,

[My] hogan is made of logs piled to make a beehive-shaped structure, and then covered with red clay. The wind is blowing so hard now that it blows in dirt and sand at the corners and crevices. At the top there is a square hole to let the smoke out. My bed is at the end opposite the door, and on one side is the firewood, while on the other are my food and equipment. In the center is the fire, with a pot of beans cooking. The hogan is on a sort of rim, above the town of Kayenta. I have been staying in it for three days now.

I will begin my narrative back at the San Juan River, on Sunday, March the twenty-second, the day after I wrote the last letter. Early that morning, after washing clothes, I took an exhilarating swim in the river, which was cold and muddy. Read "The Art of Morals" in *The Dance of Life*. Two of the boys tried the old trick of taking me snipe hunting that evening, but I fooled them properly.

On Monday, I forded the river and followed up a beautiful clear stream on the other bank. Had lunch under a cottonwood tree which was covered with young green leaves, just unfolding. Watched little stars of light on the bottom of the stream, made by the sunlight passing through bubbles. Observed a water beetle catching minnows.

Mr. [John] Wetherill made me a map of some cliff dwellings I shall visit.

There seemed to be no prospect of a job, so I got ready to leave. On Wednesday it rained all night and most of the day. We all helped to build a chimney in the house, and mudded up the walls. I smashed my finger when carrying a big slab of rock. Had a jolly time around the fireside that night.

Thursday morning, I had flapjacks cooked on a flat rock, then packed my burro and started out. In order to save a few miles, I decided to take a steep trail across the canyon. You would not think that anything but a goat could use it, but other pack animals had, and I essayed it with mine. The pack came off twice and the burro leaped over huge boulders and skidded down to the canyon floor. Halfway up the other side, he came to a shelf three feet high, and I couldn't persuade him to step up it, no matter how hard I tried. So I unloaded him, carried the pack to the top, and repacked him.

There were wonderful colors on all sides, but the clouds gathered and a raw blast blew, with a few flurries of snow. I made an early camp in Copper Creek, and cooked spotted dog (rice and raisins) for supper.

The next morning, in packing, I found that two tubes of black and one of vermilion watercolors had been crushed, and had oozed all over the others. Three Navajos on horseback stopped by my fire and watched me pack.

Soon I came to a bend in the canyon, where I could see the open desert, with Organ Rock close by. I tried to find a trail which saved a few miles, but it was obscured. One can't go straight toward his objective because there are so many gullies to cross.

In the afternoon, I had a view of the snow-covered mountains up north, and later I could see El Capitan [Agathla], the impressive, twisted rock which is near Kayenta.

By evening I was in the shadow of a mountain, and I couldn't get out of it before sunset. I traveled in the afterglow for half an hour, then made camp while the coyotes howled. Soon an Indian sheepherder came along, chanting and singing weirdly. In the canyon next to that in which I camped was an Indian hogan, and its occupants were celebrating the fact that they had plenty to eat and were generally well off. One Indian shouted at the top of his voice in a half bark and half song. He sang first to one side and then to the other, 'till you would expect his voice to break.

Next morning an educated Indian dropped in by my camp-fire, and gossiped for a while. This was March 28, my seventeenth birthday. I reached Oljato, and found that all my mail had just been sent to the San Juan, except a package. This I opened at lunch, and what a birthday feast I had!

After lunch I plodded happily along, coming in and out of the shadows with my faithful burro. I found a broken arrowhead along the trail. As I walked along, I made up a song about the brink and another about philosophy.

Next morning, there were a couple of inches of snow on the ground, and it kept coming. By the middle of the morning I came to El Capitan, the splendid rock. It has [served as] a landmark for one on many occasions. The longer I know it, the more I like it. If I were wealthy, I'd build a castle like it.

I made early camp in a big empty hogan. Cooked biscuits and gravy, then climbed a hill to watch the sunset.

On Monday, March 30, I came into Kayenta after crossing the creek. My burro does not like water, and was very skittish about putting his feet in the creek. At Kayenta I received your birthday letters and the money. I spent Mother's dollar for a lustrous green silk neckerchief, and with the rest I bought food and equipment. Everything here costs double the city price and sometimes triple.

As to the burro, I call him Everett, to remind me of the kind of person I used to be. I am careful not to contradict him, since he is my elder, being eighteen years old. He is still alive though, and can kick hard when he wants to. He looks like a Puritan with his solemn black coat, and his white nose, and white eyebrows. I've sketched him a couple of times. When the evening sun falls in just the right way, he turns a rich chocolate brown, but most of the time he is black.

I haven't painted anything which could profitably be made into blockprint, but I am keeping the idea in mind. Some time when I have the opportunity, I want to try a few ideas in oils.

I haven't been able to leave the hogan to go off on any sketching trips, because the Navajos would steal my things. They think it is clever to steal, and only laugh when found out. I had my smashed finger fixed up, and in a few weeks it will be just as good as ever, but right now it is a handicap in writing almost anything.

I am finishing this Friday morning, in time to catch the mail. Ice formed in the puddles last night.

Haven't received your letters answering mine of March 1, as yet. Will write more letters, but by the next mail. I shall be exploring some interesting canyons near Betatakin and Keet Seel. From Mr. Nurimberger's accounts, it is an unusually picturesque district, with springs of clear water, trees, meadows, and canyons. Very isolated, and hardly an Indian goes there. I may be alone a month.

Love to Everyone,
Lan

April 16
Kayenta, Arizona

Dear Bill,

I never received the reply to my last letter, but I presume it is with some other mail delayed in southern Utah. Yesterday I emerged from the

Canyon del Muerto, Arizona. *Blockprint by Everett Ruess.*

Tsegi country, where I visited the famous old ruins, Betatakin and Keet Seel. No one was in the valley there, not even an Indian, though there was some Navajo stock. One day, however, three college boys came down from the rim to visit Betatakin, the more accessible ruin.

Everett and I have been over some rather bad trails, here and there. Once we both bogged down in the quicksand and it was all I could do to get him out. I left my shoes in the mire. Another time, following a trail on a knife-edge ridge, Everett plunged down a twenty-five-foot bank when the earth crumbled. He didn't even ship the pack. He ate my handkerchief and since I have been unable to find my towel anywhere, I think it must have gone the same way. This morning he brayed for the first time since I've had him. A dog kept nipping at his heels, and after Everett misplaced a kick, he turned his head from side to side in bewilderment, looked at me with a woebegone expression, and gave a prolonged bray that seemed to go back to primal, elemental things in its essence. He is a venerable old donkey, being a year older than I (who have just passed my seventeenth anniversary).

I haven't seen much wildlife yet. The list is: crows, ravens, buzzards, owls, bluejays, bluebirds, yellow-headed blackbirds, flickers, robins, hummingbirds, kingbirds; jackrabbits, cottontails, prairie dogs, chipmunks, and a big porcupine; lizards, centipedes, a five-inch scorpion, a milk snake; tumblebugs, spiders, ants, pollywogs, frogs, etc.

I have not been at all prolific in Art, having produced only a dozen paintings worth keeping. However, I consider them my best work, and the color is much clearer.

Somehow I don't feel like writing now, or even talking. Both actions seem superfluous. If you were here, you might understand, but too much is incommunicable. If I were there—but that is unthinkable. You cannot understand what aeons and spaces are between us. I feel very different from the boy who left Hollywood two months ago. I have changed as well as matured.

This letter you may find very incoherent and inconsistent. Ponder on the proverb, "Never less alone than when alone." Thoughts are jangling within me. In a few hours, I expect to be in a very different mood, and in the next mail, shall send another type of letter. If you write soon, I may be able to answer before I leave this vicinity. I am undecided about where to go next, but there won't be any stops for a while.

Hope your next letter doesn't say that you're leading the same, humdrum existence.

> Cheerily,
> Lan

April 18

Dear Bill,

As for my own life, it is working out rather fortunately. These days away from the city have been the happiest of my life, I believe. It has all been a beautiful dream, sometimes tranquil, sometimes fantastic, and with enough pain and tragedy to make the delights possible by contrast. But the pain too has been unreal. The whole dream has been filled with warm and cool but perfect colors, and with aesthetic contemplation as I jogged behind my little burro. A love for everyone and everything has welled up, finding no outlet except in my art.

Music has been in my heart all the time, and poetry in my thoughts. Alone on the open desert, I have made up songs of wild, poignant rejoicing and transcendent melancholy. The world has seemed more beautiful to me than ever before. I have loved the red rocks, the twisted trees, the red sand blowing in the wind, the slow, sunny clouds crossing the sky, the shafts of moonlight on my bed at night. I have seemed to be at one with the world. I have rejoiced to set out, to be going somewhere, and I have felt a still sublimity, looking deep into the coals of my campfires, and seeing far beyond them. I have been happy in my work, and I have exulted in my play. I have really lived.

There has, however, been one flaw, aside from the insistent clamor of that disgusting god, money. Art needs an audience, or it will die, just as the world ceases to exist if there are none to contemplate it. I have had many sublime experiences which the presence of another person might well have prevented, but there are others which the presence of a perceptive and appreciative friend might have made doubly worthwhile. In all this country I have met but one moderately intelligent man, and he is too steeped in sarcasm. Only one hospitable family have I encountered, and with them, familiarity has bred contempt. For these reasons, and because of the corroding effects of money, I have shirked contact with humanity, preferring to live more perfectly in isolation. Yet, after all, people are interdependent, and I have felt the need of a real friend. That is all. Make of it what you will.

In the meantime, my burro and I, and a little dog, if I can find one, are going on and on, until, sooner or later, we reach the end of the horizon.

Your alter ego,
Lan

April 19

Dear Waldo,

Among the things in the three packages which I sent are: an ancient black and white Indian bowl; a modern black bowl made by the Pueblo Indians, a mother of pearl ornament of value which I found at Keet Seel, a part of a human jawbone with teeth, some corn more than 1200 years old, and many types of pottery chips.

But now to tell you of the real news. My family group has been enlarged to three! The latest is just following an ant across the hogan floor, an attempt to find out what it is. Now he is chewing a scrap of rope as if it were a wild beast attacking him. He is a little roly-poly puppy with fluffy white fur, and blue-brown patches on his head and near his tail. His eyes are blue, and his nose is short. I found him last night, lost and squealing for help. When I stroked his fur in the darkness, electric sparks flew off.

I haven't yet decided about his name, but may call him Curly, because of his tail. When he is large enough, I am going to train him to go behind the burro, occasionally nipping the donkey's heels, so that we shall be able to go faster.

It is quite amusing to watch him sniffing and digging and investigating the world. I shall take the trail again in a few days. Repassing Kayenta in ten days, I shall collect what mail there is, and then strike out for Canyon de Chelly, returning westward through the Hopi Reservation, to the Grand Canyon, then north to Kaibab and Zion.

It is unfortunate that you have been unable to find a good position, and no doubt your $40 was gone long ago. But you are probably enjoying life anyhow, even though you do not live it to the fullest. Nevertheless, when we read of the immense strides in accomplishment that some men have made in their youth, our own years often seem wasted. However, it is man's lot to be imperfect and discontented. In my travels in Arizona, I have never met anyone whose life I envied. I myself feel much freer and happier here than I did in the city, but that is due not only to a change in environment, but to a change in my mental attitude.

My little family is a peaceful one now. The puppy is taking a nap and the burro is eating sagebrush in a nearby field. The air is clear, fleecy clouds float dreamily overhead, and not a sound is to be heard anywhere, except the scratching of my pencil. I hope no unpleasant misadventures have befallen at home, and that you are not too much dissatisfied with the careless treatment of circumstance.

Love from Lan

May 2
Kayenta, Arizona

Bill, you dear old hypochondriac,

Yes, I have a dog! He is a month-old Navajo puppy, whom I found lost in the night, a couple of weeks ago. He is a ball of white with two mouse-gray patches near his tail and on his head. He has blue eyes. I call him Curly, for his tail.

A young Navajo squaw tried to kidnap him once. She picked him up, squealing, and started to walk off. Seeking to detain her, I grasped her two strands of beads, but she wouldn't stop, and they broke. Even then I had to manhandle her and pinch her fingers before she would let go of Curly.

A couple of days ago, I helped a rancher butcher a calf, for which service he gave me the skin. I made a quirt from it, to stimulate the burro.

You wonder why I do not go into the hills and get a deer. The main reason is that there aren't any. Deer were extinct long ago in this country. All through the Indian country, the game is very scarce. Then too, there is very little water for the game.

This morning I meant to leave for Canyon de Chelly, but I slept late, and have taken several hours to write a few letters, with one more to go. I seldom write letters hastily. Now it is raining, as it has frequently done in the last two weeks.

41

Maybe you have been gloating, as you promised, over your hot baths and showers, but I don't envy you. Hot baths, say the dermatologists, are bad for the complexion. At any rate, I feel more exhilaration from physical cleanliness when I swim or splash or bathe outdoors, under the wind and sun. My last bath was on a cliff top in a waterhole a yard across and three inches deep. I tried to use soapweed, but found it impractical.

I have changed my name again, to Evert Rulan. Those who knew me formerly thought my name was freakish and an affectation of Frenchiness. It is not easy to choose a name, but Evert Rulan can be spelled, pronounced, remembered and is moderately distinctive. Of course, I changed the donkey's name. He is now definitely titled Pegasus.

Don't write, or rather, hold your letters until you hear from me again, as I am not having mail forwarded from Kayenta, and shall be on the move from now on.

Your comrade of ancient days,
Evert

May 2

Dear Waldo,

It was a fine letter you wrote me, with your individuality showing everywhere through it. I feel that you are worthy of a better position than your present one. The idea put forward by some, that all necessary work is honorable and beautiful because it must be done, means nothing to me. As far as I am concerned, your work is quite unnecessary, since I can keep very healthy without Fleischmann's yeast, and do not need it for booze or bread, as I consume neither. I'll wager Uncle Alfred and his family never use the stuff either.

I myself would sooner walk a whole day behind the burro than spend two hours on the streetcar. What are your plans for the future? Are you preparing yourself for a better job, are you ignorant of your own desires, or are you leaving your life to circumstance? There is nothing wicked about either course, but I know you would dislike to imagine yourself in the same type of job ten years from now.

Somehow, I am very glad not to be home, where civilized life thrusts the thought of money upon one from all sides. With an adequate stock of provisions, I can forget the cursed stuff, or blessed stuff, for days and weeks at a time.

Your censure was quite deserved in regard to providing my needs, but remember that I have asked for no money, and that most of the equipment I asked for was unprocurable here, and necessary to my life. The brush, the shoes, the clothing, the diary, the bell, the pack sack, the paper, the plate, and many other things were real needs. I have made many efforts to find jobs, but hard times are here as well as elsewhere, and on Indian territory the government must give all the work possible to the natives. However, I expect to find some source of income in the near future. I am determined to make my own way, but each day spent in stupid labor, I shall consider wasted. You and I seem both to suffer from backwardness, not caring or not able to "sell" ourselves.

As to my plans, while I expect fortunate and unfortunate circumstances to make changes here and there, my whole life is roughly mapped out. After the Grand Canyon, Kaibab, and Zion, I shall go south for the winter, perhaps pausing in Mesa, where a friend has relations. After working in the cactus country of southern Arizona, I may go northward through New Mexico, Rocky Mountain National Park, and Yellowstone to Glacier. This, of course, is a decision left to the future. At all events I intend to spend a year or two in the open, working hard with my art. Then I shall wish for city life again, and to see my old friends if they still exist. By that time, it is imperative for something to have turned out for the better, so that I shall have funds with which to do painting on a larger scale. Some kind of studio or large room to myself, will be necessary. There I shall work with oils and watercolors, improving my work of the past and, with it as a foundation, working out new and better pictures. It is my intention to accomplish something very definite in Art. When I have a large collection of pictures, done as well as I can do them, then I am going to make a damn vicious stab at getting them exhibited and sold. If this fails, I'll give them away to friends and those who might appreciate them.

Then I am going to lead a very civilized life, getting plenty of good music, having many new experiences in reading, and having social experience. I shall find new, worthwhile friends, meanwhile continuing with art, and perhaps working in poetry.

After having lived intensely in the city for a while (it may not be in Hollywood), I feel that I must go to some foreign country. Europe makes no appeal to me as it is too civilized. Possibly some unfrequented place in the South Seas. Australia holds little allure for me now. Alaska is too cold and Mexico is largely barren, as is most of South America. Ecuador is an interesting place with its snow-capped volcanoes, jungles, and varied topography. As to ways and means, that problem will be solved somehow.

I must pack my short life full of interesting events and creative activity. Philosophy and aesthetic contemplation are not enough. I intend to do everything possible to broaden my experiences and allow myself to reach the fullest development. Then, and before physical deterioration obtrudes, I shall go on some last wilderness trip, to a place I have known and loved. I shall not return.

Love from your brother,
Evert

May 10
Chin Lee [Chinle], Arizona

Dear Father, Mother, and Waldo,
I contrived a roundelay, but found no one to sing it with:

> Prod, prod, prod your burro
> Gently near the tail,
> Merrily, merrily, merrily, merrily,
> He's a kind of snail.

Love from Everett

May 10
Chin Lee, Arizona

Dear Bill,

On the assumption that, since I heard from you last, you have not become a professor of metempsychosis, I take my pencil in hand, once more to convey to you my thoughts, aspirations, and disgusts.

It took me four days to go from Kayenta to Chin Lee, a distance of about eighty miles. One day I covered twenty-five miles, but in the afternoon, Pegasus folded his wings, and progress was very slow.

The first day, after intermittent spatterings, two rainbows appeared simultaneously. I watched them for a long time. For three days' duration there were magnificent cloud effects, with rain, lightning, and rolling thunder.

One day, there came a young Englishman of genuine intelligence, who stopped his car for an hour or two while we talked, during the rain. He is a graduate of Cambridge and has also gone to California. Was on his way to London to find some geological job in the Orient. He won't take it unless it leaves him six months a year free for exploration. He has been on two Arctic trips, is fond of good literature and poetry.

Curly, the pup, rides the pack most of the time, as he tires easily.

In Chin Lee I have met some very interesting and very generous people. Hard times prevail here as elsewhere, and I haven't been able to find any jobs. The Indians are not very lovable here. This morning, when I looked for my burro, I found that his bell and tie rope had been stolen (from his neck). Peg had evidently been mistreated, as his legs were skinned. The burro was just beyond a small hill. Experienced Indian traders say that a Navajo is your friend only as long as you give to him. Certainly none of them would go to church if the missionaries did not give them food and clothes. The missionaries are a snoopy, superfluous lot, who gossip and spread trouble, no matter how good their intentions.

The Navajos do not help one another. If one Indian is trying to corral a herd of horses, and they start to escape past another Indian, the latter will stir neither hand nor foot, but will only laugh. When a Navajo begins to be helpless and decrepit, the others cease to have anything to do with him. The government used to give such Indians a few rations once a week, but now times are hard and they only get grub once a month. In consequence they go to all the white people and beg. I saw one woman give the very coat from her back to an ancient squaw.

Tomorrow I intend to start up towards Canyon de Chelly and Canyon del Muerto. From the pictures I have seen, and from all I have heard, they would seem to be fascinating. I shall be gone perhaps two weeks, possibly making a test of my self control which I have in mind.

I look forward to the Grand Canyon.

On all sides, people are being murdered, run over, are dying and committing suicide. It may be our turn next, but if you receive this letter, write to Chin Lee so that I'll find your reply when I return from the canyons. If you try to muss up my latest appellation, by misspelling sirs, or esquires, your own cognomen will suffer in the return mail.

Love and kisses,
Desperately yours,
Evert

P.S. The miner's hat is becoming picturesque (falling apart). But the sleeping bag is still intact.

If I had the postage money, I'd send home the shotgun, which is an unnecessary burden for the donkey. I fired it once, killing a chipmunk which was too small to eat. I've seen a few prairie dogs big enough to eat, but I'd rather not have them than carry a gun all day.

Your comrade
Evert Rulan

May 23

Dear Family,

After twelve days, I've returned from the Canyon, having been stuck in the quicksand several times. I made half a dozen paintings, but as yet I've not enough to spare. They are all different and I like to have the variety to show to people I meet. Have seen nothing suitable for blockprints, but do not despair.

Today the doctor's wife bought a blockprint of the windblown cypress for a dollar. I wish you'd send more, on the yellow, wave-lined paper, as it was my only copy. Also prints of the mountain range with the line of trees in the foreground. Preferably green on white.

I did not expect you to send any groceries or any money, but of course they were welcome. I'm sorry the financial situation is so pitiful at home. I really couldn't tell you where to reduce expenses or how to earn more money.

Here's my budget:

Rent	nothing
Electricity	"
Gas for heat and cooking	"
Telephone	"
Retirement assessment	"
Savings	"
Running burro, oats, etc.	.25 (5 lbs)
Food	$10 to $20
Magazines, newspapers	nothing
Burro insurance	"
Doctor bills	"
Clothing, no allowance made (shirts are in shreds and I've but one extra)	
Family	nothing
Contributions	.10
Unexpected sundries	$1.00
Insurance	nothing
Total	usually under $20

I have bought no more than $40 worth of equipment, most of which need not be frequently replaced. The $25 prize money is not quite all spent. All attempts to find work have failed. Hard times prevail as elsewhere.

Secretly, I had wished for puppy biscuits, but never dreamed you'd be thoughtful enough to send them.

Tomorrow I am starting for the Hopi country and Grand Canyon— about 200 miles distant. In writing, specify that the mail be held, as I may be weeks arriving.

Love to all,
Evert

On a hot day in June 1931, two high school boys, Tad Nichols and Randolph "Pat" Jenks, were driving their pickup back from a rough trip to Navajo Bridge when they spotted Everett, with a burro and a small dog, trudging along the barren road near Cameron, Arizona, moving very slowly, apparently about exhausted. Nichols and Jenks stopped and offered him a drink of water, but Everett, confused at first, thought they wanted water and reached for his own canteen.

In spite of his selfless generosity, Ruess obviously needed help, so the boys suggested that they take him to a ranch that Jenks

Tad Nichols, who took this photograph, and Randolph "Pat" Jenks (background) were driving this pickup near Cameron, Arizona, on a hot afternoon in June 1931 when they found Everett wearily trudging along the dusty road. Jenks and Nichols stopped, loaded the burro into the truck, and took Everett to a mountain cabin in the San Francisco Peaks. Everett is shown at the left.

had homesteaded on the west side of the San Francisco Peaks. Just loading the burro into the tiny pickup and tying him down was a complex operation (see photograph). Jenks says that on the ride through Flagstaff and around the Peaks he discovered that Everett, even though very tired, was an interesting, artistically sensitive young man. Soon Everett found himself relaxing in a crude but comfortable cabin beneath cool Ponderosa pines, supplied with groceries by his two young friends. Jenks, who visited him at the ranch whenever school work allowed, says that Everett spent his time in leisure, with no particular aim or objective.[7]

June 8

Dear Father, Mother, and Waldo,

This letter is being sent from the vicinity of Flagstaff, not Grand Canyon. Yesterday noon I was at the Little Colorado River, about to turn westward, when along came two boys in a small Ford truck who were much interested in what I was doing. They had passed me before near Hotevilla pueblo. One of them suddenly decided to take me and the burro and Curly to a ranch of his in the Coconino Forest, among the San Francisco peaks. I was much surprised, and did not consider the project feasible, but he was confident that it could be done.

The three of us finally shunted the donkey on, after much maneuvering. The rest of the pack was lashed on the roof. Pegasus stumbled and lurched from side to side, but maintained his equilibrium. We sailed along through desert and forest, with the shadow of the donkey beside us. At dusk we reached their school, which has five teachers and five pupils. This afternoon I'll go to the ranch, and stay in the vicinity for a week or more. I expect to do some good painting and work out some blockprints. The mountain slope is covered with aspens, and wildlife is very abundant. One of the boys, Randolph Jenks, is interested in ornithology. He wants to buy my painting of a cliff dwelling if he can procure the money. There is always some catch, you know.

The first day out from Chin Lee the peanut butter can came open and spilled over the papers in my pack. Due to misinforming signs, I went a couple of days out of my way, but the territory was interesting. I managed to reach water every day or two. The pueblo of Walpi was rather a disillusionment. There is an element of incongruity in the juxtaposition of old stonework and fences made of bedsteads.

I also passed through Old Oraibi and Hotevilla. The dust and heat were extreme. When I was nearly at Blue Canyon, a young couple passed by, and saying that the canyon was dry, they gave me a gallon of water.[8] I found that they were mistaken, and in a pocket in the rocks, I discovered an excellent swimming pool, of cool, green, shadowed water, with high rock walls. It was very deep too. Curly went swimming also. I was startled to see what a tiny creature he is with his fur wet down. Half of his size is his fur. He enjoyed the puppy biscuits greatly. Everyone who sees him seems to love him.

The next day I saw a weird thing, the dance of the tumbleweeds. A small whirlwind picked them up and tossed them in large circles. They would slowly float to earth and then bounce up again. Around and around they went in fantastic spirals.

On the following day I went through Moenkopi village, another Hopi town. There were cliffs of bright vermilion, and the finest specimens of Lombardy poplars that I have ever seen. A scorpion started to crawl into my blankets, but I stopped him in time.

The next two days I paused by a stream and let the burro rest. Some Indians passed by in a covered wagon drawn by six horses and mules.

The following two days were spent in the Painted Desert, until I reached the Little Colorado. You know what happened after that. I walked about 170 miles from Chin Lee.

Love from Evert

Those were great days at your ranch—idyllic days. There I seemed to feel the true spirit of delight, the exaltation, the sense of being more than man, lying in the long, cool grass or on a flat-topped rock, looking up at the exquisitely curved, cleanly smooth aspen limbs, watching the slow clouds go by. I would close my eyes, and feel a coolness on my cheeks as the sun was covered, and then later, the warmth of the sun on my eyelids. And always there was the soft rustling of aspen leaves, and a queer sense of remoteness, of feeling more beauty than I could ever portray or tell of.

—Letter to Randolph "Pat" Jenks, 17 December

June 26
Arizona [Near Flagstaff]

Dear Father, Mother, and Waldo,

A week or so ago, I left the mountain ranch, after climbing in the peaks, felling aspens, and making fences. For several days I have been at a sheep camp in the desert. The men are interesting characters. I've chopped a truck load of wood, and assisted in various humble chores such as watering sheep and marking lambs. There are many burros here, and when the man in authority comes, I intend to acquire one. Pegasus lacks stamina, has a sore back and broken leg. He has served me well, but I think now he should be superannuated.

Two of the men generously contrived a pack saddle for me from three broken ones, and I have repaired two old panniers. A clever burro suffering from malnutrition visited my camp twice, moved off the coverings on my possessions, kicked aside some logs and rocks, then made a shambles. He ate and destroyed sacks of sugar, flour, oatmeal, rice, cornmeal, prunes, dog food, and potatoes. I've since made a cover for one pannier.

Once as I was walking along, Peg slowed down, looked to one side, then turned around, regarding me as if to say, "Do you see that?" Offside was a herd of eleven antelopes.

Somehow or other, a cheap camel's hair brush has been substituted for the two sable brushes I formerly possessed. The letters to the Canyon were never forwarded as I requested, but doubtless I'll read them eventually.

Let your worries be as few as mine.

Love from Evert

June 30
Grand Canyon

Dear Bill,

You asked for my plans for the next six months. They are rough and subject to change, of course. Having walked 300 miles (and it was worth it) to the Canyon, I expect to spend some time here. Then I'll cross by the Kaibab Trail to North Rim, continue through the Kaibab to Zion Park, and investigate adjoining country. In the fall, I'll return across the canyon, visit Oak Creek Canyon, near Flagstaff, and spend the winter months in the cactus country. There are many places I intend to see, but I can't tell which year I'll see them.

I'm as interested as you are in these virgin fields for the archae-ologist. Follow up your rumor and find out. There are many places in southern Utah which are practically unvisited because of the absence of water and the roughness of the country.

The game is supposed to be very thick in the White Moun-tains, bear and such. But I should think pretty soon you'd outgrow the lust for the hunt. It's a very primitive instinct, you know, inherited from your caveman forbears. A couple of days ago I was within ten yards of a coyote. Dove, cottontails, jackrabbits, prairie dogs are numerous in many places.

As for the shotgun, it has made the supreme sacrifice—has lost its life as a possession of mine. Being desperately in need of a burro that could travel, and not possessing the spare cash to buy one, I traded the gun for a donkey, and I'm well satisfied with my side of the exchange. The new burro, though older than Pegasus (about twenty-five), has four sound legs, a strong back, and is far handsomer. His ears are longer, too. He is a rich, warm, velvet brown with a violet tinge.

Now to bring you to my present location. I left the camp in the aspens, climbed one of the spurs of Mount San Francisco, and followed roads which aren't shown on the map. I stopped for six days at a sheep camp, where I chopped a truckload of wood, and assisted in marking lambs—a process in which blood and tar intermingle. A burro got into my provisions, nosed off a log, some stones, and coverings, and ate sacks of flour, sugar, cornmeal, prunes, dog food, rice, etc. With a new burro, a pack saddle, and dilapidated boxes, I left that camp. The superannuated Pegasus was left behind, free to kick his heels as he listed. It rained and I was wet; the sun shone and I was dry. At a lumber camp, I spent my all, purchasing a pair of shoes, a shirt, some socks, and some grub. Again it rained. I saw a double rainbow. This morning I arrived at the Canyon.

It is sometimes bothersome to have to write four letters based on my activities, but I continue to make them different. Certainly it would be impossible to confuse the authorships of the letters I receive. My grandmother wrote one solicitous letter. "When are you coming home?" she asked.

How do I manage to subsist? That's a good question. I often wonder myself. However, when I'm broke, something always turns up. First it was that $25 prize. Recently I sold a sketch to a clerk in a lumber camp for $5. One print brought a dollar. Now when my total monetary wealth is four cents, a letter informs me that a print of my mother's which she copied from a painting of mine, brought a $25 prize and I am to have $10 of it in the course of time. For two weeks at the San Juan camp I earned my board. One week at the sheep camp. For eight days on the ranch near Flagstaff, Randolph [Jenks] provided for me. I gave him a couple of prints.

> As Eddie Guest says in his rhyme about the artist,
> "Those three grim ogres of distress,
> Hunger and cold and shabby dress,

Which most men fear, he smiled upon
And never wished them to be gone,
Saying, "From all that comfort brings
But little inspiration springs."

Eddie knows all about artists.

I throw my camps in all manner of places. I have slept under cedars, aspens, oaks, cottonwoods, pinyons, poplars, pines, maples (not the typical maple), and under the sky, clouded or starry. Right now I am under cedars, with pines all round. Cedar bark is excellent tinder.

Desert rats have told me few camping secrets, but here and there I've gleaned some. I can take care of myself rather well now. Before I had the pack saddle, I used the squaw hitch, but now I throw a double diamond hitch. It wasn't hard to learn.

My burro eats grass and bushes for the most part. He can keep fit when a horse could not. Occasionally I give him oats, or leftover biscuits. The dog often rides the pack.

I've just had a bath and watered the burro. I look forward to rice pudding for supper and to explorations of the canyon.

Yours,
Evert

At the Grand Canyon, Everett saw for the first time what is perhaps the premier natural spectacle on earth. Like many poets, however, he had difficulty describing the canyon. Actually, he didn't really try—in contrast to his elaborate, lyrical descriptions of smaller-scale, more comprehensible topography found in other parts of the West. But he was highly moved, for in the short time he was in the Southwest, he managed to visit the Grand Canyon three more times.

July 16
Grand Canyon

Dear Father,

I've opened your last two letters, also the package. I never knew that moths got into dog biscuits, but they have, and have made a fine mess. If you haven't already bought the dehydrated vegetables, don't do so. No matter how they're cooked, they have no flavor.

Thanks for the $6.50. I'm about to cash the money order.

For a week I was in the depths of the canyon. The heat was over 140 degrees at one time. I followed obscure trails and reveled in the rugged grandeur of the crags, and in the mad, plunging glory of

The Grand Canyon will always be a challenge to poets, photographers, and painters. Looking downstream at Grapevine Rapid in the Granite Gorge portion. Everett Ruess hiked to the bottom of the Grand Canyon several times.

the Colorado River. Then one sunset I threw the pack on the burro again and took the long, steep up trail. I traveled for several hours by starlight. A warm wind rushed down the side canyon, singing in the pinyons. Above—the blue night sky, powdered with stars. Beside—the rocks, breathing back to the air their stored-up heat of the day. Below— the black void. Ahead—the burro, cautiously picking his way over the barely discernible trail. Behind—a moving white blotch that was Curly.

Tomorrow begins another journey to an unfrequented portion of the Canyon. Returning, I shall cross over to the North Rim.

My life has continued as I have wished. I have made two more friends, with whom I had stimulating intellectual discourse, that broadened mental horizons. They were men of fine character both. A friend is indeed a wonderful treasure.

I wish you would reread my last letter and answer some of the questions.

A cloud has passed athwart the sun, my camp is in shadow. Shreds of juniper bark dangle idly in the breeze. The burro is just rolling on his back, enjoying a dust bath. Now there is no breeze—no sound. In all directions stretches the silent forest.

Love from Evert

August 6
Kaibab Forest, Arizona

Dear Pat [Jenks],

I'm sorry I did not see you at the Canyon. I reached the South Rim on the last of June, spent two weeks there, two weeks in the Canyon, and now a week on the North Rim. I know Clyde Searl well. He said you had been doing some splendid work here, but left three weeks ago.

I did not follow the route you proposed. Mr. Roth did not know about the road, said Crater Lake was dry, and hadn't heard of Government Caves. He referred me to a man farther on who was not at home, so I kept on, following roads not shown on the map. The morning I left the Veit Ranch, I saw some sheep there, but I told your trapper friends about them, and I believe they put them out.

Forty miles from your place, I stopped for a week at a sheep ranch, marking lambs, chopping juniper wood. I traded my shotgun for a donkey, and my Navajo cinch for a pack saddle.

The new burro I call Pericles, or Perry, for, like the Greek, he is the father of a golden age. He is larger than Pegasus, has four sound legs, and longer ears. His fur is short, of a brownish grey, and he too has a white nose. He is older than Peg—about twenty-five I think, but in good condition.

I went by the Saginaw lumber camp and sold a sketch to the clerk. The ranger at the park didn't know whether or not to let in a person with a burro, at first. The Superintendent said I couldn't take Curly across the canyon, would have to go by way of Cameron and Lee's Ferry. We didn't fight about it, but I'm here and so is Curly. He endears himself to everyone with his puppyish ways.

I went down the Hermit Trail, then the Kaibab, traveling by starlight. Perry did not want to cross the suspension bridge, so I let him rest 'till evening, while I swam in the Colorado, drinking gallons of the muddy water. Then I lay on the sand watching the blue and yellow damsel flies, and rolling over to keep in the shadow of the bridge. I saw a shadow on the water, and looking up, noticed a large, yellow-headed heron flying gracefully.

At evening I banged the burro across the bridge with an old shovel. One night I slept behind Ribbon Falls.

Perry is a constant source of amusement. Once he stepped into a tin can and made an undignified spectacle of himself before he freed his foot. When he was tied to a tree, he scratched his chin with his hind foot, but then the foot got caught in the rope and he hopped about on three legs for a while. Yesterday I gave him a chunk of salt meant for the deer and he licked it delightedly.

Love from Everett

In August Ruess made a side trip northwest to Zion Canyon, where he came down with an intense poison ivy reaction. Ranger Donald Jolley took Everett to the emergency ward of the local hospital where Everett spent eight days recovering. He never told his parents about his stay in the hospital.

In Zion National Park, Everett pauses with his burro and dog. The Watchman formation is in the background. August 1931.

55

August 18
Zion National Park, Utah

Dear Father and Mother and Waldo,

Yesterday I reached Zion Canyon, the ninth day out from the North Rim. We came about 130 miles, traveling half the day and retiring during the hot part.

The first few days were spent in the Kaibab Forest, among aspens, firs, and pines, with deer and white-tailed squirrels. I lightened the load by disposing of the Dutch oven and some other things for a meal and some provisions. I did not take the main traveled road, but took a road which had not been used for so long that it was almost obscured. Then I came through Fredonia to Kanab where I bought some foods I had been craving. Next I was out in the real deserts once more, camping in a sandy hollow, with the crescent moon low in the sky.

Yesterday morning I tracked the burro to his lair before sunrise, but as soon as I unhobbled him he galloped away and I had to chase him for a mile, then drive him down and finally caught him. I had difficulty in making him go through the mile-long tunnel on the Zion-Mount Carmel highway. He only had his picture taken six times on this trip, but that was because we did not follow the main road.

Zion Canyon is all I had hoped it would be. I am not actually in the park, but half a mile below it in the canyon, camped under maple trees by the Mukuntuweap River. There is no fodder for the burro farther up, but here there is a field of alfalfa for him. I went to Zion Lodge last night for the mail, and had to walk the four miles back.

I am enclosing some maple seeds. I did have some porcupine quills, but they've disappeared.

Love from Everett

August 27-28
Zion National Park, Utah

Dear Bill,

For six days I've been suffering from the semi-annual poison ivy case—my sufferings are far from over. For two days I couldn't tell whether I was dead or alive. I writhed and twisted in the heat, with swarms of ants and flies crawling over me, while the poison oozed and crusted on my face and arms and back. I ate nothing—there was nothing to do but suffer philosophically.

Yesterday morning I managed to pry my lips far enough apart to insert food. I thought my eyes would swell shut, but not so. Even now, they are mere slits in the puffed flesh.

You may remember that last year I took antitoxin injections and bounced happily off on my vacation—within a few days I was suffering it again with dull resignation. One chap says to use saltwater, another gasoline, another claims tomato juice is a sure cure. Nothing I used in times past alleviated the raging perceptibly. Most of the dope sold is stuff you paste on your face until you are a worse mess than before. I was just recovering from a dose of poison oak when I started this trip.

I get it every time, but I refuse to be driven out of the woods. My face is on fire as I write, and I managed to make a painting at dawn of a peak that has fascinated me. I'll have to repeat it when I'm well, then send the best version to you.

My friends have been few because I'm a freakish person and few share my interests. My solitary tramps have been made alone because I couldn't find anyone congenial—you know it's better to go alone than with a person one wearies of soon. I've done things alone chiefly because I never found people who cared about the things I've cared for enough to suffer the attendant hardships. But a true companion halves the misery and doubles the joys.

It is true that I can be happy alone and many times I've felt relieved to be in solitude. I look forward to my trip tomorrow because it will take me into the solitude again. But a real friend is not an intrusion.

I've been scraping along one way and another. I told my family not to send money but they've sent some. The park is adding territory, and farmers have to move. I helped one tear down his house, but got sick with the heat and then poison ivy. I'd rather starve than exert myself physically for wages, anyhow. I make it a rule not to be concerned about filthy lucre until after I'm broke.

While I was sick I could hear the squeak and bang of boards being pounded and nails being pulled. The farmer here is a Mormon, bishop of this district. His three daughters are named Velate, Merle, and Leda. He with his wife lived on this spot for twenty-five years. The government is going to remove all traces of habitation, allowing the green fields to go barren and the fruit orchards to die for want of water. Some park employees had flowers in their gardens but the architect made them pull them out because they weren't in harmony.

I'm truly glad you enjoy the picture—as I told you once before, an artist can't paint for himself alone—he must find someone else who thinks his stuff is good.

On this whole trip I haven't met anyone who really cared for art—not even the few tourist artists I met.

I started a poem the day before I sickened—here are the first four lines:

I have been one who loved the wilderness
    Swaggered and softly crept between the mountain peaks
I listened along to the sea's brave music;
    I sang my songs above the shriek of desert winds.

Evert

Upon his recovery from poison ivy exposure, Everett rode to the southeast, then ascended through the Kaibab Forest to the North Rim of the Grand Canyon, taking eight days. He spent another week crossing the canyon by way of North Kaibab Trail, the Kaibab Bridge, then Bright Angel, Tonto, and Hermit Trails, reaching the South Rim at Hermit Rest. Again, Everett neither painted nor wrote in detail of his impressions of the canyon. He only commented that "Nothing anywhere can rival the Grand Canyon."

September 30
Kaibab Forest

Dear Bill,

Thanks very much for the compass and purse. I know they will be useful.

For eight days I traveled from Zion to the North Rim, a distance of 150 miles by my route. If only you could have seen what I saw then—but you didn't and as a picture is supposedly equal to a thousand words, I'll send you that when I reach the South Rim.

One of those sunsets will always linger in my memory. It was after a day of struggle—of violent hailstorms that beat down like a thousand whiplashes, and of ferocious, relentlessly-battling winds.

Then sunset, at my camp on a grassy spot in the sage. Far to the north and east the purple mesas stretched. Cloud banks arched everywhere overhead, stretching in long lines to the horizons. There was an endless variety of cloud forms, like swirls of smoke, like puff balls. Here and there where a sunshaft pierced a low hung cloud bar, the mesas were golden brown and vermilion.

Everett poses with his burro and dog, Curly, in Arizona, 1931.

Then the treeless western hills were rimmed with orange that faded to green and deep blue. A cold clear breeze caressed me and the full moon rolled through the clouds. The lunatic quaver of a coyote—silence and sleep.

Winter is close at hand; the maples are crimson, and flurries of yellow aspen leaves swirl about with each breeze. On many hillsides the yellow leaves have blackened, and the trees stand bare and silent. Soon the snows will be here, but I won't.

Tomorrow I start down the hole. In a week or ten days I'll be at the South Rim. After that, God knows where, except that I'll be drifting south toward the cactus country. I may not have a postal address for a month or two, again. When I reach the South Rim I am sending my parents most of my earlier paintings, some relics, and curios. Ryall means to go over and look at them.

> Your comrade,
> Evert

October 9
Grand Canyon

Dear Waldo,

I was delighted to hear from you yesterday. I'd almost given you up—thought you were tired of me. I would have replied yesterday, but I was expecting an important change which has not occurred. The season is changing—cold winds shriek ominously, and then there is meaningful silence. I expect change in my life, too.

I'm glad you don't find it unpleasant to write to me. You are right that in spite of our differences there is much that makes us near to each other. Whenever I think of you I feel glad that I have a brother like you.

Though I have not seen a bathtub since I left Hollywood, I never find it difficult to be clean. Whenever I feel futile, impotent, a swim in an icy stream, a shower under a waterfall, or in a few gallons of water in the canyons, the forest, or the desert, with the wind and sun to dry my skin, never seems to fail to lift the depressive feeling.

As to terrific physical experiences, I've had several, but recovery from each was fairly rapid. Only once was I ever too tired to eat when I was hungry.

I meet very few Mexicans. Many of the sheepherders are Basques. I learned a few words of Navajo. The Latin and French I learned in high school have never been of practical use.

My only choice between getting out on my own and going home is the first alternative. I couldn't go back—not defeated, at least. In that last letter I told you to tell Father to send no money and I wish you had made that clear to him. It might have saved me more trouble than the money saved.

It is unfair to you to be chained at home—particularly if it is partly on my account. I don't feel very guilty, because in more than eight months, Father and Mother have sent only fifty-two dollars.

You may be interested in a financial statement.

I started with fifty dollars, parents sent fifty-two, thirty-five came from prizes, I procured fifteen from various sources.

I have spent 136 dollars altogether. Considerably more than a third went for equipment—all the rest for food. Needless to say, I have earned dozens and dozens of meals.

Not for God's sake or yet for Hell's sake can I sell any of my paintings. The world does not want Art—only the artists do. Oh, I have sold something over six dollars worth of prints and I traded one sketch for a sheepskin and another for some grub—but that's negligible.

It should be superfluous to say that jobs are nearly impossible to find.

On my way across the canyon I took the Tonto Trail. No one else has been over it this year. It was always a rough trail, and washouts and landslides made it doubly so. In one side canyon that cut deep into the plateau, I found the skeleton of a mountain sheep in the middle of the trail. One horn was broken, but I have the other and am sending it home. I traveled after dark that night. Time and again the burro went off the trail, twice at dangerous places. We traveled on the edge of a cliff. I could hardly see where to set my foot. Only a white spot on Perry was visible. Arriving at Hermit Camp, I saw that the place was lighted. Some Fred Harvey employees who I had met before were preparing the abandoned camp for the use of the Fox outfit. They are producing *The Rainbow Trail*, another Zane Grey picture. I met the art director and his wife yesterday. They gave me some good advice.

Many times I have been broke. I was broke yesterday, and I met another young chap who was all but broke. He turned out to be a very likeable and intelligent person. I showed him about the canyon and gave him the first good meal he'd had in a long time. I arranged so that he had a good night's sleep. He left home in order not to handicap his family financially.

For the present I am stranded here, with no means of moving my equipment. My clothes are fairly well worn out. As soon as I can procure two good burros, which is my greatest concern at present, I'll be traveling south.

I expected to send most of my pictures home from here, but I find it desirable to have the better ones with me so what I am sending is really the dregs. However, it gives an indication of what I have seen and done. There is one picture, however, of the Grand Canyon from the North Rim, showing Brahma Temple and Zoroaster Temple, which I like above anything I've done.

Everett

October 9
Grand Canyon

Dear Waldo,

That picture is for you. I hope you like it well enough to frame it and put it in your room.

I came to the room in which I'm writing to escape the wind but a radio is nearby and baseball addicts are crowded around it. I have to leave.

Whatever I have suffered in the months past has been nothing compared with the beauty in which I have steeped my soul, so to speak. It has been a priceless experience—and I am glad it is not over. What I would have missed if I had ended everything last summer!

I'll quote part of one day from my diary:

"As soon as we were out of the town, proceeding slowly on the cow path beside the long row of poplars, the cloudburst came. The hail beat down like a thousand whiplashes. Two small boys on a horse were thrown off into the mud when the horse saw Perry. There was another violent hailstorm, then, what with the wind and the sun, everything was soon dry again. We crossed the line into Arizona.

"Curly danced and pranced about with shreds of bark and bones.

"Then the wind blew furiously and relentlessly. I was soon weary with fighting against it. It was like walking in sand. At last we left the beaten path, turning south toward the Kaibab. The wind battled unceasingly.

"The noon halt, long delayed, was in a bend of a deep gulley, where the steep sides shut out some of the wind.

"We struggled against the gale until we came to the old campsite on the hill near the grassy slope.

"Supper of fried yams, toast and cheese, and corn.

"Sunset made all the misery worth enduring. Far to the north and east stretched the purple mesas, with cloudbanks everywhere above them. Some were golden brown and vermilion when sun shafts pierced the low clouds. A rainbow glowed for a moment in the south. That was a promise.

"Clouds of all kinds and shapes arched overhead, stretching in long lines to the horizons. Some were like swirls of smoke. Then twilight—a rim of orange on the treeless western hills. The full moon appeared, rolling through the clouds."

Months ago, at the San Juan camp, I was in the tent with Johnny, Elston, and Mac. One of them remarked that it was unfortunate there was no dog to eat the meat they were throwing away. "Why not save it for my burro?", I asked. They roared with laughter. I thought they would never stop.

However, they were wrong to laugh. I knew more about natural history than they did. At Ribbon Falls I had more meat than Curly could eat, and offered some to Pericles. He ate three large tough pieces and wanted more. He always liked greasy paper, or any kind of paper.

Once I was eating cheese when Perry snatched the wrapper and knocked the cheese to the ground. He enjoyed that piece of paper.

Nothing anywhere can rival the Grand Canyon. I must come here again some day. There are things I must paint again. I think it would have given you a new lease on life to have seen what I have seen.

We both feel the lure of far places. I hope your dreams come true.

Your loving brother,
Everett

To escape the approaching cold in northern Arizona, Everett caught a ride with tourists to a lower elevation, south to the saguaro cactus land east of Phoenix.

October 23
Superior, Arizona

Dear Mother,

This evening I am starting for the Apache Trail with two new burros.

For the past two days I have been in Mexican town in Superior, which is a mining town. The Mexicans use burros to haul wood, and there are dozens of them here. I could not buy two burros with my ten dollars, so I wired you to send some money. It came this noon, and I felt much better. This is the first time on this trip that I've asked you outright for money, and I needed it. Good equipment is much harder to find than food, and it is very important to get a good start. Neither Pegasus nor Perry were good burros—they were too old, and suffered under their loads. I had to travel light and carry part of the pack myself.

I am not a haggler—it is not my nature. If I knew Mexican and stayed here a week, I might be able to buy burros for what they are worth, but I don't and I can't. I bought two burros for $11.50 ($8.00 and $3.50 pack saddle included), but when I started off today, the smaller burro fell down under his pack. I got $1.50 back and bought another burro for seven dollars. That took most of my money, but ten dollars was the price named for each, so you see I saved five dollars. I bought films and food and had my shoes repaired and now I have twelve cents. Only one of my burros is shod—all the shoes in town have been sold. Perhaps I can get back the dollar that is owing me—I hope so. One of my burros is brownish gray, with white nose, a brown streak down each shoulder, and brown bands on his legs. The other is black with a white nose and breast. I haven't named them yet—I just bought the black one an hour ago.

It hurts me to think you consider me selfish for wanting another burro. My load is too heavy for one burro to carry. This is the only place I've been where there were burros to choose from, and I could not let the opportunity go by. The only work in this country is cotton picking—men are wanted for that job—but imagine picking 100 *pounds* of cotton for sixty cents!

I intend to spend several days in a small canyon, and I expect to find interesting subjects in the saguaro forests. Write to Mesa. I will be there two or three or four weeks from now. I may not be able to get mail until that time. I wish you would send to Mesa my pup tent which I used last year. It would be very useful.

You would enjoy watching the Mexican children playing with baby burros.

I came from Grand Canyon to Mesa with two tourists—a man 6½ feet tall and his wife.

Love from Everett

November 13
Tonto National Monument, Arizona[9]

Dear Bill,

I traveled over the Apache Trail, then left it and struck across the mountains to some cattle ranches. My burros became adept at leaping across gullies, and many times they were persuaded to go down steep places, against their better judgment.

I want to survive this panic and yet have my time free for work and travel. Bill, you don't know what you're missing. This life is the only one, and the only disagreeable thing has been the financial uncertainty.

Snow has fallen on the crests of the Sierra Anchas, and several sousing downpours have drenched the valley, accompanied by lightning and rainbows.

The outlook was quite dismal for a time, but now I am assured of enough to keep me going for a month or so. Tomorrow I must wrangle the burros, shunt them into a truck, and join three New Yorkers and an easterner beyond Three Bars Ranch. There I'll pack the burros with three days' grub for the five of us, and blankets, and drive them up toward an amethyst mine back of Four Peaks.[10] It will be a three-day trip. I'll do the rough work while the easterners hunt.

In 1931 Everett wrote, "My burro and I, and a little dog, are going on and on, until, sooner or later, we reach the end of the horizon."

We went over some quite rough trails—it was a good thing the donkeys were ahead—from the land of Saguaro and Cholla to that of sycamores and willows, and of pine and alligator juniper. One cow ranch has to have supplies brought twenty-five miles by burro train.

All this time I was penniless and trying to pick up a few dollars and some grub. I managed to keep fed, but the dollars were elusive.

I circled around to the Tonto cliff dwellings and have been here for ten days, perhaps. There is an Apache guide—a generous, childish soul, and an old globe-trotter and artist who sells postcards and paintings. He wants to found an art colony here! He has been telling me all about the pyramids, the diamond mines, his ranches in the South Seas and Australia, and we've had some good discussions on scientific subjects.

My grub gave out, so I trundled the burros to the lake shore and loaded them heavily with driftwood. It was three dollars worth of wood, but I managed to get a dollar for it. Then I sold a black and white sketch for a dollar. I've met several well-known artists and got new slants on the matter with my stuff. It is improving. That criticism of your friend about comparative distance was well founded, but I am getting over that obstruction. I am confident that I can make something of my work—the problem is how to keep alive until I have succeeded in a larger measure. My plan is to amble about the Southwest with donkeys for a couple of years more, gathering plenty of material and mastering watercolor technique—then to get some windfall so I can work with oils and do things on a larger scale, perfect my field studies, and then do something with what I have.

I have been meeting all types of people—artists, writers, hobos, cooks, cowmen, miners, bootleggers. A friendly hotel keeper got me this latest job.

The bootlegger said that as soon as he sold his stock on hand he could offer me a job guarding his still in the mountains and packing barrels to the retreats.

Enclosed is a foppish photo of Pericles, Curly, and me in the Kaibab forest.

> Your old cronie,
> Evert

> December 13
> Tonto National Monument

Dear Waldo,

On canyon trails when warm night winds blow
Blowing and sighing gently through the star-tipped pines,
Musing, I walked behind my placid burros
While water rushed and broke on painted rocks below.

I have been here at the cliff dwellings for nine or ten days. First I took the Apache Trail, left it, and struck across the mountains into the rough country, with Cynthia and Percival, my two new burros. I killed a rattlesnake, and forced the burros to descend steep mountains against their better judgment. They became quite dexterous at leaping gullies and avoiding cactus. I stopped at a cow ranch which is supplied by burro trains that start twenty-five miles away.

The lore country is dotted with saguaro, cholla, cat claws, and mesquite, the canyons are brightened by sycamores, cottonwoods, and willows, and the heights are covered with pine forests, oak, pinyon, and alligator juniper.

All this time I was penniless and trying to pick up a few dollars and some grub. I managed to keep fed, but the dollars were elusive. A bootlegger said that when he had sold his stock on hand, he could offer me a job guarding his still and packing barrels into the mountain retreat.

I've met several well-known artists, and got a new slant on the matter with my stuff. It is improving.

I'm confident that I can make something of my work; the problem is how to keep alive until I begin to succeed in a larger measure. The proprietor of the Apache Lodge said he thought he would sell some of my paintings, but I would have to buy frames or mounts first.

The prospect was dismal until this evening. I sold a black and white print for a dollar, then the Apache boy invited me to supper of venison, and the hotel keeper found me a small job. I am going to pack supplies on my burros for four hunters and myself for a three-day trip. Three of the men are New Yorkers; the other owns an amethyst mine back of Four Peaks, and we are going there, by way of the Three Bars Ranch. I am assured of at least five dollars a day and my chuck. The proceeds will keep me going for another month. I want to survive the panic and yet have my time free for work and travel.

Winter has set in. For days the sky wept. Drizzles and drenching downpours were accompanied by lightning and rainbows.

Love from Everett

In late December Everett hitchhiked to his home in Los Angeles for the winter months. He remained there until March 1932, when he returned to the Salt River Valley to resume his travels.

The Burro Shoe

It protected his feet while he slid down rocky slopes of wild, cactus-covered hills; it caked with snow as he descended mountain trails between white-mantled pines; it scraped waterworn boulders as he gingerly felt his way through muddy mountain torrents. Following its imprint in the red soil I tracked him many weary miles till at last old Longears stood before me, discovered; sometimes in nimble haste I dodged it. I heard it crunch pebbles in a river bed and later over concrete bridges. Heedless of Percival's dignity, a whiskered Mexican threw him down and nailed it to his hoof. An Apache jerked it off.

So hang it over the door of your room, and look long at it, for it is the spirit of the wilderness trail.

—Everett Ruess

*From my desert nightingale to you
Comes this well worn burro shoe*

It protected his feet while he slid down rocky slopes of wild cactus covered hills; it ached with snow as he climbed down mountain trails between white mantled pines; it scraped waterworn boulders as he gingerly felt his way through armadily mountain torrents. Following its imprint in the wet soil I tracked him many weary miles till at last old long ears stood before me, discovered; sometimes in nimble haste I dodged it. I heard it clatter over concrete bridges and crunch the pebbles in a river bed. Heedless of Parcival's protest, a whiskered Mexican threw him down and nailed it to his hoof. An apache jerked it off.

So look well at this shoe, from me to you; hang it high on the wall. Its days of use are over, but now it is something of which to dream and sigh.

To his friend, Bill Jacobs, Everett wrote this first version of the "Burro Shoe" with his own letterhead.

THE LETTERS

1932

March 30
Roosevelt, Arizona

Dear Father, Mother, and Waldo,

If you are going to send any money in April, right now is the time to send it. Put money first on the list. Next in order come books. There are two that I want you to be sure to send: *The Magic Mountain*, by Thomas Mann, and *The Brothers Karamazov*, by Dostoievsky. Get them in the Modern Library series; otherwise they will be too bulky. These two will not cost more than two or three dollars. They are the ones I want most. However, you might keep in mind the following: *The Satyricon of Petronius, Gargantua and Pantagruel, Candide, Mrs. Dalloway*, and *Nana*.

We have traveled in all four directions from Roosevelt. One night, on the road to Tonto Dwellings, a rattlesnake came out near us.

Did you develop the roll of film that I took?

The hills are covered with flowers: lupines, poppies, paint-brush, daisies. A crow is clacking his beak in the cottonwood overhead. Quail are calling. A cardinal has been here.

Luck
Everett

April 20
Roosevelt, Arizona

Dear Father and Mother,

As I write I am sitting on the Roosevelt Dam, halfway up on the lower side. Wild winds are shrieking in the wires, swirling in the dust heaps, and swishing the bushes. Clouds are scudding by, and the water from the powerhouse is roaring out like a maelstrom, whipping itself to froth before it blows to Apache Lake. The turbines are humming. Now the gale grows fiercer. The lake above is flecked with whitecaps and the willow trees bend low.

Luck to everyone,
Everett

Adventure is for the Adventurous

Adventure is for the adventurous. My face is set. I go to make my destiny. May many another youth be by me inspired to leave the snug safety of his rut, and follow fortune to other lands.

—From an essay by Everett Ruess

We have no correspondence from Everett for the next two months. When he finally left southern Arizona, however, he resumed his letter writing.

June 20
Zeniff, Arizona

Dear Bozo [Bill Jacobs],

I haven't any idea where you are or what you are doing, but I hardly imagine you are at Pinto Creek. Wherever you are, you'll probably be thinking I've been having a tougher time than you. I don't think I am, but here are a few choice bits for you. Aside from the trouble Curly gave me, Pacer, my horse, broke away from me the second night and I had to chase him a couple of hours by moonlight before I could catch him. I had two light touches of poison ivy, lost the trail several times, and stepped on four rattlesnakes. In Pleasant Valley I traded my horse for a couple of burros, and one of them is about to have a colt.

I rode up to the asbestos mine and took a last look at Roosevelt Lake and Four Peaks. I thought of you two while I was up there under the pines and firs, while I read beside the stream and Pacer munched wild flowers.

I struck across the mountains to Cherry Creek, following a very steep trail. I came out at the Flying H Ranch, but the saddle blankets had slipped out, and I had to backtrack halfway up the mountain before I could find them. Old Pacer turned out to be more or less of an outlaw, full of tricks.

I found an interesting cliff dwelling in Rockslide Canyon. Only two rooms were visible from below, but the lower one went back fifty feet. The one above went back even farther, and another above that came out in a balcony on the other side of the cliff. There was no trail from there on, until near Pleasant Valley. All the lower branches are broken from the trees, by the heavy winter snows.

Near Dry Lake, a rancher befriended me and undertook to find me a better outfit. At first he couldn't locate any pack mule, but he found a Mormon who runs a dude ranch and had a stray buckskin mule which had been on his range for five years. He said he'd catch him for me, so I rode over one day and we chased him, but he jumped out of a corral twice and went through three fences, so we gave up. The Mormon gave me an old white cow horse with four brands on him, and I bought a tough old bay for six dollars. The rancher gave me an old Frazier saddle and some shoes. We had to tie the horses to a post by their hind feet in order to shoe them.

I have been striving vainly to acquire a sense of balance, but I still flop in the saddle when the horse trots. I've only been thrown once, from a horse. A steer threw me twice.

This morning we branded two hundred cows. Last week we staged a rodeo, and one rider was piled three times.

There were a few days, coming north, when I had nothing but parched corn and jerky, but here at the Rocking Chair Rancho, the food is far better than I ever had at home. We have homemade cake or cookies nearly every day, and we don't have to subsist on Mexican strawberries, as at most ranches. There is plenty of milk and butter, corn bread, honey, applesauce, and everything nice.

I saw plenty of pine trees when I was "way high up in the Mogollons" but I was glad when I left them behind. I like the aspens, and the pale, waxy yellow green of the oaks, but after a few days, a pine forest becomes very monotonous to me. Speaking of pines, I think you should really enjoy Fletcher's "Green Symphony." I've enjoyed my poetry books.

I abandoned my heavy kyaks at Cherry Creek. For awhile I used sacks, but I made a light pair of boxes. Then a storekeeper gave me a stout kyak which had been used to ship a little pig in. I made another out of a kerosene crate and put cowhide strips on them both.

I am not certain how soon or how I am going north. I have a tentative offer that looks very good to me, but I won't know anything for certain until after the rodeo at Holbrook this weekend.

Once more I am in the desert that I know and love—red sand, twisted cedars, turquoise skies, distant mesas, and, far to the south, the blue line of Mogollon Rim.

Evert

In late June, Ruess reached Ganado, one of the centers of Navajoland, both geographically and culturally. Ganado was important also for white men in that, from 1878 until 1930, John Lorenzo Hubbell operated, at Ganado, the "... most important single trading post in the history of Navajo trading." (*Soldier and Brave, Indian and Military Affairs in the Trans-Mississippi West, Including A Guide to Historic Sites and Landmarks*, Volume XII, National Park Service. New York: Harper & Row, 1963, p. 112.) In 1932, although Hubbell had died, his trading post was still in full operation. Everett does not mention stopping at the post. He normally had little interest in trading posts, which always seemed to serve as local centers of white men's culture, but instead Everett, as he wrote, "... stayed with the head man at Ganado, hoeing corn and resting my horses." He adds, "His daughter is the most beautiful Indian girl I have seen."

July 9
Ganado, Arizona

Dear Father, Dear Mother, and Waldo,

Tomorrow morning I am starting for Chin Lee, which I'll reach in two or three days. I'll expect to find some mail there. Here are a few pages from my diary:

"June 25.

"Men and boys and girls on horses and burros displayed themselves. The townspeople swaggered like mannequins. Those with ordinary clothes tried to show by their demeanor that they were of a superior sort. I met the boys I had seen at Lake No. 1. The bucking Ford went through town. After the parade I bought some dried fruit, ate, and walked out to the rodeo grounds. I sat on a roof on the outside edge of the fence. I was soon joined by a boy from Winslow, and we became pretty good friends. He told me about his horses, we smoked and sat, watching calf roping, bull dogging, steer riding, wild cow milking, pony racing, and bronc riding. No one was thrown from a bronc, but no one stayed on a steer, . . . A clown performed tricks with his mules.

"When it was over I hurried to the post office, where there was a letter from Mother with the films from Cherry Creek. Then I went back to see Tom, but he was drunk. He was riding Old Nig, with an old friend behind him, each with a bottle in hand. He cursed the natives, the cowboys, the Navajos, and the Mormons. Someone had stolen his purse with seven dollars and some papers. He was quarreling with EdHennessy, the cattle inspector, pushing his hat off, pouring beer in his hair, and haranguing about who was his friend and who wasn't.

"Ed tore Tom's shirt and Tom tore Ed's. Ed tried to pull Tom off his horse and told him to get out. Tom led Nig in drunken circles and swore he would take Ed home. It ended by vows of friendship. Tom said Ed wouldn't lose his temper at him no matter what he did. He spoke to me a few times. He seemed to be ashamed to go home and face his wife. It was the first time in fifteen years that he had been drunk.

"A sandstorm blinded us for a while. I went off to Cosby's, got my ropes and a nosebag, and walked along under the rim looking for my cayuses. I found them with the rodeo horses and I rode Whitey back. After watering them, I turned them out once more.

"I talked with Virgil. He is a pugilist, but he has appendicitis and his girl has made him promise not to fight anymore. He writes poetry of a sort. I showed him my stuff. His family certainly don't approve of what I'm doing.

"June 26.

"Mr. Cosby invited me to Sunday breakfast of hotcakes, eggs, and cereal without sugar. Barely was I through when he probed into my religious upbringing and beliefs. He invited me to Sunday School. He shaved me and we drove down. This particular house of the Lord is in the back of a drycleaning store. I was introduced to Mr. Brown, the pastor, and his wife and three daughters—the eldest rather pretty. This was the first time I'd been to Sunday School in many years, but my old training hadn't been in vain. I had difficulty finding the chapter of Paphnalius, or whatever. I read that beautiful passage in the Book of Ruth, 'Intreat me not to leave thee, or to return from following after thee, for whither thou goest, I will go,' etc. I read the Sermon on the Mount. The songs are of a revivalist sort. Mr. Brown and Mr. Cosby believe the world is about to end any moment, signs of the times coinciding with prophecies in the Book of Revelations. They were gratified when they learned that the Bank of America had just failed. There were not many present— not as many as were in the jail last night. One of Mr. Brown's small daughters made specific prayers for various absent sisters, that they might not go to Hell for being at the rodeo instead of church. We sang songs about Judgment Day, dining with Jesus, and the Royal Telephone: as, 'Telephone to Glory, Oh what Joy Divine; I can feel the current coming down the line, sent by God the Father to his blessed own, I can talk to Jesus on the royal telephone.' We all had to quote a line. I quoted 'I will lift up mine eyes unto the hills, whence cometh my help.' On the whole, it was quite interesting, and Mr. Cosby must have thought that I behaved quite well for an unbeliever. Sunday dinner was quite good. Mr. Cosby thought it worldly to attend a rodeo and I think it is a boring affair anyway, so I reclined in an easy chair for a few hours, then wrote a letter and posted it. The rodeo was just over.

"At Bible study we prayed for the little boy of one of the women. He had broken his arm and she was in hysterics for fear it would be stiff. Also for a lady who had heard the singing and wanted us to pray for her husband, who was so drunk she couldn't do anything with him. One woman wept uncontrollably because her son wouldn't come to church and was doomed to Hell. Mrs. Brown and the mother went into hysterics, then suddenly rejoiced because their prayer was answered and the boy was well. Mr. Brown explained that he was not a Holy Roller, had never rolled on the floor, but didn't believe in formal churches. He warned us against Christian Science, Universalism, and Unitarianism. Then in his sweet, gentle voice he sang *The Feast of Belshazzar*. Discussed the need of prayer. Before I left, Rev. Brown gave me some tracts and the Book of John to carry along.

"July 1.

"It had rained lightly and the sky was black. The old Indian again showed me where my horses were. I put the bridle I made yesterday on Whitie.

"We trotted up the hill, I singing lustily. We passed an Indian encampment and crossed a bridge over a deep arroyo. Then it began to rain. I put on my poncho, which covered my whole saddle. Trucks passed. The rain beat down steadily. The poncho leaked. I made a sketch and photographed a butte. The beauty of the wet desert was overpowering. I was not happy for there was no one with whom I could share it, but I thought, how much better than to be in a schoolroom with rain on the windows, or at home in my dreary bedroom. My tragedy is that I don't fit in with any class of people.

"The first day out, I felt like a hero just because I had a hat, but it is part of me now.

"I met two men in a mule cart near Indian Wells. At the trading post I bought sugar, milk, and oats. We circled a butte, magnificently colored with vermilion and black, and then came to a spring. I saw two hogans and a corral. They were empty, so I stopped at the larger hogan and turned the horses out to grass. I climbed the hill and looked at the rainbow, the red hills, cedar-capped, the distant mesas. I read, cooked, and watched the fire."

I have only two dollars and a little food now. As soon as I get more money I am going to buy a Navajo saddle blanket for three or four dollars. It will serve many purposes. I've been staying with the head man at Ganado, hoeing corn and resting my horses. His daughter is the most beautiful Indian girl I have seen. The Navajo diet of squaw bread, mutton, and coffee does not appeal to me. There were three meals when there was nothing but squaw bread and coffee. I shall go to the post office soon, and mail you *Magic Mountain* and some of the other books. I may want to tell you my plans when I decide what they are. The nights are very cold in spite of the torrid days.

Love from Everett

July 12
Chin Lee

Dear Waldo,

That day I forded the Salt River and climbed high up in the Sierra Ancha Mountains, camping in the pines by a mountain stream. The next night I had fed Curly a little and ate some of my supper when Pacer got away, galloping with his hobbles. I chased him for two hours by moonlight. When I came back, Curly had eaten my supper. I punished him and he went off. I called and searched for him next morning, but he was not to be found. A good dog is a fine companion, but Curly had disappointed me. I did not have enough to feed him and I didn't want to go back for him, so I went on, hoping he would trail me. He didn't and I heard no more of him.

Untitled blockprint by Everett Ruess.

After leaving Salt River, I entered country where people are hospitable, generous, and friendly. I stayed at several cow ranches, and bought no food for a long time.

Physically, I am not very tough. I haven't the constitution of a day laborer. I soon wear out at a job like road building, or digging and lifting. This seems to be my physical makeup, because though I have tried many times, I find I can't do a man's work in physical labor. Aside from this, however, I am well able to take care of myself, to a certain extent I know my capabilities, and I pride myself on sincerity and steadiness. I don't have much trouble getting along with people, but I have the greatest difficulty in finding the sort of companionship I want.

At Ganado an educated Indian invited me to stop at his house, rest my tired horses, and hoe corn for him. I taught him some English. He had to go to an Indian council for a couple of days and told me to stay with his son-in-law while he was gone, if I wanted to. His son-in-law lived seven miles south on the banks of the Pueblo Colorado. He could not speak English, and was staying alone. I helped him hoe weeds in his corn fields until I was on the point of exhaustion. For the first two meals we had absolutely nothing but coffee and cold squaw bread (namskadi). Then another Indian, Lefty Johnson (Sam Johnson was my host), came, and Sam walked off without a word to me. We cut hay and hoed another corn field, then had mutton for supper. The next day we hoed another corn field and a bean patch and plowed a field in which we sowed oats. Next morning I left. It had been some nightmare! The horses had plenty to eat, if I didn't. I was glad to find someone who spoke English again. While I was cutting hay I saw a rattlesnake, stepped on his head, and cut off his rattles. He is the seventh I have killed this year. None of them gave me any trouble or danger. We used scythes, not mowing machines, to cut the hay.

It took me only a day and a half to cover the forty odd miles between Ganado and Chin Lee. That was very good for my thin old horses. We camped a few miles beyond Behikatso Lake the first night. I'd have liked to camp by the lake, but grass and water are never found together in the Navajo country. The sheep eat all the grass within two or three miles of waterholes. One must choose either a dry or a grassless camp. I was glad to see the old landmarks.

Mrs. Wetherill, whom I knew in Kayenta, drove in yesterday with Grace [Frances] Gilmore, author of *Windsinger* and other Indian books.[11] Mrs. Wetherill is looking for Indians without accents to play in the picture *Laughing Boy* which is to be made near Kayenta.

I like this country very much, though at times I wish for the ocean. The country is fiercely, overpoweringly beautiful. I have not been able to paint for some time, but I am going to try some more before I admit defeat. The thing I miss, here as elsewhere, is intelligent companionship. Then too, it seems wrong that people should mean so little to one another. This certainly could be a glorious world. Neglected opportunities are piled sky high. I have not met any intelligent girls out here. Before I left Hollywood I met a very interesting Polish girl, but it might have been better if I hadn't. I have an endless hunger for good music, but it is hard to hear good music anywhere unless you are wealthy. In Hollywood I knew, and knew of, several people with fine orthophonic victrolas and whole cabinets full of symphonies, but all these people were either effeminately queer or impossible in some other way, so I did not hear their music.

Unlike you, I do not have to pay for gasoline and haircuts. However, I have to buy grain for my horses, and my clothes must be frequently replaced. My shoes wear out, my shirts and trousers tear, and occasionally equipment must be purchased. A cowman cut my hair three weeks ago. Food is extremely costly on the reservation.

My life in Arizona has much more uncertainty than it would have at home. The low spots are fearfully low, but I have learned that they do not last, and a few glorious moments make me forget them completely.

It seems rather late, but I think I shall continue to Mesa Verde by way of Roundrock, Red Rock, and Shiprock. I'll take my time going through Canyon de Chelly and Canyon del Muerto. I suppose Shiprock, New Mexico, will be my next address. I'll be here a day or so but you probably won't get this letter for a week. If you write there, be sure to put "Return after two months" or something like that, so they won't return it if I don't call for it in a week. It is over a hundred miles of rough traveling by my route, but I'll probably be there within a month, perhaps much sooner. I'll see Lukachukai, which I have heard is very beautiful. There is much wild backcountry.

The night before last, near the lake, I made camp by moonlight. Inky clouds swept across the sky, wild winds whiffed by. Lightning flashed and thunder muttered ominously. Some bulls nearby roared like lions. The storm blew, and to my ears sounded like hyenas, or a frightened heard of goats.

For the time I am among friends, in beautiful surroundings, with plenty to eat and think about. I hope you're in the same condition or better.

Love from your brother,
Everett

I have been thinking more and more that I shall always be a lone wanderer of the wilderness. God, how the trail lures me. You cannot comprehend its resistless fascination for me. After all the lone trail is the best. I hope I'll be able to buy good horses and a better saddle. I'll never stop wandering. And when the time comes to die, I'll find the wildest, loneliest, most desolate spot there is.

The Wild Calls to Me

God, how the wild calls to me. There can be no other life for me but that of the lone wilderness wanderer. It has an irresistible fascination. The lone trail is the best for me.

—Diary entry, Canyon de Chelly, 12 July 1932

Canyon de Chelly, as seen from a tourist viewpoint, looking west.
Photo by W.L. Rusho.

There was a hawk's nest in the treetop. I cooked some sweetbread and read the letters of Mendelssohn, Wagner, Liszt, W.W. Story, and Jules Breton. After it had cooled a little and the horses had grazed awhile, I grained them and went onward. The road followed the rim of Beautiful Valley. My water was quite gone. I had been misinformed about the distance to Behikatso Lake. I met a car and the occupants told me it was five more miles to the lake. They had no water. Before long I left the road and "followed the gleam." There were gullies and ridges to cross. Finally I came to a dry lake. The alkali glittered like water. Close by was the lake. I looked prayerfully across the wide waters while the horses drank. I was in another land. I could hear some horses on the other side splashing as I drank. I waded in and filled two canteens, then led my horses toward the road. Grass and water are never found together in the sheep country. I saw a small snake wiggle away. The moon rose. I stopped on a grassy knoll. There was no firewood, only a few dry weeds. Fortunately I found the remains of a summer hogan and used them for firewood. Just as I was ready to eat, it began to rain. I covered camp in a hurry and when I was half through eating, the storm passed over. Thunder still muttered and the sounds of an African jungle accompanied it. Some bulls roared just like lions and a band of goats, frightened by the lightning, sounded like hyenas, in the distance. It was decidedly weird.

—Diary entry south of Chinle, Navajo Reservation
10 July 1932

July 25
Mesa Verde

Dearest Bill,

This letter is written high up in the Lukachukai Mountains, on the New Mexico border. I have just returned from a swim in the lake below my camp. There are a hundred small lakes nearby. The mountainsides are green with aspen glades and black with firs and pines. Yesterday I saw a big brown bear ambling into the forest depths.

I wish that you could have been with me in Canyon de Chelly and Canyon del Muerto. How they would have delighted you! I'm sure you have never seen anything like them. Words are futile to describe them.

I've had a wide variety of experiences now, cutting hay with a scythe, hoeing corn, and the like. For several days I lived with the Navajos. I've now killed seven rattlesnakes this year. The fastest traveling I've done was forty miles in a day and a half— from Ganado to Chin Lee.

I went up Canyon de Chelly past the last Indian settlements, then came part way back and lived in a hogan for five days. You speak of ruins. They are very numerous in the canyons, and I saw several which were untouched, but they were inaccessible. In almost all the ruins, the walls and the cliff above have fallen down covering up most of the relics. One can find things in almost any ruin by digging, but the dust makes one sick—a mask is required. I scratched around with a stick in one kiva and uncovered dozens of soapweed cords, two headstraps, coated with pinyon pitch, abundance of corn, pumpkin shells, and pottery chips. I found fine arrowheads on the slope, but none were perfect. They were made of petrified wood for the most part.

Canyon del Muerto gave me a strange sense of unreality. For the first few miles the walls come sheer to the sandy floor. Cliff dwellings are in every cranny. There are drawings of deer and antelope, devils, snakes, scorpions, turkeys, and hand prints, in white, red, brown, yellow, and grey. I bought a saddle blanket from old Dilatsi (yellow moustache) whom I had met last year. His daughter was just adding the last tassel when I came. I went beyond the last Navajo hogans and spent a day in solitude.

Then I saddled old Nuflo, my white horse and led Jonathan (also old) up the side canyon under the dwelling where I found the necklace last year. We started up a steep trail, but halfway up, Jonathan fell down and couldn't get up. I unpacked him, but when I pulled out the pack saddle, he slid off the trail and rolled over three times before he could stop himself. I packed Nuflo and led Jonathan up the canyon a few miles to a grassy spot, and camped. Jonathan wouldn't eat. I doctored his cuts and he stood still awhile, then he walked around in circles with his head up. Finally he ran sidewise like an athlete putting the shot, but his legs buckled under, and he fell to his side in a clump of cactus. He never got up. For him, Canyon del Muerto was indeed the Canyon of Death—the end of the trail, for a gentle old packhorse.

I saddled Nuflo and galloped up the canyon, riding in the old Frazier saddle for the last time. I stopped him under a high perched cliff dwelling, shouldered the saddle, and toilsomely ascended to the dwelling where I found the baby board last year. No one had been in it since then. I cached the saddle in an old corn bin, leaving it for the ghosts of the cliffdwellers to guard. As I climbed down from the "asoaze bekin" loud peals of thunder crashed and reverberated in the narrow canyon. I was wet to the skin by the time I reached Nuflo, and the dry stream-bed was a torrent when I reached the pack. The sky opened wide, water cascaded down the cliffs in muddy floods, I took a last look at Jon, loaded old Nuflo, and waded up the canyon. By evening I was nearly at its source at Sehili. I camped in a dry cave, made a meal of mutton and namskadi, and watched the stars appear in the fir tops.

Everett

Serene and Tempestuous Days

I wandered through the Painted Desert and spent days serene and tempestuous in Canyon de Chelly, then traveled up Canyon del Muerto in the shadow of sheer, incurving cliffs, breathtakingly chiseled and gloriously colored. I passed the last Navajo encampments and stopped for a space in an abandoned hogan constructed of smooth clean-limbed cottonwood, with singing water at the door and sighing leaves overhead. Tall, gracefully arched trees screened the turquoise sky with a glistening pattern of dappled green; above and beyond were the gorgeous vermilion cliffs.

All day I would brood in the cool of the hogan, lying on the diamond-figured saddle blanket I bought from old Dilatsi. Beneath it was a swirl of crisp brown leaves, over the earthen floor. Now and again a trickle of sand pouring through a crack in the roof of logs would rustle the dry leaves, and the circle of sunshine from the skylight would move from hour to hour.

At evening I would go out into the glade and climb high above the river to the base of the cliff. I would gather scarlet flowers and come down when the stars gleamed softly. Sighing winds would eddy down the canyon, swaying the tree tops. Then the leaves would cease their trembling; only the sound of rippling water would continue, and the spirit of peace and somnolence would pervade and the red embers of my fire one by one turned black and shadows deepened into a gently surging slumber.

The time for leaving came. I decided to climb out of the canyon and ride to the Lukachukais of New Mexico. On a steep, tortuous trail, Jonathan, my meek, lovable old pack horse missed his footing and fell. For him it was indeed the Canyon of Death.

So I took a last wild ride in my old saddle, loped Nuflo to a place below a crumbling cliff dwelling that is never visited, climbed the steep slope shouldering my saddle, and cached it in a prehistoric corn bin beside a cliff-dweller's cradle. There I left it, to be guarded by the spirits of the ancient dead.

As I stalked down from the high perched ruin, lightning flashed out from the darkening sky; thunder rolled and reverberated in the narrow canyon. A vivid arrow flare of piercing brilliancy struck down at the red cliffs, ricocheting with a sickening whine, like a hurtling shell. With a grinding, grating sound, a mass of rock slid down the cliffside.

In a moment the cloudburst came. The water cascaded from the gleaming rocks and poured frothily from a thousand sources into the plunging stream. I flung the pack on Nuflo's wet back and lashed down the stiff tarpaulin. Afoot, I breasted the foaming torrent, Nuflo following obediently. For hours I trudged upstream, until at dusk I reached the head of the canyon, camping in a dry cave.

—Portion of an essay

Everett and his packhorse at Mesa Verde, 1932.

The Clouds Have Gone; the Stars Gleam Through

Pines and firs were on the canyon floor, and there was one clump of aspens. At long last the canyon walls were lower, but we did not find a way out. Finally I saw sheep tracks, the print of bare feet, and when I found a dry cave, I stopped, for we were both very weary.

There is good grass for Nuflo. I climbed out and saw a range of purple mountains and buttes—doubtless the Lukachukais. An Indian was whistling a herd of sheep. I found a trail leading out of the canyon and returned to camp. It was late. The skies were murky, and I had not eaten since morning, so I fried some mutton and sweetbread. Then I read Browning and pondered.

How strange is reality! In the morning I shall not ride. I don't think I'll buy another horse—I haven't the money and one will do. Having only Nuflo, I'll care for him more solicitously. He'll have more oats, there'll be no more rope hobblers. I put the saddle cinch on the pack saddle and left the other in the cliff dwelling.

If I had not attempted the steep hill, Jonathan might yet be serving me, but he behaved strangely the last few days.

I sang tragic songs, looked into the coals of my campfire, listened to the song of the crickets, the murmur of the water, the clatter of Nuflo's bell (yo asoyu), and the sound of the grass being munched.

Somehow Jonathan's death has not disheartened me. I feel better for accepting the challenge to proceed without him. His death was certainly dramatic. I shall never forget how he ran sidewise, as if groping for something to lean on, found nothing, crashed to earth, and rolled over.

I don't think anyone will ever find the saddle. The babyboard was where I left it last May, except that the hoops had fallen into the bin. My printing on the board—Evert Rulan, etc.—was almost obscured. The rain washed away my tracks. The saddle is well cached. The ghosts of the cliff dwellers will guard it. I do not think I will return for it, however.

The clouds have gone. Stars gleam through the fir tops. It might be Christmas.

—Diary entry, July 1932

Accident in Mancos Canyon

The trader [at Mancos Creek Trading Post] was a jovial, fat, good-natured fellow. I bought a little grub, drank cool water, and asked about the trail to Mesa Verde. I bought half a watermelon and started upstream. I'd gone a quarter of a mile when the trail led along the edge of a bank in a quite narrow pass with the high bank above and below. I supposed it was passable because it was there. Nuflo went ahead, scraped safely by, but around the turn, the ledge was narrower. There was nothing to do but go on, and Nuflo was within a few yards of safety when at a particularly narrow spot, his kyaks pushed him out and he began to slip off. He lunged up, but once more the pack pushed him off. He clawed the ledge frantically, then fell down into the current of the muddy Mancos. It was deep near the bank and he floundered about and wet his pack. When the kyaks were full of water he could not lift them, and he floundered miserably and floated downstream several yards. He could not stand up. The pack became thoroughly wet.

I stood on the bank, looked to right and left, and exclaimed, "Oh, for God's sake, for God's sake." Then I leaped into the torrent, up to my waist, and tried to help Nuflo up, but he floundered worse than before. I had only fastened the breast-strap by the neck-strap because of a sore spot on his breast. The thin neck-strap broke. Nuflo squirmed and struggled like a dragon-fly casting his skin, and finally stepped out of his cinch. He started off across the creek, but I led him back and tied him to a young cottonwood. Then I wallowed back to wrestle with the pack. I flung off the things tied on top—canteens, groceries, camera, then unhooked a kyak, bore it to the bank while the muddy water sprayed out at the bottom, then got the other. The saddle blankets were heavy. One of them, a red and gray one from Grand Canyon, disappeared. I suppose it will come out at the Gulf of Mexico. I flung the other and the saddle on shore, then heaved at the bedroll. It weighed like lead. I had to try a dozen times before I could get it on the bank.

Nuflo had skinned his legs a little, but already he was unconcernedly munching grass. I hobbled him and took stock of the catastrophe. The camera was soused. The film was wet. I unrolled a little and found that some was dry, so tied it up and put it away. The pictures of Jonathan were on it.

I hung the saddleblankets and sleepingbag on a fence, and wrung them out as best I could, but the alkali hurt my hands. Then I spread out all my spare clothes on the ground, opened my sketch-case (sorry sight!), and spread some of the papers to dry. Most of them are spoiled. The oatmeal was quite ruined. The flashlight batteries were mushy. I tied my lash rope to the lead ropes and strung a line. There was only one tree to tie the end to. The fence runs east and west, did not get the sun. The wreckage was strewn all over the field, drying, but clouds came up and it began to rain. Hastily I piled everything in a heap and threw the tarp over.

I put on my poncho, and chewing wet candy, walked in the rain to the post. There is a footbridge that sways alarmingly and has no side rails. I told my story to the trader. He is a native of North Carolina but has worked in Zuni and Phoenix. A supply truck came and I helped unload watermelons.

I borrowed a pair of socks, a rug, and canvas to sleep in, and returned to camp. I ate watermelon and peanut butter sandwiches, then turned in. Though I had not let it show, I really felt overwhelmed by what had happened.

—Diary entry, July 1932

August 18
Mesa Verde

Dear Father,

I have been staying in the ranger quarters while in the park— there are a dozen rangers, likeable young men. One of them [Fritz Loeffler] went with me over to Wetherill Mesa, where we explored several cliff dwellings. In Long House, I caught a buzzard, and we took his picture. Your letters, packages, and all reached me. You say nothing about the films. Tell me, don't you think some of them were really very good? I think those in Canyon de Chelly and del Muerto were very successful.

That is unfortunate that your salary was cut again. I cashed the Shiprock money order here without trouble. I have not really been suffering. Here in the park I have been eating at the government mess hall frequently. The meals are very good— thirty-seven cents each. I came down Ute Canyon to the Mancos River yesterday and up Navajo Canyon into the park again. Then Jim English, the horse wrangler here, helped me take off Nuflo's shoes, and I turned him loose. He is too old—his teeth are worn down so that he can hardly eat. His back was getting sore too.

If there is clear weather, I intend to hike over to Wild Horse Mesa tomorrow and spend a few days there. It has rained, the last few

Everett displays a live buzzard he caught in Long House, Wetherill Mesa, Mesa Verde, 1932.

days. While I was in Ute Canyon a cloudburst came down, the first I have seen. I heard a rumbling and roaring, and ran to the edge of the stream bed. Below was the dry canyon floor, above was a foaming, boiling, brown torrent, rolling sticks and trash ahead of it, coming down like lava from a volcano. Soon it rushed past, and for several hours there was a torrent. By morning the stream was dry again. I found a pretty little arrow point of obsidian in a Pueblo ruin on the mesa.

I don't know how much longer I shall be here, but when I leave, I'll be starting home, I expect. I am just getting to know the people here—some of them are very likeable. I don't feel in the mood for a big change now, but it is bound to come. I guess I do not feel as oppressed by poverty here as I would in the city— there, lack of money seems to paralyze one; it closes all roads. I shall look forward to concerts and symphonies, and use the library extensively. I'll want to paint, but before I could do that, I'd like to purchase a complete set of oils and camera again—that would run into money. I'd like to play tennis too, but I'd have to buy a racket. It might, as you suggest, be profitable to spend a week in Red Rock Canyon.

I don't feel that I have the right spirit for junior college, at all. You spoke of my aloofness before. That is enforced—I want friends as much as anyone, but my ideals of friendship make it very difficult to find true friends. Four of my best friends have gone to New York, and Bill, Clark, and Cornel have become estranged, while I rather outgrew Dee. That leaves me completely friendless, and it is hard to start from the bottom again.

As to careers, they are vaguer than ever before. I am not as sure that I am an artist. I might try writing my adventures, but the personal element makes that very difficult. I could never endure any position with routine, regular hours, and monotonous work. Unless I am having new experiences, broadening horizons, some sort of change, I cannot feel that life is worth living. I can't say I've ever met anyone whom I could really envy, unless it was Edward Weston. Most people's lives do not appeal to me. I'd not be willing to change places with them, great as are the shortcomings of my own position.

I've been having plenty of contrast misery that highlighted the ecstasies that would follow. For the moment, I'm feeling blithe.

Love from Everett

August 25
Mesa Verde

Dear Family,

This afternoon I returned from a four-day trip to Wild Horse Mesa and the North Escarpment. I visited several small cliff dwellings, some of them so situated as to be nearly inaccessible. However I had no accidents. There was one small dwelling which could only be reached by a ledge, from six inches to a foot and a half wide. Below was a sheer drop of fifty feet or so. I had little trouble entering it, being right-handed, but when it came to returning, matters were more complicated. I could not get by the narrow part with my back to the cliff, and if I faced the cliff, I had to go backwards and could not see where to set my foot. After three false starts, I finally reached level sandstone, by crawling on my knees. There was another dwelling near Horse Springs, which could only be reached by worming up a nearly vertical crevice, part of the way hanging by my hands. Even after that, I had to cross a wide creek and crawl under a boulder on the brink. There was a little storehouse right on the face of the cliff, which I did not enter. I found a bone awl in one house.

Usually the Mesa Verde canyons are bone dry, but it had rained heavily for several days, and there was running water in places,

Blockprint by Everett Ruess.

and plenty of pot holes on the flat rocks. There was a waterhole with cattails growing in it above one ruin.

I picked my way up to the mesa top, and followed a grassy way to the north brink of Mesa Verde—8,300 feet high. The sun was just setting behind a smokey cloud, casting a lurid glow over the olive drab terrain. Small lakes and canals gleamed up at the cloudless sky overhead. The lights of Cortez flickered in the distance. Soon a west wind sprang up, blowing a veil of fleecy clouds across the stars.

This morning I headed around several canyons and followed a trail southward on Wetherill Mesa till I reached Rock Springs. After a good rest I crossed Tony Canyon to Long Mesa, followed the narrow ridge peering down on some ruined towers, then into Wickiup Canyon, with Buzzard's Roost, a picturesque dwelling, in a cave on the opposite side. Wickiup led into Navajo Canyon, then I turned north, up Spruce Canyon, up a steep trail past Spruce Tree Dwelling, to park headquarters, just before the post office closed. There was no mail however. It seems to take four or five days for mail to reach the park from California.

I had a good shower in the ranger quarters, and a good meal in the government messhall. It seems that there are no California tourists here now, but I am watching the traffic. I have been wondering what I will do in Hollywood, and while there is no great range of possible activities, I expect to do many things I've never done before.

Tomorrow I'm going to take the trips to Square Tower House, Balcony House, and Cliff Palace again, scanning the horizon for California-bound motorists. Balcony House is an extremely interesting cliff dwelling, splendidly situated.

Love from Everett

Everett hitched rides from Mesa Verde to Gallup, then Williams and on to Grand Canyon. He worked his way to Kingman and had his belongings shipped home to Los Angeles. After being stranded in the middle of the desert and for a time in Needles, he finally got a ride into Los Angeles. Back in Los Angeles in September 1932, Everett enrolled in college, probably at the urging of his father. Although some of his high school grades were low, he was admitted to UCLA through what he called a "fluke." Whatever optimism he may have had, however, was soon dispelled as social and academic pressures closed in. In December he confided that he had not been successful in college and did not belong. His grades were good in English and geology, which was not surprising, considering his experiences, but he did poorly at history, philosophy, and military drill.

After completing one semester, he declined to re-register at UCLA in February, but waited instead for the warm weather of 1933, in which he planned long visits to the high Sierras and, later, to San Francisco.

September 29
Hollywood

Dear Cornel [Tengel],

I have just been listening to Cesar Franck's Symphony in D Minor. I turned out all the lights and danced to it—then to Saint-Saens' bacchanal in *Samson and Delilah*, until everything whirred.

I had some terrific experiences in the wilderness since I wrote you last—overpowering, overwhelming. But then I am always being overwhelmed. I require it to sustain life.

I turned homeward from Colorado early in September, but I stopped for several days at the Grand Canyon, descending alone to the depths, to submerge myself in the steep silence, to be overcome by the fearful immensity, and to drown everything in the deafening roar of the Colorado, watching its snakey writhings and fire-tongued leapings until I was entranced as with the vermilion waste of the Navajo desert and many other places. I feel I must return sometime to Grand Canyon.

But I turned my back to the solitudes and one chill, foggy dawn, I arrived in Los Angeles, where I discarded my sombrero and boots for city garb. For a week I worked intensively in black and white. Also I've been reading, and now, of course, I'm attending UCLA. I got in by rather a fluke. My chemistry grades were low, as you remember, but, in transferring credits from Indiana a *D* in advanced algebra was magically changed to an *A*, which balanced the chemistry deficit.

I am taking philosophy, geology, English history and composition—also R.O.T.C. and gym. I went swimming in the pool today. I've arranged so that I have no classes on Tuesday or Thursday—just three days a week.

Haven't you met Mr. Weston? If not, do it by all means or you are making a mistake. I think he is by far the most interesting and genuine person in Carmel. Tell him that you are a friend of mine.

If you plan to come back, I think you are foolish to pay bus fare. Send your bulky belongings by freight or parcel post, forget your timidity, and rely on the public. There are always exceptions to the general inhospitable type, if you have the fortitude to wait for them.

I expect to return to Carmel some time—mine was a rich experience there. After months in the desert, I long for the seacaves, the crashing breakers in the tunnels, the still, multi-colored lagoons, the jagged cliffs and ancient warrior cypresses. I think I will choose a fine steed and ride on the velvet beach with the waves lapping and drops splashing in the fresh ribbony edge of the surf. I may go up there during the three weeks Christmas vacation. I went up to Red Rock Canyon to paint for a couple of days. Have you been there? Why don't you call on Harry Leon Wilson, Jr.? I think he'd be interested in your stuff and he's an odd chap—own psychology and standpoint.

I'm enthusiastic about a great many things now, a natural reaction to a period not long ago when I was fearfully low, I suppose. I'd like to see you again—I'll plan to visit you if you're staying there.

Why don't you send me the best of what you've written, and I'll send you some prints.

Sweepingly,
Everett

I hope it rains. I will sit on a granite rock with my back to a twisted cypress, and stare endlessly at the fighting grey water.

Just to think of the broad expanse of the lake, mysteriously vast at twilight, soothes me.

When the Christmas vacations arrived, Everett took off for Carmel, apparently glad to leave his studies behind and become re-acquainted with the beauties of the land and sea he had learned to love on his previous trip.

December
Carmel

Dear Family,

After an adventurous trip I arrived here Sunday morning, and I'm staying at the Greene's house. Theirs is a fine family—Anne and Betty are splendid girls. Mr. Weston is busy doing Christmas orders. I sold five Christmas cards—sea horses—for ninety cents. Now it is raining so I had to stop going the rounds. I'm just as enthusiastic as ever over Carmel.

Love Everett

December 26
Carmel

Dear Bill,

On my way up here I saw a coyote on the Malibu estate, a group of beautiful egrets at Point Mugu, and an owl of some kind. I was just waking from a pleasant sleep in a haystack near Salinas when I saw the owl, perched like a carved block of wood, atop a derrick. The morning sun poked through a cloud and a level beam shone in the old bird's eyes. He turned his head around and about, then flew soundlessly off. The next moment, when I was contemplating the Pacific, the farmer drove up in a truck, to pitch away my haystack. He was quite good natured about finding me.

Today I went over to Monterey. I watched the young men of war striding jauntily down the street, and riding their spirited horses. I made sketches of some groups of hobos encamped by the railroad.

It is very interesting the way the sandpipers skitter along, always half an inch ahead of the waves. Also the quail, pelicans, cormorants, woodpeckers, squirrels, and deer are engaging. I saw a doe this morning that switched her tail like an angry cat. It looked wrong, somehow.

I've not accomplished much. It is always too cold to sketch carefully—my fingers shiver and I have paper after paper covered with wavy, erratic lines which are hard to decipher. I've been constantly occupied however, if only in absorbing my surroundings. Yesterday I was at Point Lobos.

I tried out a new dish a few nights ago—squid. After you remove the head, the ink, the white mucous substance, and the cellophane wrapper, you have what looks like a piece of flat rubber coated with white enamel. It tastes as it looks, I think. A few days ago I pruned a very tall pine tree. I sold some Christmas cards.

Everett

Sausalito, Tamales Bay, Portuguese Fishing Shack. *Blockprint by Everett Ruess.*

THE LETTERS

◆5◆

1933

Dwarf Pines of the Sierra. *Blockprint by Everett Ruess.*

March 23
Hollywood

Dear Fritz [Loeffler],

I was quite delighted to find your letter last week. I was probably just as surprised as you were to receive my print. You don't know how good it makes me feel to know that someone is truly enjoying something I have made. I appreciate the picture you sent me very much too. I have made about a dozen prints this year, all of them very different and appealing to different people for different reasons, but after looking them over I have selected one of a cypress grove at Carmel, which I'm sending you in the same mail. I hope you like it.

       Jim English sent me a card at Christmas, and said that old Nuflo was getting fat and coming down to water every day with the other horses. I have visited Doc Rice a few times at the hospital downtown, and watched him assist in an appendectomy case once. He plans to loiter through Colorado this fall before taking an internship in the Bellevue (I think) Hospital in New York.

When I left Mesa Verde, as you probably know, I got a ride to Gallup with a tourist going to Grand Canyon. I had only two or three dollars then. You may remember that certain of the rangers were amused at my idea of getting a ride with all my dunnage, but I persuaded an unwilling chauffeur to take me on as far as Williams. Then he wanted to drop me again, but helped by my magnetic personality I persuaded him that he was foolish not to take me to the Canyon, which he finally did. There I had him deposit me late at night, and I was very glad to be on my own again. I always enjoy the Grand Canyon, and I couldn't resist going down again, so I swung my pack over my shoulder and went down into the depths of the glowing furnace. I killed a Grand Canyon rattler, and camped in a wonderful little side canyon with a stream. I went along the Tonto trail and down to the writhing Colorado, then did some hiking, climbing out between mid-afternoon and dusk. I had hardly recovered on the following day, when, failing to find a single California-bound tourist who was not overcrowded or inhospitable, I accepted the invitation of an old war veteran to guide him down the abandoned Hermit Trail, for the fun of it. It turned out that he couldn't make the grade, so he stopped halfway down and I ran on down in the dark, rejoining him the next evening. He and his friends, who were prospecting, took me to Kingman, where I shipped my pack boxes and took to the road again. After enduring the inferno of the empty desert for a whole day, I got a ride the last few remaining miles of the distance to Oatman. Later I was fairly stranded in Needles, and was reduced to wiring for help, but the wire was never received and I got a ride straight through, arriving in a dense fog in a strange part of the city.

I hadn't been home a week before I heard the call again, and went inland to Red Rock Canyon for a few days. Then I followed your suggestion and enrolled at U.C.L.A., taking geology, philosophy, English history, English, gym, and military drill. I'm glad I went, but I'm glad it's over. College was a valuable episode, but I didn't let it get a strangle hold on me.

During the three weeks' vacation at Christmas, I went up to Carmel by the Sea, did some good work, and had some splendid experiences among others. I rode a black horse on the cool velvet beach at the edge of the surf, splashing through the salt water at times, and galloping beside the waves.

I went back to school in January and finished the semester last month. It seems ages ago.

I have been taking a self-prescribed course in human relations, and have taken a more than usual interest in music of late. Music means more to me than any other art, I think. Have you been enjoying your violin? I have several friends with fine victrolas and recorded music, and I have some myself and can borrow more. I've been reading heavily too—philosophy, poetry, travel, psychology, etc.

Also, I have been writing occasionally. You might be interested in an essay I wrote today. I'll quote you a portion.

"Work is a malevolent goddess, made impossibly conceited by unlimited and untempered flattery. She does not even make any effort to attract new lovers, knowing that no matter how insolent and indifferent she is to them, they will cast themselves on her sacrificial pyre unasked.

"It may not mean much to her who has everything she could want already, but I am vain enough to hope that she is nettled when, strolling insouciantly through her temple, I raise my eyebrows in amused contempt as I look at her marble eyelids, and walking with a slight swagger, feeling her hostile eyes boring through my back, I saunter gracefully out of the dim, reeking temple. When I am bowled over and trampled upon by the contemptible fools who rush madly to cast themselves upon her pyre, my face flushes to the roots of my hair, but I do not look back to see the evil leer in the eyes of the thwarted goddess as I pick myself up, flick decorously at my smirched clothes, and thread my way past the pitiable throngs swarming to her sacrificial altar.

"Although thousands are going in and I am the only one going out, I go my way firm in my inner convictions, though for a second there is a wry twist to my lips and a swifter beating of the heart in unwilling trepidation, as I pause at the portals. Then, nostrils dilated in derision as I meet the eyes of the malignantly leering goddess for the last time, I go forth alone into the outer sunlight where I meet no one save straggling contemptible fools who are hastening anxiously to the temple, eyeing me askance as they pass. It may be that I am more pathetic in my solitary independence than they in their submission, but I have left the temple irrevocably behind me. Lone and proud I fare forth into the sunlight."

That is just one section and really is not self-explanatory, but maybe it will amuse you.

In a month or so when it is hot, I am going to shoulder my pack and go up into the Sierras, with some rice and oatmeal, a few books, paper, and paints. It will be good for me to be on the trail again. A friend of mine is just preparing for a trip to Utah, and it is hard for me to stay. After the Sierras, I may stay in San Francisco and have the experience of another city. Perhaps later I'll be up the Coast. Next year I expect to spend almost the whole year in the red wastes of the Navajo country, painting industriously.

Let me end on the same note with which I began and say that I was certainly glad to have your letter, and let me hear from you again.

Your friend,
Everett

March 31
836 N. Kingsley Dr.
Hollywood

Dear Bob [surname unknown],

How little you know me to think that I could still be in the University! How could a lofty, unconquerable soul like mine remain imprisoned in that academic backwater, wherein all but the most docile wallow in a hopeless slough? You do me wrong, Robin; my noble spirit is crestfallen at the knowledge of such misinterpretation.

It seems that eons have elapsed since the academic episode was closed, though it is less than two months. I was no quitter, but stayed on the sinking ship 'till the end of the semester, acquitting myself honorably if not creditably. I was awarded *D*s in history, philosophy, and military drill, though I think I got more than most *D* students out of those classes. I did well in geology, and I was surprised to receive a *B* in English. I had not turned in any essay cards or notes and was remiss in several other respects. Needless to say, my opinion of Mr. Bock has risen greatly. I am obliged to respect him highly for his judgment and vision. In spite of all his shortcomings and handicaps he was able to see that here was a student of unusually high calibre! *Let us congratulate him* on his insight!!

I don't think you were at the school when T.S. Eliot, our poet of decadence, spoke. It was quite amusing, and he matched my conception of J. Alfred Prufrock (you should read his love song if you haven't).

Even after climbing out of the maelstrom of college, I find that life is still awhirl, though no longer a swirl. I have, however, been on several Bacchic revels and musical orgies. (Admire the irreproachable logic of my sentence and thought sequences, or else turn aside and hide your smiles.)

The Tahitian idyll died of itself. A friend invited me to stay on his plantation there, but I decided that I am too young and vital to let the lotus blood get into my veins. Furthermore, I don't have the small agglomeration of cash which would so greatly facilitate the venture. Also, I was disillusioned about the islands in several respects.

As it is, I have been passing time pleasantly, reading copiously, studying personalities, working out blockprints, and dabbling with the typewriter. I'm enclosing a recent essay which may amuse you. Also, I've had my fill of concerts, and seen Wigman and Kreutzberg gyrate fluently.

In a month or so, when the lowlands are swimming in the heat, I am hitting the trail again, this time to traverse the length of the Sierras with a few books, pencil, paper, and paints, and some rice and jerky in my packsack. After the mountains, I expect to peruse San Francisco.

If chance, will, or destiny blows me out your way, I'll visit you, be sure. Meanwhile, do you make a similar resolve regarding me, and let me know how you react to this febrile frippery.

Your friend,
Everett

While in the Sierras, Everett made first mention of the depression that was to recur, apparently with increasing frequency. In this letter he states, "Every once in a while I feel quite ecstatic, but I slip out of such moods quite easily." In the next letter he writes to his family, "No, I am in no danger of a nervous breakdown at present," as if it was a potential threat of which his parents and brother were aware. The general mood of his letters, however, was still cheery and replete with by now typical Everett Ruess lyric prose on the beauties of nature.

By June 1933, Everett was in the Sierras, fording swollen rivers, climbing trails by moonlight, and riding through rapidly-melting alpine snowbanks.

June 8

Dear Waldo,

Thus far, I have been free of watches and clocks. I never wonder what time it is, because for myself it is always time to live. I've had a number of new experiences, not all intense, but nevertheless enjoyable. I've been meeting people and climbing trails. I was in a snowstorm on a mountain top a few days ago. Life is pleasant, but things will not finally resolve

In Yosemite National Park, ascending the heights.

themselves till I hit the trail for Kern Canyon in a week or so. At the present, the high country is choked with snow. I traded a print for some credit in the store here, and I have a possible buyer for a painting I made on Sunset Rock. I've met several boys from the reforestation camps. They are not a bad lot, but I couldn't bear to be tied down. What I miss most here is intellectual companionship, but that is always difficult to find, and I have met a few interesting individuals.

Don't leave your problems to be solved by Time—the solution might be adverse.

> Your brother,
> Everett

[Salutation and date missing.]

Right now I am sitting on a hill overlooking the Marble Fork of the Kaweah River. The colors are glorious—fleecy white clouds, a clear blue sky, distant blue hills flecked with snow, tall pines all around me, monstrous grey glacial boulders, and patches of sunlit moss on the fir trees. The snowwater rushes and pounds through its rocky channel, tumbling frothily into lucent green pools.

Here I seem to be in my element. Save for the lack of intellectual companionship, which is not utter, and is troublesome wherever I am, and for a few trifling disturbances, I have nothing to lament. More than ever before, I have succeeded in stopping the clock. I need no timepiece, knowing that now is the time to live.

I have lived intensely on several occasions here. Down in Three Rivers, below in the cow country, I rode thirty-five miles in one day, fording a river so swollen with snows that I had to put my feet on the saddle horn. I rode my horse up cliff banks, over unknown canyon trails by moonlight, watched the stars as he groped over the darkened path, and climbed to a lonesome cabin on the skyline. Later I loped for miles on a winding river road, following its pale gleam under tunnels of foliage.

Again I climbed the mountain pass, fought a snowstorm, and scraped through three feet of snow to recover broken trail signs. Then I set my feet and slithered down long snowy aisles, swerving and careening past groves of writhed, snakelike, tortured aspens, and past willow trees with bark of coppery sheen, incense cedar, red fir, and white fir.

A Life

A life
        Is a mirror
Reflecting the road over which it passes.
        Sometimes
When it rains
        The mirror itself is reflected in the road.

—Everett Ruess

June 16
Giant Forest
Sequoia National Forest

Dear Family,

Yesterday I hiked about fifteen miles, up to Heather Lake, Asted Lake, Emerald Lake, and the Watch Tower where I watched an eagle in its nest. I was accompanying the ranger, and I stopped to make some sketches. The sun on the snow was blinding, and I had to squint. My

Living life at its edge.

face and arms were snowburnt. The aspens are just leafing. On the mountain slopes, they grow twisted and writhed like tortured snakes. The snowflowers are out, and the snow is melting rapidly. However, the high passes are still choked with snow, and I won't be able to start for Kern Canyon until almost July. At the present my burros are pastured in Willow Meadow, and I am camped at Lodgepole on the Marble Fork of the Kaveah. I have to move, though, and I think I shall pack up to Willows Meadow or some upland meadow, tomorrow, and stay there for a week or ten days. This morning I came down past Sherman Tree and walked through the forest around Circle Meadow. I took a plunge in a little stream in the redwoods. The sun was warm and the trees were splendid.

Things are just getting under way up here. Earl McKee drove up with Ord Loverin this morning. Loverin has the stock and pack trip concession here, and he is just preparing to bring in his horses. Spring has not yet truly arrived, here. The waterfalls are foaming and plunging down the granite slopes.

I have had little time for idleness as yet. I've been over the trails in several directions, and crossed the park boundary once. I know most of the people here and two of the rangers I find quite intelligent. I met the naturalist today. He has just come, and his two assistants will arrive later. It would almost be a good idea to carry a fountain pen and a bottle of ink, wouldn't it?

My health and complexion have greatly improved, and every once in a while I feel quite ecstatic, but I slip out of such moods quite easily. I hope everything is proceeding harmoniously with you, and let me hear something from you.

Love to all,
Everett

July 5
Giant Forest
Sequoia National Park

Dear Family,

When I came down from the back country, I found the park overrun with holiday tourists. They even came over on my side of the river with their radios and gas lamps, and it was like sleeping on a park bench in Pershing Square. Now they have all gone home, and there is peace again.

I haven't done much painting of late, but I sold a couple of prints the other day. The one of the eucalyptus and the last one of the cypresses on the coastline are quite popular. If you have a chance, you might print some more and send me them.

Today I am loading up on supplies. What with films and other expenses, I will just manage nicely. I'll have some books and things to mail back when I return.

No, I am in no danger of a nervous breakdown at present. How about you?

Love from Everett

August 20
Deadman Canyon
Sequoia National Forest

Dear Mother,

Everything has been proceeding beautifully, and at present I am in the most interesting little canyon I have found in the Sierras. Parallel to it is Cloud Canyon. They converge below to form Roaring River, which flows into King's River.

The elevation here is 10,000 feet, and above is Elizabeth Pass and the Copper Mine, at nearly 13,000 feet. Golden trout and rainbow are in the stream, which flows under snowbanks at its head. There are no fir or sugar pine at this elevation—only lodgepole pine and quaking aspen.

For the last few days, I have been camping with Andy Ferguson and his grandson. He has been in these mountains for fifty years, and was the first to plant trout in the streams. He also started the copper mine above here. In his long and somewhat checkered career, as he says, he has done everything from preaching to bartending.

Betsy and Grandma are enjoying the short hair grass. Grandma bogged down in a morass once, but struggled out again.

A pack train headed for Giant Forest is coming by, so I'll give them this note.

Love from Everett

For a couple of hours I watched the fire. I find sleep unpleasant. I do not yield consciousness without a struggle, as I sleep poorly. I call sleep temporary death.

In a while I begin to feel better. I chanted Navajo and enjoyed the thought of return [to northern Arizona]. I thought of the prints I would cut in San Francisco. Then my soul floated out in song. Cesar Franck's Symphony carried me away, and Brahms and Beethoven followed. Finally, seeing the dreamy mists in the mysterious dark lake with guarding mountains, I succumbed to sleep.

—Diary entry in the Sierra Nevada Mountains, August 28

August 30
Castle Crags

Dear Doris [Myers],

I have been feeling so happy and filled to overflowing with the beauty of life, that I felt I must write to you. It is all a golden dream, with mysterious, high, rushing winds leaning down to caress me, and warm and perfect colors flowing before my eyes. Time and the need of time have ceased entirely. A gentle, dreamy haze fills my soul, the rustling of the aspens lulls my senses, and the surpassing beauty and perfection of everything fills me with quiet joy and a deep pervading love for my world.

My solitude is unbroken. Above, the white, castellated cliffs glitter fairy-like against the turquoise sky. The wild silences have enfolded me unresisting.

Everett on burro, probably taken in 1931.

Beauty and peace have been with me, wherever I have gone. At night I have watched pale granite towers in the dim starlight, aspiring to the powdered sky, tremulous and dreamlike, fantastical in the melting darkness.

I have watched white-maned rapids, shaking their crests in wild abandon, surging, roaring, overwhelming the senses with their white fury, only to froth and foam down the current into lucent green pools, quiet and clear in the mellow sunlight.

On the trail, the musical tinkle of the burro bells mingles with the sound of wind and water, and is only heard subconsciously.

On the lake at night, the crescent moon gleams liquidly in the dark water, mists drift and rise like lifting enchantments, and tall, shadowed peaks stand guard in watchful silence.

These living dreams I wish to share with you, and I want you to know that I have not forgotten.

Love from Everett

[Salutation and date missing.]

During the last few weeks, I have been having the time of my life. Much of the time I feel so exuberant that I can hardly contain myself. The colors are so glorious, the forests so magnificent, the mountains so splendid, and the streams so utterly, wildly, tumultuously, effervescently joyful that to me at least, the world is a riot of intense sensual delight. In addition to all, the people are genial and generous and happy, and everyone seems to be at his best.

With a pack of groceries on my back, I swung irresistibly up the starlit road between the pillared redwoods. I drank at a rushing mountain stream, and strode gallantly up, singing some Dvorak melodies till the forest boomed with my rollicking song. Then the transmuted melody of Beethoven, Brahms, and the *Bolero* rang through the listening forest. I rocked from side to side of the road. I spun around in circles, looking up at the stars, and swung exultantly down the white pathway to adventure. Adventure is for the adventurous.

Oh, I have lived intensely, drinking deep! One day I rode thirty-five miles over mountain trails with cowboy comrades. We forded the swollen rivers putting our feet on the saddle, plunging through the foamy, buffeting snow water, rolling like ships in a heavy sea. We galloped up cliff sides and found our way over unknown trails in the starlight. While my horse groped his way up the darkened mountainside far above the rushing stream, I leaned back in my saddle looking at the towering ranges, the looming ridge above, the intensely brilliant stars, and the waning moon.

We delivered a horse to an outrider at a battered old cabin on the skyline, then in the dim starlight, in the hours before dawn, we came down the mountain. We loped for miles, swerving and wheeling at full speed on a winding river-road, following its pale gleam through tunnels of foliage.

Then I was in a snowstorm on the mountain top, helping a ranger from Alaska to probe for and recover [trail] signs broken and buried in the snow. We sat on our feet and slid down the snowy slopes speeding uncontrollably past mountain lakes, thickets of writhing, snakelike, contorted aspens, and cherry and willow with bark of coppery sheen.

I swam in a deep pool below one waterfall and above another. The granite sides were so slippery that I could hardly draw myself out when I had frolicked enough.

With great enjoyment I read of the unrestrained exploits of Gargantua, Granzousiers, Picrochole, and the monk. The other night

I ate a Gargantuan mess of sandwiches and fried yams while I read about Pantagruel and Panurge, how they discomfited Impgarva and his giants.[12] When the fire faded the embers took on a more intense glow, the trees loomed higher, and the starlight poured straight down.

So now you know how I deport myself. Do you, in your turn, inform me of your various adventures. I hope you two also are on the crest of the wave, or at least not in its trough. Tell me anything.

Irrepressibly,
Everett

September 6
Lake of the Fallen Moon
Sierra National Forest

Dear Father and Mother,

I have been filled for three days with a dreamy intoxication from the serene beauty and perfect solitude.

The lake is almost invisible from above, and only a faint, very steep path leads down to it. Grey cliffs rise sheerly from the other side of the lake, which is deep green, mysterious, and unfathomable.

On a little promontory nearby, I watch the moving panoramas of clouds, the gray mountains dotted with trees, and the long, undulating cloud shadows moving over distant forests. A little waterfall rushes musically down from the cliff. The reassuring tinkle of burro bells sounds nearby.

I shall probably reach Yosemite by October.

Love to all,
Everett

Storm Clouds over the Sierras

I reached the windy cliff ledge just as the first red light gleamed in the east. A smoky-gray light spread along the cloud fringes, and a smoldering orange glowed at the tops of the distant peaks. Then black storm clouds swept down dramatically from the north, enveloping the valleys. One cloudbank detached itself and blew over Mount Hoffman and me with a flurry of snow. Soon it was gone and the westerly sky was clear. I looked down on the western brink, at lakes and snowbanks on the northern cliff, at peaks and stormclouds on the southern slope, to Yosemite Valley, and Tenaya Canyon, walled in by Clouds Rest and Half Dome, and on the eastern escarpment, upon May Lake, Tenaya Lake, like a bronze shield in a flash of sunlight, and the snowy peaks of Tioga.

—Diary entry, 8 October 1933

Despite the frosty morning, Everett is found making a watercolor painting.

The Haunting Beauty of It

The morning sun peeped from behind a cloud to wake me, then hid again. The skies do not worry me now, for I'll soon be below the snowline. I found two good ropes while donkey-wrangling. Soon we were down in the Glen, and how I gloried in it! The stream was wide and quiet, full of deep, green pools, and the banks were lined with aspens in October plumage. The wind, like a cry at my heart, plucked at the yellow leaves and flung them swirling across the path. How I felt the beauty and the transience of it! I remembered September in the Kaibab with sober old Pericles, and the tall aspens raining down gold upon us. Oh, the haunting beauty of it!
—Diary entry, 9 October 1933

October 4
Glacier Point

Dear Family,

The post office clerk discovered a batch of mail which he had been hiding from me, including many letters from you. I have enjoyed the short descriptions you clipped for me. I still have the poem on Solitude you sent, and like it well. I found the prints, and the second five-dollar order. No use to send more prints now, I fear. I tried to make a deal with the film people here, but though they were very enthused over the prints, they could not afford to trade for work.

That night I climbed out of the valley by moonlight and found my way through the dark forests to my meadow at Lost Lake.

Yesterday I was wakened by the lunatic howling of coyotes in broad daylight. I climbed up Half Dome and lunched on an overhanging rock, above the sheer drop fronting Tenaya Canyon. Mirror Lake was a disappointing reddish-brown mud puddle, and the valley was dry and yellow.

This morning I have circled the valley's rim from Nevada Falls to Glacier Point. I had my first good view of Illillette Falls, a white filmy tracery on wet granite. Vernal Falls is a single narrow jet of spray.

Here at the hotel I met Mr. Cuesta, my old friend from Little Yosemite Valley in 1930.

Last night by the fire I was thinking again about San Francisco, and I thought how jolly it would be to rent a little garret on some hilltop, and spend a month or so in devil-may-care wanderings about the city and sea front. I'll make color studies of the tropical fish in the aquarium and hear a few concerts. I have a friend there who is studying medicine at the Stanford U. hospital.

Both my trousers are quite worn out, so please mail the striped grey ones that fit me (not the baggy ones) to El Portal, with instructions to hold a week or two. I'd also like to have another 200-page diary book if you can find one reasonably. You might send five dollars of the October money to El Portal.

I'll put in some aspen leaves when I reach camp at Lost Lake. My bed on the edge of the meadow is encircled by three tall aspens, some lodgepole pine, a white fir, and two or three junipers.

Love from Everett

With his arrival in San Francisco, Everett began what was to become his richest cultural experience, one that was to affect his emotions, his painting, and his writing. He was to be enthralled and enlightened, but also shaken and disturbed. He entered the city as a sensitive youth; he left it four months later as a more mature adult, hoping to make an artistic mark on the world. And if he did not find a clear identity, he at least began to see dim outlines of his rough road ahead.

What Everett was embarking on in San Francisco was a Bohemian life in association with many other artists, where ideas, original concepts, and creativity flowed as the heady wine of California.

107

Granite Towers. *Blockprint by Everett Ruess.*

He once stated that he was living "with an undercurrent of starvation and an overtone of magnificent music." Into it, young Ruess
was swept up and carried along, stimulated and renewed by contact with other sensitive and accomplished individuals. Everett, as
a child, had undoubtedly met artists in company with his mother,
but it is doubtful that he was sufficiently trained in art himself for
these to have made much of an impression. His association with
photographer Edward Weston in 1931 and again in 1932, however,
made a lasting imprint on his awareness. By late 1933, when he
arrived in San Francisco, he had three years of difficult artistic field
work behind him, and he was certainly ready to absorb and
evaluate comments and recommendations of painters,
photographers, musicians, and art gallery administrators.

Typically, Everett showed no reluctance in introducing
himself to those who he thought would be interesting. One cannot really accuse him of excessive ambition or even social climbing, since neither trait is apparent in his letters. More likely it was
simply his old tradition that allowed little awe, and certainly no
reticence, with strangers. His letters do not specify how he met

these people, but he probably just knocked on their doors and introduced himself.

Berkeley
October 17

Dear Family,

I am sitting on the back porch of the Whitnah's, looking out across the Bay. Mrs. Whitnah is in the city, attending a class in interior decorating, but she and Mr. Whitnah and I are going to hear Lincoln Steffens lecture at International House this afternoon.

In a day or so I am going over to locate in the city, and it may be that I'll find a very nice place and new friends on Telegraph Hill.

In El Portal I received your letters, but I did not find time to reply. As I was climbing up from the post office Saturday morning, I went to look at the burros. They were standing in a shadow on the hillside, and two little girls were close by. They were afraid of the donkeys, but at the same time fascinated, and unable to go very far away. I persuaded them that Betsy and Grandma were harmless, and they began petting them, but could not get over the fact that Grandma had no tail.

So I brought down the saddle and they both sat in it, parading ecstatically up and down on the hillslope. Before long, ten more little girls arrived, bubbling over with excitement. They were all delightful children, and it was a pleasure to watch them enjoying the burros. Everyone had a ride on each burro, and wanted more. Toward noon, when it was hot, I let the burros rest, and made the children find something for them. They all went running off and came back with boxes of apples, bags of bread crusts, rabbit oats, and soda crackers.

Then at noon, three small boys came in from their hunting expedition, and had to have their rides. After that we took the burros down to the road and tied them in plain sight in the shadow of an oak, to wait for the buyer. While we sat there on the river bank, one of the boys said he thought he knew where there was a water ouzel's nest, and we went down to look.

We could not find it, but the water was so tempting that we all went in swimming. While I was splashing, I heard shouts from the roadway. The burro buyer had arrived.

He is a school teacher in Visalia whom I met in Sequoia Park. He told me then that he wanted the burros, and finally he decided he would come for them with a trailer, and meet me at El Portal. He gave me what I paid for them. All the children crowded around while we crammed the burros into the trailer.

We reached Merced in the evening, and I bid my friend goodbye. After freighting my kyaks to the city I went over to one of the cheap restaurants frequented by the cow men and the most picturesque characters of the town. I had a good meal for twenty cents, then sat back to watch the show. There were two or three drunks who were very amusing. One of them, a Filipino, kept posturing and wheeling around and around, waving his arms like a dancer. He insisted that he would go home if they'd give him one more drink. After obtaining fifteen or more drinks in this manner, he was still there.

I struck up an acquaintanceship with one of the panhandlers. We walked about the town and went out to the gambling hall together. In front of the pool halls, a big limousine drew up. The barker shouted, "Come and watch those galloping dominoes." We climbed in and were swiftly carried out to the city limits where we entered the den. The men running the different games were all slick and well-dressed, with masque-like faces. One of them shouted all evening, "High, low, up they go, sometimes high and sometimes low." One game interested me. You placed some sort of bet with the operator. He gave you a narrow metal strip, and you put dimes under and over it. Then a Chinaman poured out part of the contents of a bowl of beans on the table. With a curved bamboo stick, he grouped them in fours, and your luck was dependent on the number left over at the last.

At eleven o'clock I went out in the yards and caught the "hot shot" to Sacramento. I struck up with a young cowboy going back to the ranches. For several hours we rode on top, as there were no "empties" or "gondolas." It was a thrilling ride, though cold. At Modesto, we had to do some fast work to keep from being left. At every stop the freight shunts cars back and forth on the sidings, taking on some cars, and leaving others. When we pulled out, one of the fellows found a reefer, and while the cars were gathering speed, we ran the length of the train on top, leaping from one car to another, till we reached it. A reefer is a cooler in a refrigerator car. There is one at each end. This car was full of cantaloupes, so there was no ice in the reefers and the hatches were open. Four of us climbed in and swapped yarns for awhile. At Stockton two of them left, my cowboy friend and an elderly wanderer. A Canadian boy stayed with me. He had been down to Mexico and lost his pal. Now he was homeward bound for Calgary. He is in the militia there. His company is the crack troop in all Canada. They could load a machine gun on a pack horse in two minutes.

We reached Roseville, the division line, at dawn. The crescent moon faded, and stars paled as we climbed down into the yards. I bought my companion a breakfast, and we waited for our freights while he remade my pack, hobo style. The northbound came first, and I watched my friend out of sight.

In due time, only two hours behind schedule, the Oakland freight was ready. I had watched them making it up in the yards, for some time. I climbed on a gondola with a New York bum. A gondola is a flat car, without a roof. This was empty. We rolled along at a smart rate when we approached the Bay in the afternoon. On the open stretches, we did better than forty miles per hour, and the wind from the salt marshes fanned our faces and blew back our hair. I dismounted in Oakland, and climbed up the hill to the Whitnah's.

Love from Everett

October 24
San Francisco

Dear Family,

The last week has been rather trying, and I have but just succeeded in establishing myself. Now, however, all is optimism. I have a pleasant room at the Broadway Apartments on Polk Street at Broadway. I could not find any rooms near Telegraph Hill, where Mrs. Whitnah had directed me.

I enjoyed my walk in the morning sunlight, on my way here to the post office. Here I found an accumulation of letters. I'm glad that all is well at home. Glad you are sending the package, though perhaps I asked for more than I need. I forgot to request pajamas, however.

Two nights ago I watched the sunset from the tower at Telegraph Hill. It was certainly splendid, with the skyscrapers, which I missed in Los Angeles, and the islands in the sunset sea.

I met Maynard Dixon in his studio, and shall see him again. I have liked his work for a long time, and the man himself is interesting. He has been through much of the Arizona country that I covered, and knows some of the same old-timers.

To educate myself, I heard Mischa Elman at the Opera House and saw Paul Robeson in The Emperor Jones, my first movie since May. Both were fine. There were some excellent shots of Robeson, though I felt the producers neglected many opportunities for artistic effects.

This morning I am securing a library card and getting one of my kyak boxes at the freight depot.

All's well.

Love from Everett

October 24
2048 Polk St.

Dear Father and Mother,

I was glad to find your letter and Mother's package waiting for me this evening.

This has been an interesting day. This morning I went to a couple of galleries with my prints, which I had mounted, and Paul Elder took them all on consignment.[13] They seemed pleased to have them.

Then I went to Cornel Tengel's place on Telegraph Hill. I met him at the library the other day and we had a jolly time together. He has been here since September. He has quite the fictive sort of residence, in a little shack on stilts above a chicken-littered courtyard, off an alley. An Italian murderer has the shack built onto his. If I can borrow a bicycle, we are going on a two- or three-day trip into Marin County.

Then I met Mr. Schermerhorn and George Brammer, and we drove to Watsonville with a couple of boys. We went over the Skyline

Granite and Cypress. *Blockprint by Everett Ruess.*

Boulevard, and I got some good snapshots of oak trees and horses. The three of us had great fun together.

On Tuesday, Mrs. Dixon [Dorothea Lange] and I went to Berkeley to hear Rockwell Kent. We enjoyed seeing the cuts and paintings shown very large on a screen. Much of my time has been occupied making mounts for my prints. The Eopa seemed to work.

On Sunday I plan to see *Le Coq d'Or*, Rimsky-Korsakov's opera.

I have one print design nearly ready to cut, and have been rehashing two others.

Love to all,
Everett

Without doubt the two people that most influenced Everett during his San Francisco visit were the painter Maynard Dixon and Dixon's wife, photographer Dorothea Lange. During these Depression years American artists were struggling financially, but Dixon, age fifty-eight, was at his career peak, painting many murals and paintings using scenes from the desert Southwest for subjects.[14] Among all of the nation's artists, Dixon was one of the better known, and Everett was acquainted with his work. Moreover, Dixon's painting subjects were scenes similar, and often close in proximity, to those sketched by Everett in northern Arizona.

Dorothea Lange, then thirty-eight years old, was fairly well-known regionally, but she had not yet established the reputation she made in the late 1930s as one of a team of Farm Security Administration photographers who recorded the human tragedy of the Depression in the Dust Bowl.[15] In Everett, Dorothea apparently recognized talent and ability worthy of her time and attention. She may also have felt that young Everett could use a little mothering.

October 28
San Francisco

Dear Family,

The packages reached me all right a few days ago. Some of the inclusions were very thoughtful. I also discovered the cookies in the other package.

Write from now on to 2048 Polk St., Broadway Apartments.

The fog has closed in during the last few days. I did some work at the Aquarium, also at Telegraph Hill. There were some good exhibits of woodcuts and prints at the museum—Paul Landacre, Mason, and others. I've been reading with great enjoyment the *Autobiography of Lincoln Steffens.* Have you read it?

Love from Everett

October 29
2048 Polk Street
San Francisco

Dear Family,

All's well, and I'm on the crest of the wave again as I hope you are, too. I have finally found myself, and have been busy painting all day.

Yesterday I heard four symphonies, and then spent the afternoon and evening with Maynard Dixon, his wife Dorothea, Ernst Bacon, a musician, and some other artists. I had a grand time, and it was certainly good to be among friends and artists again.

Last night, with the Dixons, I ate my first cooked meal in over a week. I have been living on raw carrots and banana sandwiches.

I've not heard from you since the day before receiving the packages. In regard to the remittance, I suggest that you put $10 of the October money (if you haven't already sent it) in the bank for me against the desert trip, and send on the other $15 odd as soon as you can. I'll pay my own rent (ten dollars) and I think I can make out on the rest.

It has been raining all day.

I've had great fun exploring the city and running up and down the hills. By now I know my geography fairly well. I enjoy the fog, too. I'm beginning to make friends now, and I think I shall enjoy the city more and more.

Love from Everett

October 31
San Francisco

Dear Father, Mother, and Waldo,

I have just returned from a concert, which I heard with Uncle Emerson.[16] He is as jolly as ever, and it was an intensely enjoyable evening I had with him. He sends his regards to you all. The concert was the music of Italy, chamber music at the Community Playhouse. There was a very fine piece by Pizetti, a modern Italian composer.

Uncle Emerson lives just two or three blocks away from me. He is in the city now for the first time in three weeks. We talked about music, conservation, and economics. He is so busy that I probably shan't see much of him. He expects to leave soon again, too.

Today I made a few unsuccessful attempts to hawk my wares. People admired my stuff, however, and gave good criticisms. Uncle Emerson gave me something to chew on, too; his was quite a thorough criticism. Ansel Adams waxed very enthusiastic about my black and white work.[17] He could not exhibit it in his gallery, but he gave me a number of suggestions which I am following out. He is going to trade me one of his photographs for one of my prints. The photograph I chose is of a mysterious lake at Kaweah Gap, where I was this July. Sheer granite walls shelve into a dark lake with ice at the base of the cliff. It is very fantastical.

I finished the first volume of Steffen's autobiography. You were telling me about Kristin Lavransdatter. What sort of book is it? I have been wanting to read one of Sigrid Undset's books, but did not know which one to begin with. They are written in a sequence, are they not?

I did a little writing last night, and this morning I made another plan for a print, a bold design of Banner Peak at sunrise.

Tomorrow night I shall have dinner with the Ormonds, people whom I met in Yosemite. They are people full of vitality. Mr. Ormond is in the Education Department in some capacity.

On Thursday I have a sitting with Dorothea Lange, who wants to make some photographic studies. On Sunday I am invited to dinner with the Jory's in Mill Valley. Mr. Jory works for the American Trust Company here. I met him and his wife in Kern Canyon in July. They were vacationing with a couple of pack burros from Mineral King.

It's hardly likely I shall continue to be in such demand, but for the present I am quite busy, and full of plans and ideas to keep me going some while. Whenever I stop working, I have plenty of reading I have been wanting to do.

The climate has been cool and bracing. It rained hard yesterday. I had to wear my sombrero and slicker.

The children had a Halloween parade down Polk Street tonight. They were having a gay time with much excitement.

Love to all,
Everett

November 2

Dear Family,

Your letters have been a pleasure to read. Often, if I am in my room all day, old Julius brings them up to me, and the other day he brought me one from Waldo.

I sold a couple of prints the other day, but what with concerts, rent, and art materials, it was gone in less time than it takes to tell. I took Cornel to see Rimsky-Korsakov's opera, *The Golden Cockerel.* I was not able to go with him on his trip up the coast. Yesterday I had a delightful time at the Schermerhorn's. Tonight I am taking George Brammer to see *Dr. Faust,* a puppet play of Perry Dilley's. I traded a couple of prints for the tickets.

I have been having worthwhile experiences here in the city, and I'm very glad to be here instead of in Hollywood. I've had the opportunities to know this city fairly well, in many aspects, but much remains to be discovered. As yet I've not had time to go back to Berkeley, and I probably won't for some while. I have to get busy with my linoleum cuts now. I've cut one, but three more remain, and also two or three small things that must be done before Christmas. I hope you have more of the envelopes, cardboard, and mount paper that I used last year, as I shall need them soon. I may send you a small block to print on post cards for me. It was Waldo who borrowed *Ulysses.* Ask him to return it to Mrs. Southard. I went to Paul Elder's today, and they haven't even got around to putting my stuff up, so naturally they hadn't sold any.

Of the list of books you sent, I have read and enjoyed *South Wind, Candide, Green Mansions, O'Neill's Place, The Brothers Karamazov, The Dance of Life, Magic Mountain, Arabian Nights,* and others. Some on the list, like *The Golden Ass,* I do not consider literature.

I have been enjoying my poetry anthology and lending my other books. I am reading now a book of *Nine O'Neill Plays* which Charles Schermerhorn lent me. I have a phonograph in my room, lent me by the plumber, so I am enjoying my music and sharing it.

I went over to Cornel's early this afternoon, and after some fun at his place, we climbed from Telegraph Hill to Russian Hill, and have been listening to music in my room. I just let him take a bath in the tub here, as he has none in his shack.

Edwin Markham is speaking here tonight, but I won't be able to hear him.

The Hospital Association wants me to pay them $1.65 December 1. Their physician told me that my complexion is due almost

116

entirely to overaction of the skin glands, and has nothing to do with diet. He, like the other doctors, thinks the condition is unavoidable. Raw carrots, he said, are extremely hard to digest, and should not be eaten.

Clouds are gathering here, but it has not rained yet. The moon is nearly full.

Love from Everett

November 2

Dear Mother and Father,

I was glad to find your letters, yesterday and the day before.

Mother asks about my room: I have just acquired a Japanese print, an old one of Hiroshige, for it. I traded one of my prints to the Ormonds for it, and mounted it yesterday. Three of my prints are up also, and before long I shall have a photograph or two. My sombrero, too, is on the wall.

In a corner are my kyaks, and on the floor is my Navajo saddle blanket. The table at which I work is between the two big windows, which overlook the street. At night, the reflection from a neon light casts a rosy glow on the curtains.

There are no cooking possibilities, and I do not have to eat out all the time either. I have eaten three cooked meals in the last two weeks. I get along famously on fruit, sandwiches, and milk.

I have now made about a dozen India ink sketches for blockprints. Half a dozen of them are worth cutting, I think. Yesterday I met Stanley Helmore who has a blockprint press and will print mine for me if I say. What are Mr. Bryant's rates for my five by seven blocks?

I am all out of the prints of the Morro Bay oaks. Look in my file of prints, and send me eight or ten. Also a few of Radiation, Monument Valley, and several of Wild Conthine (the last Monterey print, like yours). You might send two or three more linoleums with blocks, also one small block and piece of linoleum, about this size. Send also the Kitikata papers in my files. It might be well to send more too. It may be difficult to obtain here.

I have done two good watercolors and a couple of black and white crayon sketches. I use a china marking pencil and it gives plenty of gradation without smudging. There is a studio on Telegraph Hill where they hold life classes for fifty cents an evening. It is good practice, and I may go sometime to brush up on my drawing.

I met Mr. Burrell, who won the prize last year for the fifty best prints of the year. (I'm not sure what prize. His was an etching of a windmill.) He admired my stuff and said I should have had it exhibited in the American Etchers and Print Makers Society.

The other day I went through the Legion of Honor Building. Nothing outstanding, though, except some things of Warren Newcombe, most of which I saw down South. (Los Angeles is way down South, now.) Wolo's stuff is being shown at Courvoisier's.

I bought two little glasses of blue and purple, made in Mexico. They are like wine for the soul when held up to the light, the colors are so beautiful.

Love from Everett

November 5

Dear Mother,

The other day I had perhaps the best art lesson I ever had; a lesson in simplicity from Maynard Dixon. That time I really did learn something, I think, and I have been trying to apply what I learned. The main thing Maynard did was to make me see what is meaningless in a picture, and have the strength to eliminate it; and see what was significant, and how to stress it. This he showed me with little scraps of black and white paper, placed over my drawings. You should try it and follow up the suggestions it gives you.

The Dixons are going to move into a house in a month or two, and I may help them and earn a room in it. They have a phonograph, but hardly any records, so I wish that you would send me my album of the twelve or thirteen records which I bought this spring, unless you are really using them yourself. I'm enclosing half a dollar for postage; I hope that will be enough. Insure them for twenty dollars, and, naturally you will try to pack them so they don't break. You might wrap them in my black trousers.

This afternoon I had a delightful ride with the Jorys along the coast near Muir Woods and back at sunset over a shoulder of Tamalpais. They have a pleasant little home in a wooded canyon in Mill Valley. I came back in the moonlight, across the bay.

Last night Melvin Johnson, a friend from San Jose whom I took on a pack trip in Sequoia, stopped in to visit, and we had dinner together in Chinatown.

In a few days, I'm going to start cutting my designs.

Love from Everett

November 12

Dear Family,

I have been reading of late: Nikolai Gogol's *Taras Bulba*, a swashbuckling historical story of the Russian Cossacks on the border marches of the Ukraine; *Green Hell*, an Englishman's narrative of exploration in tropical Bolivia; the *Jurgen* of James Branch Cabell, full of sparkling satire; and the poetry of Robinson Jeffers, Edna St. Vincent Millay, and Elinor Argile.

This afternoon I walked up the hill to the park between Laguna and Gough streets. On the way I passed a splendid array of fuchsias in bloom. There were many varieties, and I was quite interested, as I had never observed the plant before. On the hill I started work on a study of an old watertower and a eucalyptus, but was forestalled from my colors by sunset.

Last night, having spent a dollar for standing room in the balcony, I too went to Grand Opera, *Tristan und Isolde*. Between the acts I threaded my way among the plutocrats of society, studying orchids and roses. I had never seen so many orchids before. The theatrics and staging of the opera annoyed me. To feel the full beauty of the music and the voices, I sat on the floor with my back to the wall and closed my eyes. The final song of Isolde mourning Tristan's death always seems to me the finest thing in music when I am hearing it.

As to the duration of my stay, I am not yet certain. It depends partly on when I go to the desert, and how much time I spend in Hollywood before leaving. I would like to spend a whole year in the desert, but I might not go until March or April. While I am here I would like to take a jaunt up the Del Norte Coast, where the redwoods meet the seacliffs. Probably I shall be here through January at least.

Love from Everett

December 4

Dear Father,

I have been asking myself some questions latterly, and I wrote some of them down, thinking you might be interested. Most of them I can answer one way or another to my own satisfaction. But you would probably have a different reaction, and I would like to know how you would answer them, so I enclose a list.

I spent Sunday with the Schermerhorns, and in the evening, Charles and I went to Fiske's church, then with him to another church where a Socialist Methodist spoke on what religion could do and had to do if it were honest to its own tenets, for a better order. His name was Roy Burt, or Burke, I think, and he spoke very stirringly. Afterwards I asked him what limits, if any, there were to the patience, tolerance, apathy of the mass of American people with their present abominable situation. He said candidly that he thought there were none, and though some might resist feebly, we were headed hopelessly for fascism. If the people are hungry and weak with suffering, they have not the strength to revolt, and if any modest lessening of their hardships occurs, they at once resume their former complacency. He pointed out that the N.R.A. [National Recovery Act] is an effort made solely for the maintenance of the owning class and of the things that contribute to their welfare.

He said he had known of many men with no religious professions who in time of strikes made themselves and their children live on potatoes and "rock soup" because they were willing to sacrifice for a principle, and that by comparison, most "religious" people should be ashamed of themselves. He also told of an old fellow who, criticized for his cynicism, replied, after a tug at his moustache, "Wal, I'd rather be a pessimist than a liar." How many people would?

Love from Everett

The unusual letter that follows was written not by Everett, but by his father. It is Christopher Ruess's answers to a number of astonishingly deep philosophical questions that Everett had asked in the previous letter. Christopher's equally well-thought-out and well-expressed answers give us some measure of the type and depth of communication between father and son. In each case, Everett's question is listed first, followed by his father's answer.

December 10

1. *Is service the true end of life?* No, but rather happiness *through* service. Only as we play our part, as a part of the whole, aware of the interrelationedness, do we really and fully live. You and I are like the right hand or the right eye or the big toe—we are grotesque when living apart.

2. *Can a strong mind maintain independence and strength if it is not rooted in material independence?* Yes, as many great souls prove. They were not independent. Dependence and independence are alike harmful to the best life. No dependent or independent man can play a high part in life—but only the interdependent man. Great souls today have issued a Declaration of Human Interdependence.

3. *Do all things follow the attainment of Truth?* No, not unless you create a new definition of the truth. It takes *all* three "ideas of the

reason" to define the whole of culture or to define God. He whose life is exclusively devoted to Truth, or to Goodness, or to Beauty, is a very fractional man. This age is in trouble because it has exaggerated *truth*—it is lopsided. There is no ultimate conflict when all three are stressed and, as Aristotle says, we ". . . see life sanely and see it whole."

4. *Is bodily love empty or to be forgotten?* No, it is a part of life. It is not all of life. I do not see that it should ever be outgrown, but it changes form; it begins animal and always remains healthily animal, but it is refined and sublimated.

5. *Can one ask too much of life?* Yes, many do. We should have faith in life, in cause and effect, in action and reaction. We owe much more to the past than any one of us can give to the present or to the future. It is not for us to play highway robber and hold up life. The great souls probably never ask such a question. But the greatest givers have got most from life, whether Jesus or Edison.

6. *Does life have infinite potentialities?* Yes, so far as we can conceive infinity. Certainly incalculable, immeasurable is the contribution and joy open to you or to me. As Tagore says, Life is immense.

7. *Must pain spring from pleasure?* Not always. Not equal pain from equal pleasure. Psychologically, we seem to know pleasure largely by contrast and contrast seems necessary for our minds to make distinctions. No black, no white. No high, no low.

8. *Are pain and pleasure equally desirable and necessary?* They are both good for us if we have the will to extract the sweet from the bitter. No one need seek pain, he will get plenty without searching. He need not seek pleasure, he will get more if he gets it indirectly. He needs rather to go his way regardless of both pain and pleasure. Pleasure is perhaps the wrong word—joy or ecstacy may be better. Ecstacy is the highest of this family of words. It means such happiness that we literally seem to stand outside of ourselves in exaltation.

9. *Is pleasure right for all, but selfish for one?* There is no sin or wrong in pleasure except it be at the cost of another soul or life, to aggrandize ourselves by the degradation of another. Selfishness is not evil, it is good, but it must be the larger and not the narrower selfishness. A man's real self includes his parents, his wife and children, his friends, and neighbors, his countrymen, all his fellowmen. He should be selfish both at the center and at the circumference, selfish for *all*. I doubt that there is a real conflict, but there is a harmony. It is not beautiful for a man to sacrifice himself for his child and thus spoil his child. Parents who do not practice give and take, fairness, in this relation make pigs and tyrants out of their children. These children are not being brought up to face reality, are they?

10. *Can one be happy while others are miserable?* Yes, a callous man can have a callous happiness. But a noble man cannot be nobly happy while others are miserable. In that sense a man like Jesus never except for moments of rest and retreat can be happy, for he had com-passion upon the multitude. Great lovers have a happiness higher than our ordinary happiness. There is a happiness in identification of oneself with others, in bearing their burdens, even their sins. Great souls are not worried much about happiness. "Wist ye not that I must be about my Father's *business?*" Jesus and Socrates and Lincoln were not con-stantly concerned about their pleasure or their happiness.

11. *Can one be fine without great sacrifice?* Not the finest. For such a one has been spared great experience. Such a one has not really lived. He has just played at life. Yet he need not be maimed by sacrifice to know reality. Sacrifice is in quality as well as quantity. Sacrifice may be so great as to amputate life and may be silly or futile. There is sacrifice and sacrifice. One need not be sadist or masochist; neither are sound persons.

12. *Can one make great sacrifices without submerging onself?* Yes, wives of many great men, mothers of great sons, teachers of leaders, have found their lives by losing their lives. "He that loseth his life for my sake shall find it," says Jesus. You would now begin to find great things for your opening soul in a good modern version of the Gospels. Get one and read it slowly like any other book, and receptively. A seed fulfills itself by losing itself in the ground. So did the men at Thermopylae.

13. *Should one submerge oneself in sacrifice?* That depends. Not for the sake of sacrifice, that would be masochism. He that loseth his life for my sake, said Jesus, shall find it. So says the Great Idea or the Grand Old Cause at any time. A man should follow the gleam. He should be wise, not a fool, but a man must sometimes be a fool for the glory of God. There are no better words in which to express the thought.

14. *Does not one serve most by doing what one does best?* Yes, if the world needs that or can use that service. On the other hand, it may be selfish, where it is done to please oneself solely, without regard to the needs of one's time or one's fellows. As to art, beauty, the world always needs that, but it flourishes best when one is part of a world that has found itself and is going somewhere, when art is the expres-sion of the time.

15. *Is it possible to be truly unselfish?* No, because even Jesus fed his ego: a man who dies for a cause does express himself, achieve his

goal, perhaps. God does not ask unselfishness in an absurd sense. Asceticism and self-mortification, and all that sort of thing, are abnormal attitudes. A man must be first a healthy animal. Then he must be more than an animal, too. He must be a human.

16. *Is there any fulfillment that endures as such, besides death?* I doubt if death fulfills. It seems to end but I doubt that it ends much. Not one's influence or the influence of one's work. Perhaps even the echoes of your voice may go on forever. Some instrument might pick them up years or ages hence. Beauty is an ultimate fulfillment, as is Goodness, as is Truth. These are ends in themselves, and are for the sake of life. Many things are worthwhile that are not enduring. Eternity is just made of todays. Glorify the hour.

17. *Is there anything perpetual besides change?* Yes, the tendency to change, to unroll or evolve, and possibly the direction of change. The fact, if so, that things hold together, make sense, is perpetual. Why should we object to change? Maybe it is the essence of life.

18. *Is passage from the sensual to the intellectual to the spiritual a correct progression of growth, and if so, should that growth be hastened?* Why not live in all three at the same time? Why such sharp demarcations? A house has a foundation, a first story, and a second story. Why not all three at the same time? "Nor flesh helps spirit more now than spirit flesh," or the like, is a saying of Browning's. The Greeks separated flesh and spirit. We moderns tend not to do so, but to respect all parts of creation, each in its place.

Now you tell me, where did you get all these mind-twisters anyway?

Love,
Father

December 13
San Francisco

Dear Father,

I was very pleased with your carefully considered replies to my questions, and I think you have answered them very well.

The other day, I was talking with Alfred Fiske, and he believed, and won me over to the idea that we are not asking enough of life. When people find that we do not expect fine, splendid things of them, or that we do not appreciate them and scoff at them, naturally they cease to aspire. If more people felt that fineness was hoped for from them, and would not be scorned, they would respond and the world would be more beautiful. As it is, many people are ashamed of deep feelings when they have them, and always try to hide them. Don't you think this is true?

As to Briffault's statement that no first rate mind in this day of crisis can possibly be interested in beauty or in art when the world is going through death throes and birth throes, I naturally say that he is wrong, because if I agreed with him, I would contradict my whole life.

His thought is not new to me. A year ago my Communist friends were firing it at me when I told them that beauty and friendship were all I asked of life. I am not unconcerned with the crisis of our civilization, but the way of the agitator, the social leader, and the politician is not my way. It is not in my nature to deal with masses of people and be an organizer, and I don't propose to make any fundamental changes in my nature. I couldn't change that anyway.

Meantime, suppose a year past, I had heeded my friends, and thrown myself into the struggle. What would I have now to show for it? Most probably, if I had gone into the thing with any intensity, I'd soon have been just one more of the hundreds of political prisoners who are so utterly without any real influence on the stream of things. If, on the contrary, I had been cautious in my enthusiasm, what could I have accomplished in that way? And, as I said before, I consider it a hopeless, thankless task to struggle with the blind apathy of the masses. Neither can we persuade the leaders, the capitalists, to cut their own throats, so there you are. Am I right?

So, instead, during this last year, I have continued to seek beauty and friendship, and I think that I have really brought some beauty and delight into the lives of others, and that at least is something.

Love from Everett

December 13
San Francisco

Dear Waldo,

You must have been surprised at the rather senseless letter I remember sending you last. It was very good of you to send me that Thanksgiving letter. Doubtless my landlord was thankful for the green paper. I have been living a life of wild extravagance and utter penury, with an undercurrent of starvation and an overtone of magnificent music. Thus far, I've always managed to pay my debts sometime, and I've been trying my best to bring beauty and delight into the lives of others, with varying success.

In many respects my life here in the city has been a fulfillment. At last I have been able to turn to some account many of my hard won experiences in the past. I have some fine, sincere men, and several fine women, and one girl with whom I am intimate.

In short, I often feel in a conquering mood, and I am proud of my life, for I believe that I have really lived life at its most intense, and that I shall continue to do so.

Everett

In the last letter Everett says that he has "one girl with whom I am intimate." This girl was undoubtedly Frances. Who she was or how Everett met her, remains unknown. But for a brief period, at least, romance had entered Everett's life. In earlier years Everett referred to other girls in his life—a "Polish girl" in 1932 and Doris Myers in 1933—but neither seems to have made the impact that Frances did. See also two letters to Frances written from Arizona in May 1934.

December 14
Polk Street

Dear Frances,

I have just acquired the most heart-rending symphony you ever heard. You must come out to my mean hovel Saturday night to hear it, for I have to share it with you. In addition, there are two things I want to read to you, and a new picture I want you to see. Don't refuse, for I must see you, and I have laid in a store of Roquefort cheese as a special inducement. Yesterday and today I have been working spasmodically, and then drowning myself in music. I saw two girls on the streets this morning who reminded me of you.

I'm going out to Charley's tonight, but I'll try to call you sometime tomorrow. Meanwhile, don't despair, for I'm trying not to.

Love from Everett

Monday Afternoon

Frances dear,

Teresine dances tomorrow night at 8:20, so sleep sweetly tonight.

Everett

December 19

To Frances,

I wish the most blithe and serene Christmas that anyone could wish.

Everett

Though not swept up by radical organizations, his thoughtful discussions with friends gave him a pessimistic turn.

An abundance of social, political, and moral ideas, many of them contradictory, led Everett to question his own emotional stability, especially in regard to his frustrated need to express himself artistically.

December 22
2048 Polk St.
San Francisco

Dear Waldo,

I did not answer your letters earlier because most of the time I have been in a very restive, unstable mood, and did not feel like writing. I feel particularly that way tonight, but Father remarked that you were hurt by my silence.

Perhaps, as someone said the other day, it is just because I am nineteen and sensitive, but it is small consolation to be told that. I have been discovering new moods, new lows, new and disturbing variations in myself and my feelings for individuals, and people as a whole.

On the other hand, there is a lot of fun in me yet, and I have had some unusually gay times that were not feverishly so. But for the most part there has been an undercurrent of resentment or unrest.

I am sorry I could not send you anything at Christmas. I did have a gift for you, but I decided it was unsuitable. Your check rather embarrassed me; my first feeling was that I did not want it. I know too that you could ill afford to spare it. I have been spending what is, for me, a good deal of money lately. I sold a couple of pictures today, and spent the money already. Half the time I am broke or without money for carfare and telephone. I am not sure what I will do next month. I am tired of the place where I am staying. I shall probably spend a week in Berkeley, and then go up the coast, but probably I will hit the worst of the rainy season and sleep in mud puddles most of the time. I thought a while ago that I might be able to loosen up and really do a quantity of good work, because I was able to see some very splendid things; but I have not been able to loosen up for some while.

HAPPY JOURNEYS

Blockprint and greeting on Everett's Christmas cards he mailed from San Francisco in 1933.

After various turnings, twistings, and recoils, I still have not been able to find any proper outlet for my feelings. Perhaps there is none and perhaps it is necessary for my feelings to die of weariness and refusal.

I won't apologize for my emotions because I don't feel completely responsible. I can trace certain reactions in them when I am analytic, but I do not care to now. I don't expect you to understand them any more than anyone else, nor would it matter much if you did, because it seems to be up to me.

Don't let my straying from normalcy disturb you; doubtless it is part of a somewhat symmetrical scheme which I seem to see dimly.

> Your brother,
> Everett

December 29

Dear Uncle Emerson,

I want to tell you again how keenly I enjoyed the symphony last Saturday and how much I appreciated your taking me. I have since taken great pleasure remembering some strangely vivid phrases from the Mozart symphony, and the very delicately beautiful string passages in *L'Oiseau de Feu.* And the Wagner too; there are things in Wagner that always make me feel like flying. The music itself certainly soars.

Yesterday I went to the opera house and talked to Merola and to Mr. Ross, who, refusing to trade, generously gave me tickets to the next two concerts. I am taking Mrs. Maynard Dixon tonight. Last night I talked with Mr. Bem, and I expect to be able to hear his concert, too.

This afternoon I am downtown to get some fine photographs from Mr. Dassonville, in exchange for some prints I gave him the other day.

So you see, I am having a glorious time of it, and I'm glad I followed up your suggestions about the concerts.

Best wishes for a most joyful new year.

Your nephew,
Everett

THE LETTERS

1934

Oaks, Morro Bay. *Blockprint by Everett Ruess.*

January 2
235 Grenville Way
San Francisco

Dear Father,

On Sunday afternoon when the rain stopped for a while, I went for a long walk on the north side of the city. I watched the clouds shifting on the skyline, the stevedores loading tons of copper on a freighter, the gulls wheeling over the Bay, the clean, wet grass on hill slopes, the shacks and slums of the poor, and the mansions of the rich. I paused for about a quarter of an hour to admire the trunk of a symmetrically towering old eucalyptus on Russian Hill. I never saw more vivid or more beautiful coloring in a eucalyptus before.

  This afternoon I went back there and made a painting of it, finishing at sunset. I knocked at the door of the house to show it to the owner, a woman, who was very interested. It turned out that her house is the second oldest in San Francisco, being built in 1852. All sorts of famous old characters have lived in it. I was invited to return and see the place more thoroughly.

This evening I just finished reading Pitkin's introduction to the *History of Human Stupidity*. It is a long book and occupied me much of my time in the last few days. I was quite enthused for the first three hundred pages or so, and enjoyed the mental stimulation of it. It was strongly recommended to me by a boy I met in Sequoia, and it happened to be in at the library. I think I've had enough of Pitkin's style for a while, but I'll ask again at the library for the *Psychology of Achievement*. Do you know any other really good books on psychology that would be in the library?

I think you would be interested in this book if you have not read it. I enjoyed it for its range, and made a number of notes from it. Here are some that might interest you:

"The ability to perceive objects starts to decline as early as the seventeenth year. At fifty a man perceives things around him about as well as when he was fourteen, and at eighty, no better than a six-year-old.

"The commonest and mildest form of stupidity caused by the ego is the habit of talking too much.

"Whitman (Walt) had a peculiar lack of normal motor reactions, especially on social relations. He also lacked the normal aggressive behavior of the erotic male. The one positive, creative urge in his nature was his narcissism. (Pitkin gives a lengthy exposal of Whitman's stupidities.)

"Relatively as many people succeed in criminal careers as in non-criminal careers.

"The Church is the easiest way for frail and sickly stupid people, while the State is the easiest way for healthy, active dullards.

"In submission due to weakness and inability is the origin of the lure of Church and State, monastery and army, hierarchy and bureaucracy.

"The Golden Rule builds on a silly psychology, assuming, first, that people know their own minds, and secondly, that they can penetrate the minds of others.

"Things do not work themselves out for the good, as imbecile optimists say; they work out their own natures, whatever these happen to be, under conditions at hand, whatever they may be.

You say that an artist must live deeply before he can achieve, but a person capable of it can achieve in music from eight until eighty. I contest that. There has been no great composer who has not lived long and deep, and to a large extent, you can trace improvement with the years. I think the same thing is true of performers, though in a lesser degree, for it requires less to interpret than to create. If you study the dates of the great musical compositions, you will find they were not written by eight-year-olds, nor, on the other hand, by eighty-year-olds. So I don't agree with Pitkin that music (the composing at least) is very different from the other arts in respect to age.

For myself, I am doing my best to have variety and intensity of experience, and largely succeeding, I think. I see no grounds for complaint on that score. There is no need for fearing that I will be a "one-sided" freak artist, to use your phrase, for I am interested almost equally in all the arts and in human relations and reactions as well.

As to this half-baked pother about my always feeling inferior in the presence of college graduates, that fear is groundless too. I am not nonplussed in the presence of anybody, and I am seldom at a loss with anyone I am interested in.

As to the million-dollar endowment of going through the college mill, I have three million dollar endowments already, that I am sure of, and I don't have to go begging. I have my very deep sensitivities to beauty, to music, and to nature. In addition, thanks to you and Mother, I have an intellect that is capable of analysis and of grappling with things almost anywhere I turn.

I am learning things all the time, and I certainly have never felt any handicap with Fiske and Schermerhorn. I could not do the things they are doing, but on the other hand, they are shoved into such a rut by their work that they cannot follow any of the broadly cultural lines that I follow, and I certainly do not regret my freedom. On all sides I meet people who are not able to follow things up as I am doing, and it is not I who envy them.

You can be ashamed of me if you like, but you cannot make me feel ashamed of myself, in that direction at least. Waldo has an entirely different problem, and I don't think it is profitable to compare us as you do.

As for me, I have tasted your cake, and I prefer your unbuttered bread. I don't wish to withdraw from life to college, and I have a notion, conceited or not, that I know what I want from life, and can act upon it.

Concerning my return, I want to spend about a month in Hollywood anyway before leaving for Arizona, but I may not go there until March or April. Meanwhile, I can hardly pretend to have exhausted the possibilities of San Francisco in three months, and several considerations incline me to prefer it to Los Angeles. Not only does it still have something of newness to me contrasted with the (yes) staleness of L.A., but I sense a vitality here which is totally lacking in the people down there.

Furthermore, I really have more friends here than I do there, and there are many leads remaining to be followed up.

I would have sent you one of Mrs. Dixon's photographs, but she did not think they were good enough, and wants to make some others.

I hope you will send the boots up, repaired as I asked. I will be glad to get the money order but I must ask you to send the other too, as ten dollars barely pays my rent, and I can't commute, telephone, buy art materials, eat, etc. on the differences between ten dollars and ten dollars. I spent my last three cents today for a postage stamp for you. I could send the letter postage due, as you and Mother often do, but I prefer not to.

As to the way I've spent my money, I think it *has* done credit to my emotions, and I don't regret it. On occasion, I have calculated things to a very fine point, but you may well cease hoping that I will ever be practical in the accepted sense. I would sooner die.

However, I have used my ingenuity in such a way that four pairs of tickets to various concerts have been gladly given to me, and I traded for three fine photographs the other day. I took Mrs. Dixon to the first of the concerts. It was Roland Hays, and she said she would remember his song "Der bist die Ruh" all her life. It was sung as beautifully as anything I have heard.

I had dinner with the Schermerhorns yesterday. Charles asked me to give you his regards.

Love from Everett

January 7

Dear Father,

Your letter of the third reached me the other day. Three dollars seems an exorbitant price to pay for repairing the boots, and I can ill afford it. I had an excellent job done on them in Arizona, when they were in worse repair, for $1.50. However, if you've done it, it is all right. Send the rest of the money now; I need it.

I have had two beautiful new ideas today, and it may be that I can do something with them. A few days ago, the owner of a shop for rare books and old prints took eight of my prints on consignment, but I won't get much out of it, even if he does sell them. A while ago I was reliably informed that Paul Elder's are and have been on the verge of bankruptcy for a long time, and that I should take my stuff out as soon as possible, as they would not pay me anything even if they sold all my stuff. This from a man who had let them have 200 dollars worth of stuff, and had no returns from them.

Mother told me that you saved the eucalyptus tree growing on Lemon Grove Street. I'm proud of you.

Last night I heard a fine concert in company with a poet friend. Some nocturnes of Debussy were beautifully rendered, as was also the *Death and Transfiguration* of Richard Strauss.

I have been reading Dunsany and Sven Hedin.

I now intend to start my trip up the coast the first week in February. I feel the need of doing some first-hand work. I hope the February allotment reaches me in time for an early start, before I have to pay more rent.

I have been having some interesting and valuable experiences here in San Francisco. I cherish them, for I know that there will never be another period in my life like this.

I hope you are all busy and happy.

Love from Everett

January 27

Dear Father,

I returned from Berkeley today and found your letter of the thirteenth. The article in the *Unitarian* was quite interesting, I thought, and surprisingly clear and unprejudiced. After I had heard considerable fanfare from various quarters, I went to a Christian Science meeting with the Boyntons and was very much disappointed. The church especially seems a refuge of weaklings. I mean to visit one of the Catholic churches here some morning. Last night I read part of *Transition* and found it rather depressing.

At the Turner's the other day I was reading *The Sense of Beauty*, and was startled by the resemblance between an essay of his on work and play and a much-criticized one I had written on the same theme.[18]

The boots reached me all right, and doubtless you were right about their condition. I have never had a shoe or boot that would last more than a month, or two at the most, of outdoor service without resoling and heeling. These boots lasted for only a month of Sierra wear.

It will be fine if you will send the twenty dollars now, as I will then be able to plan more skillfully. I expect to leave this place next Saturday.

I certainly enjoyed transforming my room today. Before even opening my mail, I took all my belongings from the storeroom, eliminated the blank, staring look of the walls, put spots of color here and there to relieve the drabness, and changed the place from a coffin to a place that could be lived in. It is quite homelike now.

What you say is partly true, in your remark that I have done what I wanted most in spite of the world crisis. I found three letters today from friends in various quarters, of whom it is by no means true. They have been wallowing in the shallows of life this past year—not growing or having new and enlarging experiences; driven partly or wholly by circumstances into lives that they themselves consider ignoble, stale, and depressing.

A few nights ago, Joe Whitnah, Ed Bates, and I had a jolly discussion, and went to bed serene in the belief that the world is hell bent for destruction, writhing from one snare into another, becoming more and more hopelessly involved in vicious, unbreakable circles, and gaining momentum on the wretched road to Ruin. One feels the need of believing something, and this is less repugnant to the intellect than the other outlooks, or so it seems to me.

Love from Everett

February 9
Tomales Bay

Dear Family,

For a week I have been staying at the sheep ranch of Khan Alam Khan, formerly of Afghanistan. His wife is German, and there are three boys fostered here—Italian, American, and Negro. There is also another woman who is a pianist. I first met Khan through Schermerhorn.

The ranch is on the ridge of a vast hill, looking down upon the sea. Lines of lacy eucalyptus and twisted cypress break the wind. On the slopes are large rocks and into their crevices are fitted the laurel trees, their crests shorn by the winds.

In addition to several hundred sheep, there are chickens, turkeys, dogs, cats, horses, and cows. There has been every kind of weather, but now the wind, rain, and fog have left us for a while. I've made several pictures.

In a few days I shall continue on up the coast. This morning I am going up the ridge to photograph a rock.

Love from Everett

February 12
Valley Ford

Dear Family,

I'm on the northward trail again, riding to Monte Rio. Last night was a beautiful experience. I walked mile after mile, over vast, rolling hills, down canyons with rushing streams. At sunset I started back to the ranch, but I had started a bigger circle than I thought, and walked for an hour or two until I topped a rise and heard the roar of the surf and the bleating of sheep and saw the lights of home. Northward now.

Everett

February 18
Rockport

Dear Father, Mother, and Waldo,

Since yesterday I have been staying here at Rockport. It is an abandoned lumber town; there are rows and rows of empty houses and disused machinery. I walked here from a ranch near New Haven, where I had spent a night, and one of the three caretakers invited me to stay with him. Being rather footsore, I was glad to accept, and it has been rather pleasant. This morning we were out spearing salmon in the creek, and my friend caught three big ones. He and one of the other men are curing them in a smokehouse.

I have been interested in studying the people as I go up the coast. I have been curious to observe what various people get out of life, but most of them are disappointing under close observation. Also I've been observing reactions to the economic situation. I was startled by the intelligence of one of the ranch hands, but most of the people are living the super simple life and have no energy for thinking.

My host here says that on the first of this month the government will take over this and all other companies that have not paid them back taxes and cannot.

The sea has been gloriously beautiful these stormy days, grey-green combers rolling in—white foam reaching over the dark beaches. The surf crashes against the cliffs, leaps into the air, and slowly, gracefully subsides into the sea. At other places, there are long strips of foam racing in ahead of the combers far out at sea. Sometimes on the dark stormy sea the hidden sun shines through and makes an unearthly radiance. Other times the grey waves glisten like new metal under the crests when they topple.

So it has been a jolly time; life has been quite adventurous and highly irregular. Tomorrow I expect to go over to the redwood highway. The maximum daily travel north on this coast road is about ten or twelve cars, and sometimes there are none. I expect to go as far as Crescent City.

Love to all,
Everett

February 26
San Francisco

Dear Father and Mother,

I am burning all three candles as I listen to the magnificent music of my Beethoven's Fifth Symphony. I am fairly well established in my new room; it is better than the other, and I had a jolly time making it my own.

The city seemed senselessly hideous and squatted when I reentered it today, after the clean spaciousness of green hills and blue seas. But it was good to see and hear from my old friends. I know some fine people in this city.

As I strolled downtown today, I noticed a theatre bill for Walter Hampden, and stopped in to buy inexpensive tickets for *Macbeth* and *Hamlet*. As I walked away I felt that I had done quite well.[19]

This will be a busy week, but I think that on Monday I will be ready to mail or freight my belongings and be on the road south. I am not sure yet whether or not I want to stop off at Carmel and Morro Bay. I'm not sure how my finances will hold out either, but I may sell a picture or two this week, and I'll probably have ample more.

Love to you both,
Everett

March 2
San Francisco

Dear Father, Mother, and Waldo,

I am writing this at the Dixon's tonight. Mrs. Dixon and I are driving up to Khan Alan's Sunday, to photograph the Khan. I sold her on his profile.

Last night I sold a picture, so this afternoon I bought a ticket on the southbound boat. It is the *Emma Alexander* and leaves Tuesday, arriving in Wilmington at Berth 153 at five o'clock Wednesday. It cost

136

me four dollars. I get my meals and berth, but I don't know just what the accommodations will be. Could one of you plan to meet me with the car? I will have a good deal of luggage. I haven't had any mail since I arrived here, but I presume everything is all right. Ben Boynton tipped me off about the boat. Mr. Boynton wished you well. He is working now on the Tevis case. Tevis wants to go bankrupt, and have an income of $37,000 per annum.

Love from

Everett

Back at his parents' home in Los Angeles, Everett spent a month making preparations for his forthcoming trip to northern Arizona. Waldo, who was expected home shortly, offered to drive Everett to Monument Valley.

March

Dear Waldo,

I was happy to find your letter when I returned home last night. I spent the evening with my friends who planned to drive me to San Bernardino. I know they would be glad to take me, and I should like to make the last trip with a friend, but your plan sounds much simpler and more convenient, and I shall tell them about it.

I won't take many of my pictures, as they are hard to carry—only prints, a few photographs, and blank paper. I'll remember your shoes. I went to the flower show at Dudley's on Saturday, and had a delightful time. I met Mr. Epling, a botany professor at UCLA, who was very interesting, and rode in with Miss Weir, who bought one of my prints. There was a gorgeous display of golden iris.

As to my prophecies about the Flagstaff country if I were on foot, they were rather obscurely presented, I suppose. What I meant was, the arrangements would be difficult and expensive, and I'd probably have to hitchhike to Tuba City or beyond for burros, then drive them on foot all the way back to the railroad where my stuff would have been left, load them there, and drive them back again on foot—which, you may imagine, would not be the pleasantest or most profitable use of time. It is hardly likely that I'd be able to hitchhike with the burros—although I did once.

These last months in the cities have been very strange; there have been many beautiful moments. I have seen more of beauty than ever before, and my relations with people have been riper, with more complete understanding than before.

A few nights ago I went to a Young Communist League demonstration. There were posters with captions like "We Can't Eat Battleships," and sound talk about the stupidity of armament and the wretched condition of the lower classes. But in about five minutes, the Red Squad came with six men, who leaped out of a car, laid about with their clubs, snatched the posters from the boys and tore them up, seized all the papers, kicked the girls in the legs, and chased the boys and girls for several blocks, trying to separate the group. Such are Free Speech and Free Assemblage in America.

I look forward to the time when we will be going places, together on the road. You are surely a good brother to me.

Love from Everett

April 6

Dear Waldo,

As to car troubles peculiar to Arizona—in all the traveling I did there in at least a hundred different cars and on all sorts of roads, I remember only two misadventures—a flat tire, and running out of gas. Which, of course, proves nothing.

So, Waldo, this amounts to asking you to change your decision if you feel you can do it without being half-hearted. If you cannot, let me know if you will drive me across the border, as it is crucially important for me to get started. I have made most of my purchases already, and I will meet you in San Bernardino next Thursday evening at the appointed place unless you have thought of a better one.

This morning I was reading an interesting book called *The Fantastic Traveler*, of a boy who creates a dream world more real than his actual world.

I'm enclosing a list of some books in the library. Susanna Ott of the History Department is a friendly, interesting woman. She took me downstairs to show me some pillars in the library from the palace of Croesus, Crete, built some 2,500 B.C.

Did you ever read Schliemann's biography? He was a man who believed that the *Odyssey* and the *Iliad* were based on fact, not legend and fable. He believed that there really had been a city of Troy, and though no one else would believe in him, he finally uncovered the city itself. *Arabia Felix* is an interesting book too, excellently illustrated.

Let me have a reply soon.

Love from Everett

Battlements of the Colorado. *Blockprint by Everett Ruess.*

When Waldo dropped Everett off at Kayenta in April 1934, it was the last time that the two brothers ever saw each other.

April 14

Dear Father and Mother,

We arrived here safely this afternoon after a very adventuresome day yesterday. Am starting back now.

Love from Waldo

April 19
Dinnehotso, Arizona

Dear Father and Mother,

Yesterday I walked here from Church Rock, near Kayenta, with a pack on my back. It was eighteen strenuous miles, but I stopped once to make a painting of a distant mesa. I am giving it to the trader here, in return for which he is bargaining for my burros, and providing hospitality. I expect to have a couple by tomorrow. They were rather scarce near Kayenta, and language was a barrier. However, I did have a jolly day riding the range with Dog Ears Begay, lunching at different hogans and inquiring for kellys (burros).

Today I rode with Charley Ashcroft, the trader's son, in his Ford. We went over the rock and sage and sand to Twisted Water and Mexican Water. Once we stopped to gather garnets. They are common on some of the sand hills, but good ones are rarely found.

Waldo enjoyed his part of the trip very much, I think. I was sorry I could not show him more of the country.

The saddle blanket came Tuesday, and I was very glad. The country here is all that I could wish it to be, and I am happy again.

Love from Everett

· One of Everett's favorite passages from Willa Cather's Death Comes For the Archbishop—and marked by Everett in the family copy—is the following:

It was the Indian manner to vanish into the landscape, not to stand out against it. . . . [The Indians] seemed to have none of the European's desire to "master" nature, to arrange and re-create. They spent their ingenuity in the other direction; in accommodating themselves to the scene in which they found themselves. This was not so much from indolence . . . as from an inherited caution and respect. It was as if the great country were asleep, and they wished to carry on their lives without awakening it; or as if the spirits of earth and air and water were things not to antagonize and arouse. When they hunted, it was with the same discretion; an Indian hunt was never a slaughter. They ravaged neither the rivers nor the forest, and if they irrigated, they took as little water as would serve their needs. The land and all that it bore they treated with consideration; not attempting to improve it, they never desecrated it.

May 2
Kayenta, Arizona

Dear Mrs. [Emily] Ormond,

Vilhjalmur Stefansson, the Arctic explorer, says that adventures are a sign of unpreparedness and incompetence. I think he is largely right, nevertheless I like adventure and enjoy taking chances when skill and fortitude play a part. If we never had any adventures, we would never know what "stuff" was in us.

So last night, I had quite a satisfactory adventure. I have had Leopard and Cockleburrs, my burros, for twelve days now, and they are beginning to learn how to play the game. Yesterday was about the longest day we have had; we came fully twenty-five miles. At dawn I watched the red moon set. There was a ring around the moon and I remembered the *Wreck of the Hesperus*. Shortly after sunrise I saddled the burros and rode off against blustering winds. The peak of Agathla and the buttes of Monument Valley were almost obscured by sand-storms. Vast seas of purple Loco Bloom were buffeted by the wind. The vermilion sand spread in ruffles over our tracks, obscuring them almost at once.

At morning we fought the gale, and in early afternoon I stopped to rest and lunch. After a few mouthfuls of oats, the burros cropped the grass tufts. Forage is plentiful this year. While I chewed jerky I read a chapter in *Death Comes for the Archbishop*, a well-written book about the early Southwest.

Then I rode on again, and for a while I was very blithe, singing lustily into the wind and remembering some magnificent music. Then the sky grew inky and I urged the burros onwards, shouting, "Sintlo, Kelly, dill yage!" We passed right under the towering bulk of Agathla, popularly called El Capitan, and I had to make a painting. It is a splendid rock, with spires and pinnacles of black volcanic stone. I did not trouble to finish the sketch, but even so it was almost dark, and it was five or six miles to a campsite.

So I soon dismounted and drove both burros, shouting until they fairly loped. Soon it was dark and we were in the middle of a broad level valley. I kept the burros at a fast walk, and finally we topped the farther ridge. It was not black dark and a mile or so to the hogan I knew of, so I urged them on. Just as I reached the rock pile where I meant to turn off a few hundred yards, the burros suddenly bolted into the night.

It was probably Leopard's idea, but Cockleburrs took the cue instantly, and they were off like a shot. I gave chase at top speed, until my lungs were afire, and I heard the pack thumping along in the darkness. The burros had certainly made their getaway at a strategic time. I followed along the trail, stumbling in the dark, and picking up a couple of saddle blankets which had slipped out.

I kept on to the creek finding no trace of them. The desert might have swallowed them up; they might be anywhere. I thought of the smashed saddles, the broken kyaks, their contents flung broad-cast, the camera crushed, my paintings lying in the rain, and the burros kicking their heels miles away. I knew Cockleburrs could not strip off his pack without smashing it. And while I hunted for the burros the

Navajos, who have no moral sense, would collect my scattered belongings and take them home.

I started to walk to Kayenta, thinking that a Mormon I knew might be willing to come in his car at dawn and pick up the stuff while I tracked down the burros. Within a mile of the trading post I made an about-face. It was not that I couldn't stand being laughed at by the whole town, for it really was funny, and such things don't bother me; but it would be asking too much from these people, and since for some time I had flattered myself that I could "take it" and always had, without complaint, I thought this was a good time to show myself. So I went back, circling around in the rocks, but finding no trace and hearing nothing but the scream of the wind I took my saddle blankets and felt my way back to the hogan. Soon I had a fire going, and watched the stars through the sky hole as they appeared and disappeared. Since there was nothing to eat or drink, I smoked a cigarette and lay on the sand with a blanket for a pillow. The moon rose murkily, and shone dimly through the racing clouds. I would sleep until the fire died down, then build it up again. After four or five naps the dawn came, and as I went in search it began to rain.

A mile or two away I found tracks on the sand, and before I knew it, I was face to face with Cockleburrs, who was standing stock still and looking foolish and tired. I had bundled better than I knew; his pack was intact! Nearby was Leopard equally sheepish, his saddle under him but unhurt. The camera and canteen were lost from it, but in half an hour's circling, I recovered them both, little harmed.

So I cinched the saddle down, mounted, and we three went back through the rain to last night's point of departure. As we approached the hogan, the fire blazed up, the smoke curled out on top, and I felt quite delighted with everything. I gave the burros an extra ration of oats, hobbled them out, and put on the supper and breakfast pot.

Though not all my days are as wild as this, each one holds its surprises, and I have seen almost more beauty than I can bear. Many times in the search for water holes and cliff dwellings, I trusted my life to crumbling sandstone and angles little short of the perpendicular, startling myself when I came out whole and on top.

So tell Mabel what kind of burros I have; they are grazing peacefully now, like good little donkeys, and haven't strayed all day.

Love from Everett

Monument Valley, Arizona. *Blockprint by Everett Ruess.*

The Lone Trail

Three or four years ago I came to the conclusion that for me, at least, the lone trail was the best, and the years that followed strengthened my belief.

It is not that I am unable to enjoy companionship or unable to adapt myself to other people. But I dislike to bring into play the aggressiveness of spirit which is necessary with an assertive companion, and I have found it easier and more adventurous to face situations alone. There is a splendid freedom in solitude, and after all, it is for solitude that I go to the mountains and deserts, not for companionship. In solitude I can bare my soul to the mountains unabashed. I can work or think, act or recline at my whim, and nothing stands between me and the Wild.

Then, on occasion, I am grateful for what unusual and fine personality I may encounter by chance, but I have learned not to look too avidly for them. I delve into myself, into abstractions and ideas, trying to arrange the other things harmoniously, but after that, taking them as they come.

—Everett Ruess

143

May 5
Chilchinbetoh, Arizona

Dear Mother,

Returning to Kayenta the other day I found your letter and was delighted with your poem. I liked the longer version much the better.

I am staying now with Jose Garcia, Indian trader whose brother Camilio I knew in Chin Lee. When I came here last night, Jose's kindness and courtesy almost brought the tears to my eyes, for there is something very fine about him, and I have not met many of his kind in this country. His father, a wizened old pioneer of the Spaniards, is here too. They are good, simple people without sophistication, living happily in this at present untroubled part of the world. Jose speaks four languages—English, Spanish, Navajo, and Zuni.

Before I leave here, I am going to make for Jose a painting of the Three Fingers, familiar landmarks on a promontory of the unexplored Black Mesa. You should see the glorious color when the first light of dawn spreads on the golden cliff tops and the blue-grey pinyon-clad slopes.

Cockleburrs and Leopard are the names of my two burros, and they are pals with each other and me now.

Love from Everett

May 5
Chilchinbetoh, Arizona

Dear Frances,

The negatives from you reached me in Kayenta a few days ago.

I am staying now with Jose Garcia, Indian trader whose brother Camilio I knew in Chin Lee. When I came here last night, Jose's kindness and courtesy almost brought the tears to my eyes, for there is something very fine about him, and I have not met many like him in this country. His father, a wizened old pioneer of the Spaniards, is here too. They are good, simple people with no sophistication, living happily in this at present untroubled part of the world. Jose speaks four languages—English, Spanish, Navajo, and Zuni.

There are some handsome, lithe young girls among the Navajos here. The Indians have many vices, but they are a kindly people, and I like them and admire their fine qualities.

Before I leave here, I am going to make for Jose a painting of the Three Fingers, familiar landmarks on a promontory of the unexplored Black Mesa. You should see the glorious color when the first light of dawn spreads on the golden clifftops and the grey-blue pinyon-clad slopes.

To one aware of the strangeness of life, my life in the cities was as strange as it is here. In many ways, toward the last, it was a fulfillment. I had many gloriously beautiful experiences, as well as the wild and intense adventures which seem to come without my searching. I do not know if I shall ever return to the cities again, but I cannot complain that I found them empty of beauty.

I was sorry, though, that our intimacy, like many things that are and will be, had to die with a dying fall. I do not greatly mind endings, for my life is made up of them, but sometimes they come too soon or too late, and sometimes they leave a feeling of regret as of an old mistake or an indirect futility. I like to be able to be perfectly open and sincere, and yet it is impossible to be sincere to all of one's self at once, so for the deepest understanding one must seek those with whom one can be most truly one's self. And never be blind to the ineffable drollery of it all.

So here too I have been leading a life of strange contrasts, violent indeed when considered separately, yet flowing naturally enough into one another. There has been deep peace, vast calm and fury, strange comradeships and intimacies, and many times my life and all my possessions have tottered on the far side of the balance, but as yet, from each such encounter I have in the end come away, unharmed, and even toughened.

But much as I love people, the most important thing to me is still the nearly unbearable beauty of what I see. I won't wish that you could see it, for you might not find it easy to bear either, but yet I do sincerely wish for you a little at least of the impossible.

Love from Everett

May 5

Dear Bill,

Once more I am roaring drunk with the lust of life and adventure and unbearable beauty. I have the devil's own conception of a perfect time; adventure seems to beset me on all quarters without my even searching for it; I find gay comradeships and lead the wild, free life wherever I am. And yet, there is always an undercurrent of restlessness and wild longing; "the wind is in my hair, there's a fire in my heels," and I shall always be a rover, I know. Always I'll be able to scorn the worlds I've known like half-burnt candles when the sun is rising, and sally forth to others now unknown. I'm game; I've passed my own rigorous tests, and I know that I can take it. And I'm lucky too, or have been. Time and again, my life or all my possessions have swung on the far side of the balance, and always thus far I've come out on top and unharmed, even toughened by the chances I've taken.

"Live blindly and upon the hour; the Lord, who was the future, died full long ago." Among others, I've tried that way, and found it good, too. Finality does not appall me, and I seem always to enjoy things the more intensely because of the certainty that they will not last. Oh it's a wild, gay time! Life can be rich to overflowing. I've been so happy that I can't think of containing myself. I've no complaints to make, and time and the world are my own, to do with as I please. And I've had it up and down; no tedious, humdrum middle course has been mine, but a riotously plunging and soaring existence.

Again I say, it's a wild gay time. I've slept under hundreds of roofs, and shall know others yet. I've carved a way for myself, turned hostile strangers into staunch friends, swaggered and sung through surplus of delight where nothing and no one cared whether I lived or died.

The things I've loved and given up without a complaint have returned to me doubled. There's no one in the world I envy.

Around me stretches the illimitable desert, and far off and near by are the outposts of suffering, struggling, greedy, grumbling humanity. But I don't choose to join on that footing. I'm sorry for it and I help it when I can, but I'll not shoulder its woes. To live is to be happy; to be carefree, to be overwhelmed by the glory of it all. Not to be happy is a living death.

Alone I shoulder the sky and hurl my defiance and shout the song of the conqueror to the four winds, earth, sea, sun, moon, and stars. I live!

May
Northeast Arizona

Dear Edward [Gardner],

I fear it is rather impolite to write to your office address but I could not remember your street in Alhambra.

For five days I have been in this canyon. I have not seen an Indian, and it is a week since I saw a white skin. Day before yesterday I narrowly escaped being gored to death by a wild bull, and there was a harrowing sequel when he discovered my camp that night, somewhile between midnight and dawn. Yesterday I did some miraculous climbing on a nearly vertical cliff, and escaped unscathed from that, too.

One way and another, I have been flirting pretty heavily with Death, the old clown.

Now the shadow of a mighty cliff has fallen on my camp to remain until dawn. On the opposite canyon wall, towering sheer above, I watch the fantastic gyrating shadows of two buzzards, that wheel and slant in the upper sunlight.

Strange, sad winds sweep down the canyon, roaring in the firs and the tall pines, swaying their crests. I don't know how you feel about it, Edward, but I can never accept life as a matter of course. Much as I seem to have shaped my own way, following after my own thinking and my own desires, I never cease to wonder at the impossibility that I live. Even when to my senses the world is not incredibly beautiful or fantastic, I am overwhelmed by the appalling strangeness and intricacy of the curiously tangled knot of life, and at the way that knot unwinds, making everything clear and inevitable, however unfortunate or wonderful.

Here are a couple of things I dashed off today. You might ask to see the letter I wrote Bill, and show him this for contrast.

"The love and perception of beauty are real, but they do not lead to happiness. Happiness lies in a large measure of self-forgetfulness, either in work, accomplishment, or in the love of others.

"When analyzed, both work and love are shown to be futile, and the joys imaginary and evanescent. All accomplished works or deeds perish or are forgotten eventually. No love lives forever, and no two can completely understand one another, or if they do, it kills their love, which is in reality only a projected form of self love.

"Realizing the transitory quality of happiness, and knowing that the intervals are filled with doubt, misery, or mere empty existence, how can we value it, knowing how it deceives the recipient? And can one feel otherwise than contemptuous towards those who blind their analytic faculties by submerging themselves in work? For whether they know it or not, the pleasure so bought is falsely grounded on a complicated built-up system of self-deception, and their lives are lies.

"The chief danger to an even semi-intelligent happiness lies in being analytic. One who is truly analytic cannot possibly be happy unless there is some great contradiction in his nature—some side of himself where the cold mind never probes. For to think is the beginning of death. And as cold as thought is purely perceived beauty. Love not beauty, for she will certainly betray you.

"Beauty isolated is terrible and unbearable, and the unclouded sight of her kills the beholder. His only refuge is in insignificant things, in labor that keeps the mind from thought, and in companionship that gives back to the ego some of its former virility.

"But he who has looked long on naked beauty may never return to the world, and though he should try, he will find its occupation empty and vain, and human intercourse purposeless and futile. Alone and lost, he must die on the altar of beauty.

"The absorbing passion of any highly sensitive person is to forget himself, whether by drinking or by agonized love, by furious work or play, or by submerging himself in the creative arts. Sometimes, if his will is powerful, he can pretend to himself that he does not know what he knows, and can act a part as one of the rest. But the pretense cannot endure, and unless he can find another as highly strung as himself with whom to share the murderous pain of living, he will surely go insane. Moral: Do not develop your faculties."

Such and so have I written. Now the last light lingers on the topmost rim of the red sandstone cliffs, touching a lone tree with gold. Now that has faded. The flowers are closing and the cicadas sing shrilly.

Edward, you do not know how ridiculous life is unless you have had strange experiences and seen the ineffable absurdity of it all.

I'm enclosing for you a single gay blossom of a Scarlet Bugler. Doubtless it will be wan and faded when you see it, but remember that it was once as fair and fresh as you.

Give my well wishes to your sister and Alec and the rest of the family. Was the final performance of the Ninth as good as the rehearsal?

I don't know if I'll be able to mail this before I reach Lukachukai. Best write to Kayenta with instructions not to forward to Lukachukai as I'll be there in two or three weeks.

> Sincerely,
> Your Friend,
> Everett

P.S. From up the canyon, I hear an ominous muttering and bellowing, rapidly coming nearer. Evidently black Sir Taurus and I are going to have it out again, and I'll leave you in the suspense I'm in. But if this letter reaches you, the chances are I will have ousted him. Now he is much closer; what ugly long horns he has, and how unbelievably horrible his furious bellowing! Meanwhile a melody of Brahms recurs to me.

The following, one of the most sensitive, image-filled letters that Everett ever wrote, was addressed to Frances, the girl he had loved in San Francisco, and for whom he still had deep feelings.

May
Near Lukachukai, Arizona

Dear Frances,

I was surprised and pleased to receive your letter a couple of days ago. Glad too that you are getting something out of life. It shocked me slightly when you spoke of my greed for life. That is a harsh word, but I guess it is true. I am not willing to take anything but the most from life. Then too,

"You know how little while we have to stay,
And once departed may return no more."

I certainly don't like to let opportunities for living slip by ungrasped, and I never liked the game of sitting back in a corner and wishing. And when people interest me and I like them, I nearly always follow up until I know them well. There are too many uninteresting people—like the trader at Lukachukai. He certainly made me feel like hitting him. He is a typical moron, only interested in food, business, and home. I was telling him about Canyon de Chelly and del Muerto, and with no provocation he remarked that he had lived here a long time and had never been to them and never expected or intended to. Obviously his decision was right for a person like him, because wherever he might go, he would see nothing beautiful or interesting.

So the other night at twilight, unwilling to drown my consciousness in slumber, and dissatisfied with life, I packed and saddled my burros, and left my camp by a rushing stream at the edge of the desert.

The half moon had an orange glow as I rode on the trail up the mountains. Behind us, thunder boomed on the open desert, and black clouds spread. Moaning winds swept down the canyon, bending the tops of the tall pines and firs, and clouds hid the moon. Silently old Cockleburrs, my saddle burro, carried me upward through the night, and Leopard followed noiselessly with the pack. Grotesque shapes of trees reared themselves against the darkening sky, and disappeared into blackness as the trail turned.

For a while the northerly sky was clear, and stars shone brilliantly through the pine boughs. Then darkness closed upon us, only to be rent by livid flashes of lightning, and thunder that seemed to shake the earth. The wind blew no longer and we traveled in an ominous, murky calm, occasionally slashed with lightning. Finally the clouds broke, and rain spattered down as I put on my slicker. We halted under a tall pine, and my sombrero sheltered the glow of a cigarette. The burros stood motionless with heads down and water dripping off their ears.

In half an hour the rain was over and the skies cleared. By moonlight we climbed to the rim of the mountain and looked over vast silent stretches of desert. Miles away was the dim hulk of Shiprock—a ghostly galleon in a sea of sand.

We turned northward on the nearly level top of the mountain, and winding through glades of aspen we came to three peaceful lakes, gleaming silver in the moonlight. Under a clump of low sprawling oaks we stopped, and there I unpacked, turning the burros out to graze on the tall meadow grass.

In the afternoon I went for a long leisurely ride on Leopard, skirting the edge of the mountain, riding through thickets of rustling aspen, past dark, mysterious lakes, quiet and lonely in the afternoon silence.

Two friendly horses were belly deep in a pond, swishing their tails and placidly chewing rushes and swamp grass. Flowers nodded in the breeze and wild ducks honked on the lakes. No human being came to disturb the brooding silence of the mountain.

Last night I came down the mountain, and as the sunset glow faded it was weird to see the orange moon seemingly falling down, down, through the pine boughs as I descended.

Now I have accepted the hospitality of a Navajo head man, and paused at noon to rest and write to you. I enjoyed your letter, and I know I did not mistake myself when first I liked you. We did have some moments of beauty together, didn't we?

It is that feeling of comradeship and sharing that I miss most out here. True, I have had many experiences with people, and some very close ones, but there was too much that could not be spoken. I had a strange experience with a young fellow at an outpost, a boy I'd known before. It seems that only in moments of desperation is the soul most truly revealed. Perhaps that's why I am so often so unrestrained, for always I sense the brink of things. And as you say, it is impossible to grasp enough of life. There is always something that eludes one.

I've not heard the recording of the Emperor Concerto, but I heard it rendered a couple of times by the New York Philharmonic. Though there is a lot of superfluous stuff, the heart of it rings through magnificently. I have greatly enjoyed Beethoven's Fifth, Seventh, and Ninth symphonies, also Brahms' First and Third. I enjoy them here, too. The night before I left the city I went to hear the final rehearsal of Beethoven's Ninth with full chorus. (A girl I knew was singing.) Then I realized the gap still remaining between any recording and the reality of a thing like that. Oh, it was utterly sublime, enough to make the hair stand on end and to lift the soul out of the body.

Oh but the desert is glorious now, with marching clouds in the blue sky, and cool winds blowing. The smell of the sage is sweet in my nostrils, and the luring trail leads onward.

Love from Everett

May

[Addressee unknown]

I have been fighting my way up tall hills, between canyons of skyscrapers, hurling myself against the battling night winds, the raw, swooping gusts that are like cold steel on my cheeks. I am drunk with a searing intoxication that liquor could never bring—drunk with the fiery elixir of beauty, the destroying draught of power, and the soul-piercing inevitability of music. Often I am tortured to think that what I so deeply feel must always remain, for the most, unshared, uncommunicated. Yet, at least I have felt, have heard and seen and known, beauty that is inconceivable, that no words and no creative medium are able to convey. Knowing that the cards are stacked, and realized achievements are mere shadows of the dream, I still try to give some faint but tangible suggestion of what has burned without destroying me.

But I realize that what I have felt must grow within one, and it is folly that will be scorned and misinterpreted to seek to tell of it.

Such is my cry, such is my plaint, and I know there is no reply. Mine seems a task essentially futile. Try as I may, I have never yet, that I know of, succeeded in conveying more than a glimpse of my visions. I am condemned to feel the withering fire of beauty pouring into me. I am condemned to the need of putting this fire outside myself and spreading it somewhere, somehow, and I am torn by the knowledge that what I have felt cannot be given to another. I cannot bear to contain these rending flames, and I am helpless to let them out. So I wonder how I can go on living and being casual as one must.

Here Everett unleashes a skillfully written blast at white residents of the Indian country. Of all the people Everett disliked, he seemed to have special antipathy for Indian traders. Traveling as he did through the Navajo country, he encountered these white men fairly often, but he rarely liked them. Everett never complained specifically about John Wetherill, the trader at Kayenta, but he undoubtedly included Wetherill in his disapprobation. On the other hand,

it has been reported that Wetherill had little respect for Everett, whom he considered a "pest" who would simply hang around for days seeking information and conversation, but who would buy nothing.[20] Obviously the old trader-explorer and the young artist were worlds apart in their thinking, their objectives, and their basic philosophies.

Two Rules In Life

I thought that there were two rules in life—never count the cost, and never do anything unless you can do it wholeheartedly. Now is the time to live.

—Diary entry for 11 June 1934

June 17
Kayenta, Arizona

Dear Bill,

Your letter reached me a couple of days ago and I enjoyed it. I did feel more than a twinge of conscience in writing that letter, but I couldn't help it. It's fun to imagine that one has an effect on others—the will to power, I guess. Often, alone in an endless open desert, I find it hard to believe that the rest of the world exists, and yet, letters sometimes establish an intimate connection which actual contact could not.

Do you know, it is in a way rather sad that you could not have had some of my wild experiences, for you have the desire to use such things, and I have not. Perhaps it is your craving for material security or perhaps for the world's recognition. Maybe you hunger to project and perpetuate your personality, in fear of the awful finality of death.

Personally I have no least desire for fame. I feel only a stir of distaste when I think of being called "the well known author" or "the great artist." I fear, or rather, the rest of the world should fear, that I am becoming quite antisocial. I have no desire to bend my efforts toward entertaining the bored and blase world. And that's what writing amounts to—or at least, your kind, I think. Your stories, if polished and published, would serve to divert various morons and business people. They would help them to occupy a few hours of their lives in reading about the imagined activities of fictitious characters. Then, more thoroughly satisfied with their own more peaceful or otherwise superior lives, they would use the magazine to start a fire or sell it to the junkman.

I hope this gets you down, for I feel like puncturing the stupid satisfaction and silly aspirations of the world this morning. And not because I am wounded by it either, for I am myself in fine fettle. This despite the fact that night before last I nearly kicked the bucket from poisoned food.

Beauty has always been my god; it has meant more than people to me. And how my god, or goddess, is flouted in this country, which to me is the most beautiful I've known in all my wanderings! It has come to the point where I no longer like to have anything to do with the white people here, except to get supplies and go on, and I think I shall not say any more what I do here.

Living in the midst of such utter and overpowering beauty as nearly kills a sensitive person by its piercing glory, they are deaf, dumb, and blind to it all. Behind bars in their dirty, dingy, ill-lighted trading posts, they think of nothing but money. When they question me, it is, how much do you make, where do you sell your stuff, what prices do you get? Not that they entertain any passing notion of acquiring a painting; it is only their single-minded interest in money. And when they have it, they seem to be comfortable enough in their stupid way, but they do not live.

A while ago I spent all my money for a bracelet and was broke most of the while since. It is a beautiful thing; I had never thought of owning one, but it seemed to fit so well, and I liked the design and the three turquoises so well, that I have never regretted the purchase. By day it is like a bit of the sky on my wrist, when my hand is on the saddle horn, and by firelight, the stones have a rich greenish luster, as they reflect the leaping flames.

But one of my trader friends asked as soon as he saw it, "How much did it cost?" He saw it only as merchandise.

Three evenings ago, after a depressing experience at a post, I rode out into the open desert and the sage, with vast reaching vermilion mesas and distant blue mountains, glad to be alone and free.

I painted at sunset—dark, towering buttes, with pure clean lines, and golden light on the western cliffs as the sun went down. Then I rode on while the new moon, a silver crescent, gleamed in the deepening blue of the night sky. A fire winked and blazed a mile or two away, at the foot of a lonely butte. As it was in my direction, I steered my course by it, thinking I might stop for a cup of coffee. The fire disappeared as we descended little dips, but always appeared again, burning steadily. At last we reached it and I dismounted and entered the circle, making a greeting. There was an old grandmother not thin, with straying locks of white hair, and the old man, her husband. Two younger women, their babies, and a young buck.

When I asked Shimassohn, the grandmother, for some coffee, she beamed, asked me questions, gave me tea and coffee, pushed namskadi (bread) toward me, and urged me to eat.

I can't tell you how her kindness warmed my bruised heart. I felt an overflowing of tenderness for those people. They are so childlike and simple and friendly when left alone.

I have often stayed with the Navajos; I've known the best of them, and they were fine people. I have ridden with them on their horses, eaten with them, and even taken part in their ceremonies. Many are the delightful encounters, and many the exchange of gifts I've had with them. They have many faults; most of them are not very clean, and they will steal anything from a stranger, but never if you approach them with trust as a friend. Their weird, wild chanting as they ride the desert is often magnificent, with a high-pitched, penetrating quality.

The people I stopped with were Utes, come down from the north. After breakfast of hot goat's milk gravy, mutton, and Dutch oven bread, I brought in my burros as the two men and the grandmother were preparing to ride to the post fifteen miles off. Grandmother led her horse over the hill, as the Indian women will never mount in the presence of a white man.

I rode all morning over sunny dunes of vermilion sand with broom and sunflower on the ridges, and nodding grass plumes. Finally I reached a little unnamed canyon where I had camped before, and rode to the very end of it, hoping against hope that the waterhole would not be dry.

There was just enough for me and my burros. Some loose horses came in, and would have drunk it all if I had not been first. There were other holes farther off which they could find.

So I unpacked under a tall, arched pinyon tree, unfastened the diamond hitch, took off the kyaks and saddles, gave the burros some oats, curried them, and turned them out to grass in a spacious bend of the canyon. There are two cliff dwellings there, one barely accessible.

After a refreshing bath at the edge of the little dwindling pool at the foot of the cliff, I wandered in the canyon and watched the burros, then worked over my equipment. This trip has been longer than I expected, for I have been in many beautiful places, and did not wish to taste, but to drink deep. I have wandered over more than four hundred miles with the burros these last six weeks, paying no attention to trails, except as they happened to serve me, and finding my water as I went. I never went two days without discovering it.

Tomorrow I shall start for Navajo Mountain and the wild country near it. At Oljato (Moonlight Water) an old timer will help me shoe my burros in preparation for the miles and miles of bare sandstone ridges that must be traversed.

Here in Kayenta, I have been staying with Lee Bradley, my best friend here. He is a tall, commanding figure of a man, half white, and combining the best qualities of both races. He is influential in the tribe, and has the mail contract and several other government contracts. His wife is Indian.

Lee's house is a rambling adobe structure. There are several pets—a baby prairie dog, rabbits, a young goat, cats, and Kisge, who is undoubtedly the father or grandfather of Curly. He is an enormous shaggy dog, with the same brown eyes and wide face.

Jose Garcia, my good friend at Chilichinbito, whose rare, old Spanish hospitality I enjoyed last month, was killed a few weeks ago, riding the load on a truck. A wheel came off, and the whole load fell on him.

There is an archaeological expedition in town now. Some pretty likeable and intelligent young fellows are in it, and I expect to visit their camp when I come back from the mountains.

Summer draws on, the shrill song of the cicadas is over, and the scarlet cactus blooms are gone. Columbine and Sego Lily have vanished from the canyons. Now only the sunflower, and in damp, shaded places, the Scarlet Bugler, are found.

In the throbbing heat of desert noon, siestas are in order, and I have been traveling at dawn and sunset, and by moonlight.

Did you get *The Purple Land?* I liked your line about "the kingly insolence of desert battlements."

I shall be returning to Kayenta in a month or so, before finally leaving for El Canon Grande, and you can reach me here. So, until then, live gaily, live deeply, and wrest from life some of its infinite possibilities.

Love from Everett

June 19
Near Oljato
(Moonlight Water)

Dear Father and Mother,

Your letters and packages reached me a few days ago. The bridle has been useful, and I enjoyed the dried plums. I had never tasted them before. I was glad to have the magazines. I was thinking of asking you for a resume of political and economic events and trends, but they serve the purpose. I gave one that I finished with to a trader.

The other day I mailed you a few things I was through with. I think Mother would enjoy *Death Comes For the Archbishop*. It is a beautifully written book about this country. I think the Shiprock papers would interest you, too.

I met some of the young fellows from the Berkeley expedition. They are likeable fellows. When you heard they were calling for volunteers, what they really said was that they wanted volunteers who would pay three or four hundred dollars for expenses in addition to carrying on scientific work.

I am on my way to Navajo Mountain now, and probably will not get back until July or August, so I will be pretty low in supplies when I do get back to Kayenta. There are a couple of things I wish you would send me; *Don Quixote*, a Modern Library book which you can get for ninety-five cents, and eight of those half-pound chocolate bars which you can get downtown for eight or nine cents each. Get half of them plain, and half with raisins and peanuts.

I thought it would be a good time to read *Don Quixote*, and it is a long book that will last me a while. Some writers rate it as one of the greatest pieces of literature, along with the *Odyssey*. Have you ever read Cervantes unabridged?

The Sense of Beauty was interesting, but in a way, rather painful. I am always interested in psychology and yet it disgusts me to think of people as puppets pulled this way and that by every force to which they are susceptible.

I have made a few good paintings and others that I need to work on.

I've had to buy considerable equipment—ropes, leathers, etc. Tomorrow I'm going to shoe my burros, to take them over the rocks.

The wind is blowing now; sandstorms yesterday, but no rain for three weeks.

Love from Everett

June
Monument Valley, Utah

Dear Carl [surname unknown],

You could not guess in what a fantastic place I am. I sit in the shade of an ancient, dying juniper tree, cushioned on my Navajo saddle blankets. On all sides, the burning sun beats down on silent, empty desert. To right and left, long walls of sandstone mesas reach away into the distance, the shadows in their fluted clefts the color of claret. Before me, the desert drops sheer away into a vast valley, in which strangely eroded buttes of all delicate and intense shadings of vermilion, orange, and purple, tower into a cloudless turquoise sky.

Here I am truly alone. The faint tinkle of the bell on one of my burros is the only sound. The nearest water is many miles away.

This is near the end of a long trip—some four hundred miles of desert, canyon, and mountain. I have often thought of you and regretted that something similar could not be happening to you. For I have had all and more than I ever desired. I have constantly known beauty so piercing as to be almost unbearable. I have led a wild gay life of fantastic adventures that seem to crowd upon me without my searching for them.

As a child I used to dream of such a life as this. Little did I imagine that all my dreams would be realized and all surpassed in every direction. Thinking of you, it has seemed almost wrong that one person should have such utter fulfillment while another leads a life of poisonous denial.

This time in my wanderings I have had more reckless self-confidence than ever before. I have gone my way regardless of everything but beauty. Trails I have used only when they led my way. I know the Indians now—have lived with them and exchanged gifts, and enjoyed the hospitality of the finest of them, riding their horses and taking part in their weird ceremonies. I know the white people too—all the traders in this locality, and strange experiences I have had with them, but I like the Indians better. I had two true friends among the whites, but one was driven from the country by misfortune, and the other was killed a week ago. A truck lost a wheel and the load fell and crushed him.

Hundreds of times I have trusted my life to crumbling sandstone and nearly vertical angles in the search for water or cliff dwellings. Twice I was nearly gored to death by a wild bull. But always, so far, I've escaped unscathed and gone forth to other adventures.

Summer draws on, the shrill song of the cicadas is over, and the scarlet cactus blooms are gone. Columbine and Sego Lily have vanished, too. Now only the sunflower, and in shaded canyons, the Scarlet Bugler, are found. In these last few days the heat has been intense, and siestas have been in order. I have traveled only at dawn and evening, often after sunset, under the stars. I shall never forget coming down the Lukachukai Mountains at dusk, with the blood-red moon falling through the pine branches as I descended.

Your good friend,
Everett

In mid-June he determined to make a trip to Navajo Mountain, clearly visible as a ten-thousand-foot-high forested dome in the west. Its Navajo name was *Naatsis'aan*, or Head of the Earth Woman,[21] and it is one of the most significant sacred mountains of the Navajos. He also wished to visit Rainbow Bridge, which spans one of the small creeks—flowing northward in a side canyon from the heights of Navajo Mountain.

Everett's route from Monument Valley to the south side of the mountain led him over high mesas and across deep side canyons tributary to the San Juan River, a few tortuous miles to the north. On the way he nearly lost one of his burros when the animal fell backward and rolled to the brink of a "yawning gulf." The following letters were written from his camp at War God Spring, located at about the 8,700-foot level, two miles south of the Navajo Mountain summit.

Everett does not understate the character of the trail along the west side of Navajo Mountain to Rainbow Bridge. When the trail was first opened in 1922 by personnel of the Charles L. Bernheimer Expedition (including John Wetherill, Indian trader and guide; Zeke Johnson, famous guide and Custodian of Natural Bridges National Monument; and Earl H. Morris, well-known early archeologist in the Four Corners area), they were forced to use dynamite to break through some of the rock "fins."[22]

June 29
War God Spring
On Navajo Mountain, Utah

Dear Bill,

A high wind is roaring in the tops of the tall pines. The moon is just rising on the rim of the desert, far below. Stars gleam through the pine boughs and the filmy clouds that move across the night sky. Graceful, slim-trunked aspens reach upward under the towering pines. Their slender, curving branches are white in the firelight, and an occasional downward breeze flickers their pale green leaves.

The beauty of this place is perfect of its kind; I could ask for nothing more. A little spring trickles down under aspens and white

Navajo Mountain rises over 10,000 feet just south of the Colorado River, which flow in Glen Canyon left to right across the center of the photograph. At lower left is the knife-edged escarpment that terminates Kaiparowits Plateau. Photo September 1982 by Gibbs M. Smith.

fir. By day the marshy hollow is aswarm with gorgeous butterflies; Tiger and Zebra Swallowtails, the Angel Wings, the Mourning Cloak, and others. There are a hundred delightful places to sit and dream; friendly rocks to lean against—springy beds of pine needles to lie on and look up at the sky or the tall smooth tree trunks, with spirals of branches and their tufted foliage.

Two small bands of handsome bay horses, each with a bell mare, water here. Often I hear from opposite directions the deep-toned music of their bells, against the sharper tinkle of the burro bell. No human comes to break the dreamy solitude. Far below, the tawny desert, seamed with canyons, throbs in the savage desert sun. But here it is lofty and cool.

It is hard not to be sentimental about my burros; they are such droll, friendly creatures. On the trail, particularly when they do the wrong thing in a tight place, I am often impatient with them. But when they stand up to their knees in wildflowers with blossoms in their lips and look at me with their lustrous, large brown eyes, cocking their furry ears and switching their tails at their fat sides—then who that knew them could help loving them?

I had to laugh, a few mornings ago on the desert, when tracking the two foolish looking pals, I saw their trail leading up to an abandoned hogan and heard a snort and scuffle inside. With all the spacious desert around them, they had chosen to bed down in that little hogan, which just comfortably contained the two of them!

We followed a steep trail out of Copper Canyon opposite No Man's Mesa. Near the rim it was just a scramble, and Leopard, whom I was packing, in attempting to claw his way over a steep place, lost his balance and fell over backwards. He turned two backward somersaults and a side roll, landing with his feet waving, about six inches from the yawning gulf. I pulled him to his feet. He was a bit groggy at first; he had lost a little fur, and the pack was scratched.

Now the moon swings clear of the treetops. The wind is in the pine trees; what other sound is like it!

The perfection of this place is one reason why I distrust ever returning to the cities. Here I wander in beauty and perfection. There one walks in the midst of ugliness and mistakes. All is made for man, but where can one find surroundings to match one's ideals and imaginings? It is possible to live and dream in ugly, ill-fitting places, but how much better to be where all is beautiful and unscarred.

With plenty of money, the way is smoothed, and it is fun to create a place to match your personality. Sometimes too it is fun to tinker away in a picturesque hovel, but the struggle for a mean existence is not worth it.

Here I take my belongings with me. The picturesque gear of packing, and my gorgeous Navajo saddle blankets make a place my own. But when I go, I leave no trace.

The post where I last got supplies is a costly place to trade. The owner has to haul his stuff 350 miles by truck, over the worst of roads. In this remote place he never sees a tourist, and seldom a dime crosses his counter in a year. All his business is trade; in wool, sheepskins and blankets. Gallup, New Mexico, is the nearest place where he can dispose of them. He has been offered seventeen cents a pound for the wool which cost him twenty, if he will haul it to New Mexico.

I baked a cake in my frying pan this noon. It was really a success. I wish you could have tasted it.

The beauty of this country is becoming a part of me. I feel more detached from life and somehow gentler. Except for passing flurries, it has become impossible for me to censure anyone. I wish harm to no one and occasionally try to be kind, though it seems futile striving. I have some good friends here, but no one who really understands why I am here or what I do. I don't know of anyone, though, who would have more than a partial understanding; I have gone too far alone.

I have always been unsatisfied with life as most people live it. Always I want to live more intensely and richly. Why muck and conceal one's true longings and loves, when by speaking of them one might find someone to understand them, and by acting on them one might discover one's self? It is true that in the world such lack of reserve usually meets with hostility, misunderstanding, and scorn. Here in isolation I need not fear on that score, though the strangers I do encounter usually judge me wrongly. But I was never one to be content with less than the most from life, and shall go on reaching, and leaving my soul defenseless to attacks. I seldom retaliate, for I perceive too well the ultimate futility.

And meanwhile, I have used my body mercilessly, seldom giving way to it until forced, so that I should not wonder if it will turn traitor to me some time. Anyway, as Omar says, "If the soul can naked on the air of heaven ride, wer't not a shame for him in this clay carcass crippled to abide?" That is a big if, but may the time never come when I have to minister to my body.

I was thinking when I wrote you last how I refused you that picture of the old watertower, and I meant to give it to you then, but felt awkward about saying it. You don't even have to frame it unless you want to, but it would look vastly better, and you ought to in fairness. It is not the soul of the desert, bare and glorious, nor yet that of the forest or the mountain. But it is an old watertower on a hilltop, in the last light, and its windows look westward to the old, mysterious sea. Perhaps you will be able to imagine that and more that is in it—even if no one else can.

Now the aspen trunks are tall and white in the moonlight. A wind croons in the pines. The mountain sleeps.

Peace to you.
Everett

June 30
Navajo Mountain, Utah

Dear Father and Mother,

The sun is beginning to set, and at last my camp is in shadow. The desert still throbs with heat, but below in the canyon, frogs have begun to croak, heralding the cool approach of Night. I am a day's journey from Rainbow Bridge. Yesterday I came down the mountain, over a steep and rocky trail. The days on the mountain were delightful, and I cannot remember a more beautiful camp than the one I had there, under the tall pines and the aspens, with swarms of butterflies at the little trickling spring.

Seen from the mountain, the country between here and the San Juan and Colorado rivers and beyond them is as rough and impenetrable a territory as I have ever seen. Thousands of domes and towers of sandstone lift their rounded pink tops from blue and purple shadows. To the east, great canyons seam the desert, cutting vermilion gashes through the grey-green of the sage-topped mesas.

I remember well the tortuous trail leading out of Copper Canyon opposite No Man's Mesa. A vast expanse of brown country lay between the mesas. Far north was the silent, nearly empty canyon of the San Juan, with a vivid green strip of willows. Opposite me the mile-wide canyon was banded with blue-green, grey-blue, and delicate purple, surmounted by dull vermilion, which grew more vivid until at the rim of the mesa, the color was almost blindingly intense.

It has not rained for a whole month now, and most of the canyons and waterholes are dry. I have been lucky and diligent in my search for water. The burros have never had to go two days without it. Here there is fine clear water under cottonwoods. I enjoyed a splash this afternoon, and afterwards washed my shirt and socks.

The saffron of the clouds that lie low on the skyline is turning to a soft blue-grey. The orange turrets and pyramids opposite me fairly glow against the paling sky.

I reread *A Dreamer's Tales* of Dunsany on the mountain, and appreciated them more than ever. How beautifully Dunsany writes, and how rich is his imagination! I thoroughly sympathize with his hatred of the commercial, the ugly, and the unimaginative.

I hope you sent *Don Quixote* and the chocolate. With the rest for July. I wish you would send me one very sturdy pair of shorts, size 32, as they are not to be had here, and mine are in shreds. If you could find some, I would appreciate a couple of pounds of dried apples. They make delicious applesauce, with a little cinnamon. Dry dates too, if you can get them easily.

The last trader with whom I dealt has to haul his supplies 350 miles over some very rough roads, so you can imagine what the prices were.

I expect to be back in Kayenta in a couple of weeks or thereabouts. Then off again southward and westward.

Love from Everett

Rainbow Bridge, looking north, as Everett Ruess first saw it when hiking in from Navajo Mountain in July 1934. Photo October 1959 by W.L. Rusho.

From War God Spring he descended to the trail circling south and west of Navajo Mountain. He stopped at Rainbow Lodge, then proceeded on to Rainbow Bridge, which he must have reached about 2 July 1934. But if he described the natural bridge in any of his letters, those letters have not been located.

[Addressee unknown]

I just reached Rainbow Lodge tonight and found the people very friendly and likeable.

In the last two days I have traversed the longest continuous up-and-down broken trail that I ever went over. It was tremendously dramatic to stride down steep sandhills in shadowed canyons only a dozen feet wide at the bottom with towering walls above. I don't see how anyone was ever able to even plan the trail; there is such a maze of narrow winding canyons, many of them blocked at one end or both, and all buried down in the confusing jumble of towers and turrets, so that you can never see where they lead until you get there. It was a real thrill to go through that country.²³

Before he left Kayenta, Everett met some young archaeologists and helpers associated with the Rainbow Bridge—Monument Valley Expedition. Sponsored by the University of California and the Museum of Northern Arizona, this group investigated Anasazi ruins along the Utah-Arizona border during 1933 and 1934. Although he was not offered a job, or even encouraged to visit, Everett was intrigued by their work and was determined to join them. Since he knew that they planned to excavate cliff ruins in high tributaries of Tsegi Canyon, he was able to head directly for their camp. Ten days after leaving Rainbow Bridge, Everett was with the expedition.

> July 14
> Camp Anasazi
> Degosha Boko,Tsegi

Dear Father and Mother,

For five days I have been with the expedition, having a good deal of fun. The packer for the outfit was a friend of mine at the Grand Canyon three years ago. Several of the fellows are from Berkeley and know friends of mine there. The packer paints, and the young fellow who makes architectural drawings of the cliff dwellings sketches, too. Ben Wetherill is partly in charge. I met Hargrave, the archaeologist, at Mesa Ranch school before. Yesterday I went out with Mr. Barton, the biologist and plant man, and explored a nearby canyon.²⁴

I worked all morning today, hewing logs for a table and carving slabs for a floor. This afternoon I went down the canyon to a side canyon and climbed into Bat Woman House, a nice little cliff ruin above a spring with Douglas fir. I made a painting of one of the rooms and the Bat Woman pictograph.

I am writing this in the supply tent at night, using the light of the six paper players. The burros are getting a good rest. I don't know how long I'll stay here. All I get is my meals. Some of the fellows are well worth knowing, and the canyons are a delight to explore.

Too bad I didn't have some money last month. I had to pass up some fine saddle blankets. I may be able to get a blanket for you this month or next.

> Love from Everett

A few days after his arrival, Everett was asked to serve as cook for a small team headed by Clay Lockett that planned to excavate a

Everett (center) and two men with the Rainbow Bridge-Monument Valley Expedition examine one of Everett's burros in July 1934. At right is archaeologist Clay Lockett. The other man is unidentified.

Archaeologist Clay Lockett and Everett's burro climb a "mule ladder" in Tsegi Canyon, Arizona, in July 1934.

ruin in a high, almost inaccessible cave. Wishing to avoid daily climbs and descents from this cave (each of which consumed almost an hour), they were able, using Everett as a cook, to remain in the cave almost two weeks. A highly unusual cave of the Basketmaker II period, it contained several half-buried mummies that had to be carefully excavated, photographed, and crated.

Everett did not impress Lockett with his interest in archaeology, for Ruess spent most of his free time, which was considerable, in gazing out over the landscape. Lockett noticed also that Everett seemed careless about his own safety when climbing around cliffs, citing as an example the time Everett wanted to make a watercolor sketch of rain-spawned waterfalls shooting off from several points. According to Lockett, Everett nearly got himself killed finding a good vantage point on the wet slickrock. Needless to say, the rain-streaked watercolor sketch was not one of his better efforts.

July 22
Lasker Marker Cave
Skeleton Mesa, Degosha Boko

Dear Mother and Father,

At present I am in a cave below the rim of Skeleton Mesa, looking out over the canyons of the Degosha Boko. This cave is in the Navajo sandstone a few feet under the rim. About three hundred feet below and some eighty feet back under, is Twin Caves cliff dwelling, but this cave is far more interesting. The culture here goes back to the first quarter of the Christian era, and presents many unsolved problems.

I have been in this locality about two weeks, working with the expedition. With me in the cave are an archaeologist, his assistant, and a photographer who also digs. Below in the canyon are ornithologists, entomologists, botanists, zoologists, geologists, and the like, each with plenty of problems unsolved.

We have been in the cave for four days now. There is a very precarious way down the face of the cliff with footholds in the stone hundreds of years old. The only other way is the horse ladder, six miles up the canyon. We came that way with pack burros, passing the carcass of a horse that slipped. After two days wandering on the mesa top, in the trackless forests, we crossed the bare rock ledges in a heavy cloudburst and came here.

We have found twelve burials here, with two fairly well preserved mummies. One mystery lies in the fact that all of the skeletons are headless, though there are two lower jaws. Evidently the graves were robbed perhaps by the Pueblo I people, but it is a difficult problem to ascertain the facts. There are traces of Basket Makers III, and Pueblo I and II on the surface.

The Basketmakers are the oldest people who have been definitely traced back in the Southwest. They used the *atlatl* or throwing stick and had corn. Pottery was first invented by the Pueblo I, and the bow came into use. Later beans and squash were used, and the turkey was domesticated. In Pueblo II, pottery was of a finer grade with different design types, and color was used.

Twin Caves, below, is Pueblo III, with a further advance. In the whole Tsegi drainage there is no Pueblo IV. All the cliff dwellers were driven off by the eighteen-year drought that began in 1290.

I have been doing the packing and the cooking here. Clayborn Lockett, the archaeologist in charge here, is a grizzled young chap of twenty-eight, widely experienced, and a magnificent humorist. He is an ethnologist and something of an artist as well. His two helpers are boys of nineteen and twenty from the University at Berkeley. We have great fun up here by ourselves, discovering something new every day, and looking out over everything from our sheltered cave.

I'm going down the cliff now to get our mail and a few camp luxuries.

Love to all,
Everett

Rugged country near Tsegi Canyon where Everett worked with an archaeological expedition in July 1934.

Upon termination of the archaeolgical excavation, Everett headed cross-country for the Hopi villages, where he wished to witness the annual August rain dances. Not only did he watch them, but he was actually invited to participate, at Mishongnovi, in the Antelope Dance, a signal honor to a white man.

August 25
Hotevilla, Arizona

Dear Mother and Father,

Yesterday I saw the Snake dance here, and now it is beginning to rain. I have been having great fun with the Hopis here, and just finished a painting of the village. The children were clustered all around me, some helping and some hindering. I have just bought a Hopi plaque for you, which has really a fine design, I think. You can probably use it on the dinner table. I was going to get a kachina doll, but decided you would have more use for the plaque. This morning I mailed a package with some Hopi prayer sticks, a rim shard from a prehistoric bowl, and a clay cow and calf (to replace your Chinese horse that was broken. They are even more fragile, however, and you will have to be very careful where you place them). A little Navajo boy made them. I stopped with his family one night in Blue Canyon, and he ranged his whole menagerie in the firelight for me. He had a whole band of clay horses, one with even a clay saddle, and a forked stick for a rider. The cow and calf are decidedly original, and I think you will like them.

I left the expedition more than a week ago, as its work was terminated. My last work was cooking and excavating for and with seven, in a Pueblo II dwelling dating 1127 A.D. I left the group and crossed the Comb Ridge, stopping at White Dog Cave, where the sandstone block had fallen and crushed the cliff dwellers.

At Kayenta I had very little time to spare. I made one trip through Monument Valley and decided to cross Black Mesa and see the Snake Dance. I rode up from the desert floor to the rim of Black Mesa by moonlight, camping in the pines. Then I beat my way southward, steering by the sun, and following a canyon as far as was practical. The whole country slopes southward, there are no landmarks of any kind, and there was hardly any water. I did not see a human being until the third night. After that I passed a number of Navajo camps, beat my way through the timber and the high sage until I reached Dinnebito (Navajo water) wash, and rode into the pueblo at daybreak on the day of the dance. Here I met the expedition members and other friends. They left last night, but one of them is staying behind with me to visit another pueblo for the next dance, tomorrow. He, Vernon DeMars, is from Berkeley. [He] sketches, does architectural work, and performs Indian dances. This afternoon he has been trading turtle shells and parrot feathers, for gourd rattles, kilts, and other trappings of the Hopi dancers.

Probably this won't reach you for a while, as the mail service is very irregular here. My next address is Cameron, Arizona.

Love from Everett

August 29
Gallup, New Mexico

Dear Waldo,

I rode here from Mishongnovi with a Hopi silversmith who is selling turquoise to Indians and traders.

The Inter-Tribal Indian ceremony is being held here, starting today. I saw Oliver LaFarge and the Kaiser's niece at the snake dance. She certainly knows how to take care of herself. I hope your plans are working out.

Affectionately,
Everett

Old Chief Tewaquaptewa, holding his prayer stick and kachina as defense against the camera, was Hopi Chief of Oraibi when Everett visited the villages in 1934. Photo by Dr. David E. Miller, 1958.

August 29
Gallup, New Mexico

Dear Mother,

I rode here from Second Mesa with a Hopi silversmith, who was selling turquoise along the way. Vernon and I spent a night in a Hopi Kiva at Mishongnovi, watching Indians practice the Buffalo and Antelope dances. Now we are going to see some of the dances at the Inter-Tribal Indian ceremonial. Yesterday I sent you a Hopi bowl from Hotevilla.

Love from Everett

September 1
Gallup, New Mexico

Dear Mother,

I'm starting back for Second Mesa with some Hopis today. My friend and I have been learning Indian songs. I got a fine blanket for my saddle.

169

How do you like these San Domingo women [on the opposite side of the postcard]?

Love from Everett

September 10
Grand Canyon, Arizona

Dear Father and Mother,

Arrived here at Desert View last night. Found your combined letter today, about your own trip north. Lost a burro (Leopard) down Little Colorado Canyon the other day, with some of the pack, but have already replaced him with a bigger burro. My camp is next to that of an artist from Tahiti. Since Gallup I have been at Mishongnovi, where my Hopi friends painted me up and had me in their Antelope Dance. I was the only white person there. Killed two rattlers the other day. One struck before I saw him. I caught the other alive. Sold a print yesterday.

Love from Everett

When the archaeological excavation was finished and the team was breaking up, Lockett had cheerfully invited Everett to drop by his home in Flagstaff, if the occasion should ever arise. "I wasn't home but about three days," Lockett says, "when here came Everett to accept my invitation." (Actually, the time between the invitation and the acceptance was closer to three weeks.) Clay Lockett's income, in 1934, was only about $30 a month, supplemented by his garden and a few chickens. Everett's big appetite was not welcomed, especially by Lockett's wife, Florence, who informed her husband, half in jest, after a week of having Everett as a guest, "Either he leaves or I do!" Lockett then tactfully suggested to Everett that he visit Oak Creek Canyon—immediately.

A few days later, after his trip to Oak Creek Canyon, Everett stopped briefly to give Lockett a gift—a book of Navajo stories, and to give Florence a copy of *Anthony Adverse,* which cost five dollars—a large sum at the time. Lockett concluded that Everett was not trying to take advantage of them but was simply a "free spirit," who did not worry about the complexities of social behavior, and who simply "loved the Navajos and everybody, loved animals, burros, dogs, kids, and everything." Everett himself, says Lockett, was a "strange kid."

September 27
Flagstaff, Arizona
Grand Canyon

Dear Ned [Frisius],

I was surprised and pleased to find your letter at Grand Canyon the other day. I have spent the past week vacationing. I left my burros, Cockleburrs and Chocolate, under the care of an artist friend at Desert View, and took the highway down here to visit a friend with whom I did some archaeological work this summer. It was fascinating work— up almost sheer sandstone cliffs, clinging by worn footholds hundreds of years old, or on narrow crumbling edges, was more spectacular than anything in the Sierras.

From Flagstaff I went south to Oak Creek, and painted some brilliantly lighted vermilion cliffs against inky storm skies. Came back and saw the first snows on the San Francisco Peaks, and the slopes golden with yellowing aspens.

Evidently you overheard something of my adventures with my friends the Indians. I have a great time with them, especially the Navajos. I once spent three days far up in a desert canyon, assisting and watching a Navajo sing for a sick woman. I drove away countless hordes of evil spirits but after I went away the girl died. The sand paintings, seldom seen by white men, were gorgeous.

In my wanderings this year I have taken more chances and had more wild adventures than ever before. And what magnificent country I have seen—wild, tremendous wasteland stretches, lost mesas, blue mountains rearing upward from the vermilion sands of the desert, canyons five feet wide at the bottom and hundreds of feet deep, cloudbursts roaring down unnamed canyons, and hundreds of houses of the cliff dwellers, abandoned a thousand years ago.

Glad you are getting a good start at college.

Your friend,
Everett

September 1934
Flagstaff, Arizona

Dear Mother,

Yesterday I returned from a sketching jaunt in Oak Creek Canyon, and now I am visiting with a friend [Clayborn Lockett] in Flagstaff who is doing archaeological work for the museum here. I'm going back to Desert View, Grand Canyon in a day or two.

171

Untitled blockprint by Everett Ruess.

In Oak Creek Canyon I painted a couple of striking effects of brilliantly lighted buttes against inky storm skies. Also a massive tower, calmly beautiful under shadowing clouds.

Chocolate is tentatively the name of Cockleburr's new companion. He is young, strong, and good natured, inexperienced, but bound to learn from his experienced comrade. I bought him from a Navajo woman for the vast sum of nine dollars, and a currycomb thrown in. I had to teach him to eat grain, bread crusts, and salt. He was a young barbarian!

I have been replacing some of the things lost from the pack. I built a new kyak, and decorated both boxes with cliff dwelling designs, painting them all over. Their like has never been known, I'm sure.

I've sold a number of pictures lately, and you won't have to worry about me much longer. In fact you can discontinue money orders any time you want to. I received the one for fifteen early this month, but nothing since.

I could copy the Indian songs, but the rhythm is one of the main elements, with the melody, and almost no white man can sing in the high pitch which is natural to the Navajos. One of my favorites is:

Wey ah hah neyah heyah heya heyoh eh hijah

Yoh eh hyah, yoh eh hyah, heyah, heyoh oh o

Heyah heyoh heyanah hyah, heyah heyoh

Heyoh eh hayah, Yah eh hayah, yah eh hyoh yah

Naturally I did not try to take photographs of the Hopi dances, as that would be like taking a flashlight picture of communion in some church.

The San Francisco Peaks soar high in the afternoon sunlight. The slopes are golden with yellowing aspen.

Love from Everett

October 1
Desert View
Grand Canyon

Dear Father and Mother,

I'm back at the canyon now, and received your letter of the twenty-eighth with the money order. Evidently you didn't have my last letter. I don't want you to send any more money, as I can get along all right, and you really need it. I have twelve dollars due me for a picture I made a while ago.

I sent you an oil of the outer houses at Hotevilla. It is pretty large, and I don't suppose you can do anything with it unless you put it at the top of the hallway.

In a day or so I am going to send you a small Navajo blanket.

The burro bell is tinkling merrily. In a day or so I am going down in the canyon. Here is a curious fact. It is only ten miles across the canyon, but by car, it is 350 miles to the other side, and by mail, or rail, one thousand miles. The squirrels and other little animals on each side have developed into different species.

I haven't had poison ivy this year. I used up my medicine in the Tsegi country, and neglected to get any since, so I was anxious to have some more. Oak Creek has poison ivy, but I stayed clear of it. I'm going into lower country where I would run a risk.

Love to all,
Everett

October 15
P.O. Ruby's Inn, Utah

Dear Mother,

Today I climbed up from Indian Gardens to get mail and supplies before starting for Utah. The date cookies reached me all right, and thanks, but the chocolate cake was not discovered under the crackers until there was a beautiful green and yellow mold inside. Thank Mrs. Ryall nevertheless.

One new accomplishment I have added to my list! I can shoe a burro! Last week I shod both donkeys, and neither had ever been shod before. It was some battle, and none of us came off without a few bruises.

A *kiva* is an underground ceremonial chamber of the Hopis and the cliff dwellers. Some are round, some square, some rectangular, with the one entrance through the roof. The bones are human sacrum, one male, the other female (more curved), about 1500 years old.

I'm glad you liked the pictures. Those I sent you were only sketches, though. I'll send you some better ones soon.

Autumn is here, with a sharp tang in the air, but below in the canyon I have been enjoying a second summer. The cottonwoods are just beginning to be touched with yellow and orange.

Down into the canyon again!

Love from Everett

With autumn well underway, Everett left the Grand Canyon and headed north, toward the rugged lands of southeast Utah that he had never visited. Whether he had a specific objective or was simply following his wanderlust from place to place is not clear. Probably he wanted to see Bryce Canyon, as well as much of the nearby desert, plateau, and canyon country. His route must have taken him and his burros northward to the Colorado River, where they crossed Navajo Bridge. Everett may also have visited historic Lee's Ferry, just five miles upstream from the bridge. After leaving the river he probably followed U.S. 89 across the Kaibab Plateau, through Kanab, and on to Bryce Canyon National Park. Although obscure trails did lead from Lee's Ferry northward along the Paria River to the village of Tropic, Utah, the fact that Everett does not mention traveling this adventurous route suggests that he must have reached the park on conventional roads.

By the middle of October, Everett was roaming about Bryce Canyon, stopping normally at tourist viewpoints and following narrow trails through the eroded formations. In the following letter written two weeks later, he reported that he was staying with a National Park Service ranger, Maurice Cope, and his family, who lived in Tropic, a few miles to the east. Since Cope had nine children, Everett was probably not too much of a disruption.

November 4
Tropic, Utah

Dear Father and Mother,

I have been having great fun here today with a Mormon family. There are about nine children, of all ages, and the father is a ranger in Bryce Canyon. This morning I rode out with one of the boys to look for a cow. We rode all over the hills, and stopped at an orchard to load up with apples. Then I went to church, my first time in a Mormon church. It was an interesting experience, and about my first time in church since I was in San Francisco. In our class we had quite a talk about crime, economics, juvenile court, etc. A frank discussion of the national crisis. One of them said that the war and turmoil prophecies of their Mormon saints would be fulfilled next year.

A while ago I sold a couple of pictures to Charlie Plumb, a cartoonist, who owns a ranch in a dramatic situation at Cave Lakes. He works about three months a year and gets $1500 twice a month the rest of the time. He is drunk or blotto at least half the time. One of the ranch hands tried a little gin and nearly died of a heart attack; he could hardly breathe.

I enjoyed riding down from Bryce Canyon, through the grotesque and colorful formations. Mother would surely enjoy the trees; they are fascinating, especially the twisted little pines and junipers. I had never seen the foxtail pine before. It is a ridiculous caricature of a tree, with gangling limbs and most amusing foxtails lopping about in all directions, with no symmetry at all. There is a natural bridge called Tower Bridge.

Hotevilla is a modern Hopi pueblo, founded in 1908 as the result of a bitter quarrel in Oraibi concerning the old and the new way. Oraibi is said to be the oldest continually inhabited town in America— seven hundred years, I think. It was left almost deserted after the quarrel. My painting is of some end houses on the rim of the mesa, near the snake kiva.

The Hopi woman in the upper right house makes pottery containers, and for some superstitious reason, always two at once. They hang mutton jerky out to dry. They did not like me to paint the old man, but I pacified them.

I sent back the kodak because it has not been working well and is an extra expense and weight.

The weather has mostly been delightful, although I was in one snow flurry on the Paunsaqunt Plateau. Now I am heading across the pink cliffs toward Escalante and the lower country toward the river.

Later in the day we had more fun—apple fights, church, and until about morning we amused ourselves with some Navajos who were camped nearby.

Love from Everett

Having been told about the spectacular canyon country along the Escalante River drainage, he first moved thirty-eight miles farther east, to the town of Escalante. He entered town in his usual manner, riding one burro, and leading another, his feet almost touching the ground. His appearance was a novelty that men and women remember to this day.

In Escalante he camped out under the cottonwoods along the Escalante River, while he spent his days visiting local young people. He also poked into some of the nearby side canyons of the Escalante.

November 11
Escalante, Utah

Dear Father and Mother,

After a truly delightful trip over the mountains, finding my way without any trails, I have reached the Mormon town of Escalante. No mail awaited, and I think my ranger friend forgot to tell the postmaster to forward it. I am going south towards the river now, through some rather wild country. I am not sure yet whether I will go across Smokey Mountain to Lee's Ferry and south, or whether I will try and cross the river above the San Juan. The water is very low this year. I might even come back through Boulder, so I may not have a post office for a couple of months. I am taking an ample supply of food with me.

I have had plenty of fun with the boys of this town, riding horses, hunting for arrowheads, and the like. I took a couple of boys to the show last night, *Death Takes a Holiday*. I liked it as well as the play, enjoying the music especially. This year the pinyon nut crop is unusual, and everyone occupies his leisure time in eating them. This year, the severe drought and the grasshoppers have made a critical situation for the farmers.

I promised you some pictures and I am sending a few of them now, as it will lighten the load, and they are getting travel stained. They all have faults, but those I like best, and mean to frame for my room later, are Betatakin, Short Cedars, The Pinnacle, Desert Light, Agathla, and Desert Noon.

I have sold away a few more lately, but I hope you will like those I am sending. As I have more money than I need now, I am sending you ten dollars, and I want both of you to spend five for something you have been wishing to have—books, or a trip, but not anything connected with any kind of a duty. Let this be the first installment on that nickel I promised you when I made my first million.

I'm also enclosing a couple of clippings which I thought would amuse you. The one about Dwight Morrow made me think of Father, but I think he has outstripped him.

Tonight I have been sitting by the fire with two of my friends, eating roast venison and baked potatoes. The burro bell is tinkling merrily nearby as Chocolatero crops the alfalfa. I took their shoes off yesterday. Chocolatero is a good burro by now. It was hard to get him across the Colorado River suspension bridge, as he was very frightened by it. A packer dragged him across behind his mule, and he left a bloody track all the way across. Later it was hard to teach him to make the fordings where the water was deep and swift, but now he does not mind.

So, tomorrow I take the trail again, to the canyons south.

Love from Everett

In the next letter, he states, "If I had stayed any longer I would have fallen in love with a Mormon girl, but I think it's a good thing I didn't. I've become a little too different from most of the rest of the world." No doubt he was attractive to the many young Mormon girls who must have seen in him a youthful, adventurous stranger from outside the remote village. But Everett felt compelled by his nature to frustrate all these women.

The following letter is also the last—so far as is known— to be received by anyone. We know from later evidence that Everett found his way into Davis Gulch, one of the deep, spectacular side canyons tributary to the Escalante River. Not only was the canyon scenic, it had grass and water for the burros, high sandstone arches, pictographs, and petroglyphs, and it had Indian ruins in large number. It would have been a fascinating place to spend the winter.

November 11
Escalante Rim, Utah

Dear Waldo,

Your letter of October twelfth reached me a week ago at Bryce Canyon.
Since I left Desert View, a riot of adventure and curious experiences
have befallen me. To remember back, I have to think of hundreds of
miles of trails, through deserts and canyons under vermilion cliffs and
through dense, nearly impenetrable forests. As my mind traverses that
distance, it goes through a long list of personalities, too.

But I think I have not written you since I was in the Navajo
country, and the strange times I had there and in the sunswept mesas
of the Hopis, would stagger me if I tried to convey them. I think there
is much in everyone's life that no one else can ever understand or
appreciate, without living through the same experiences, and most could
not do that.

I have had a few narrow escapes from rattlers and crumbling
cliffs. The last misadventure occurred when Chocolatero stirred up some
wild bees. A few more stings might have been too much for me. I was
three or four days getting my eyes open and recovering the use of my
hands.

I stopped a few days in a little Mormon town and indulged
myself in family life, church-going, and dances. If I had stayed any longer
I would have fallen in love with a Mormon girl, but I think it's a good
thing I didn't. I've become a little too different from most of the rest
of the world.

Tell your friend K.O. Duncan that the burro has been a saddle and pack animal for centuries in almost every country of the world.
I have ridden more than a thousand miles on burros myself. Both of
my burros were saddle animals of the Navajos when I bought them.
In the winter, they ride burros almost exclusively, as the horses are then
too weak from lack of feed.

Do you remember that Sancho Panza rode an ass? If you poke
back into the recesses of your mind, you may remember that Christ
once rode a donkey. So I'm not the only one.

As to when I shall visit civilization, it will not be soon, I think.
I have not tired of the wilderness; rather I enjoy its beauty and the
vagrant life I lead, more keenly all the time. I prefer the saddle to the
streetcar and star-sprinkled sky to a roof, the obscure and difficult trail,
leading into the unknown, to any paved highway, and the deep peace
of the wild to the discontent bred by cities. Do you blame me then

for staying here, where I feel that I belong and am one with the world around me? It is true that I miss intelligent companionship, but there are so few with whom I can share the things that mean so much to me that I have learned to contain myself. It is enough that I am surrounded with beauty and carry it with me in things that are a constant delight, like my gorgeous Navajo saddle blankets, and the silver bracelet on my wrist, whose three turquoises gleam in the firelight.

Even from your scant description, I know that I could not bear the routine and humdrum of the life that you are forced to lead. I don't think I could ever settle down. I have known too much of the depths of life already, and I would prefer anything to an anticlimax. That is one reason why I do not wish to return to the cities. I have been in them before and returned to them before, and I know what they contain. There would have to be some stronger incentive than any I know now to make me want to return to the old ways.

You said that you could not think what to write of, but I could write pages for every day of my life here.

A few days ago I rode into the red rocks and sandy desert again, and it was like coming home again. I even met a couple of wandering Navajos, and we stayed up most of the night talking, eating roast mutton with black coffee, and singing songs. The songs of the Navajos express for me something that no other songs do. And now that I know enough of it, it is a real delight to speak in another language.

I have not seen a human being or any wildlife but squirrels or birds for two or three days. Yesterday was a loss as far as travel was concerned for I got into an impasse in the head of a canyon system, and had to return almost to where I started. Last night I camped under tall pines by a stream that flowed under a towering orange yellow cliff, like a wall against the sky, dwarfing the twisted pines on its summit and the tall straight ones that grew part way up the face of it. It was glorious at sunrise. Today I have ridden over miles of rough country, forcing my way through tall sage and stubborn oak brush, and driving the burros down canyon slopes so steep that they could hardly keep from falling.

At last I found a trail and have just left it to make dry camp on what seems like the rim of the world. My camp is on the very point of the divide, with the country falling away to the blue horizon on east and west. The last rays of the sun at evening and the first at dawn reach me. Below are steep cliffs where the canyon has cut its way up to the rim of the divide. Northward is the sheer face of Mount Kaiparowits, pale vermilion capped with white, a forested summit. West and south are desert and distant mountains. Tonight the pale crescent of the new moon appeared for a little while, low on the skyline, at sunset. Often as I wander, there are dream-like tinges when life seems impossibly strange and unreal. I think it is, too, only most people have so dulled their senses that they do not realize it.

It is true that I have been making out pretty well of late. It has been fun to have plenty of spending money, and be able to celebrate and make presents whenever I want to. I have disposed of a good many paintings at odd times. This has been a full, rich year. I have left no strange or delightful thing undone that I wanted to do.

When my Mormon friends asked me to what church I belonged, I told them that I was a pantheistic hedonist. Certainly you and I have always been hedonists, wishing happiness for each other, as I do now for you.

It may be a month or two before I have a post office, for I am exploring southward to the Colorado, where no one lives. So, I wish you happiness in California.

Affectionately,
Everett

Wilderness Song

I have been one who loved the wilderness:
> *Swaggered and softly crept between the mountain peaks;*
I listened long to the sea's brave music;
> *I sang my songs above the shriek of desert winds.*

On canyon trails when warm night winds were blowing,
> *Blowing, and sighing gently through the star-tipped pines,*
Musing, I walked behind my placid burro,
> *While water rushed and broke on pointed rocks below.*

I have known a green sea's heaving; I have loved
> *Red rocks and twisted trees and cloudless turquoise skies,*
Slow sunny clouds, and red sand blowing.
> *I have felt the rain and slept behind the waterfall.*

In cool sweet grasses I have lain and heard
> *The ghostly murmur of regretful winds*
In aspen glades, where rustling silver leaves
> *Whisper wild sorrows to the green-gold solitudes.*

I have watched the shadowed clouds pile high;
>   Singing I rode to meet the splendid, shouting storm
And fought its fury till the hidden sun
>   Foundered in darkness, and the lightning heard my song.

Say that I starved; that I was lost and weary;
>   That I was burned and blinded by the desert sun;
Footsore, thirsty, sick with strange diseases;
>   Lonely and wet and cold, but that I kept my dream!

Always I shall be one who loves the wilderness:
>   Swaggers and softly creeps between the mountain peaks;
I shall listen long to the sea's brave music;
>   I shall sing my song above the shriek of desert winds.

—Poem by Everett Ruess

EVERETT RUESS IS MISSING

UTAH: CLUES AND FRUSTRATIONS

Bement Arch, in Davis Gulch, upstream from Everett's 1934 campsite, clings to the north wall of the canyon. Its opening is 100 feet high and 80 feet wide. It was called Ruess Arch for some time but was later renamed. On the horse is Don Griffin of Escalante. Photo taken September 1982 by W.L. Rusho.

March 1935

Dear Mrs. Ruess,

That is certainly distressing news. But wanderers like Everett have disappearing habits—and he may yet show up. We wish you luck in your search.

Yours truly,
Maynard Dixon

Not yet mid-winter, it was nonetheless cool that Sunday morning, 11 November 1934, Armistice Day, in the little town of Escalante, Utah.

Most everyone had attended the service or Sunday School at the Church, Mormon, to which virtually the entire village population belonged. In the afternoon, following time-honored routine, women cooked several courses of rich food, children played games, and men prepared their large, farm-type yards and homes for the winter.

Everett Ruess, a visitor in Escalante on that day, prepared to leave the next day on yet another adventure. Tempting though it was to participate in the social life of the close-knit Mormon community, he felt he should move on. "I would have fallen in love with a Mormon girl," he wrote, feeling he needed to justify his continuing break from organized society. Just the evening before he had treated Norm Christensen, one of his new-found young friends, to a showing of *Death Takes a Holiday* at the local movie theater. He then spent his last night in town, camped under the cottonwoods down by the river, where his two burros munched happily on the long grass, as they had for the past ten days.

Everett was flattered by the attention he received in Escalante— and in nearby Tropic, before that—from the young boys, from the pretty girls, even from the adults, who opened their homes to him. But Everett was not yet ready for a quiet life of comfortable contemplation, if indeed he ever would be. His choice, perhaps even his destiny, was to be moving on.

"Following his dream," he called it in a poem, and his dream was to articulate the wilderness, either in visual works or in words, preferably both. Routine life in the town of Escalante, however friendly, must have seemed the very antithesis of his inner need. So he departed on a bright Sunday morning, through the quiet village streets, riding southeast over rolling, sandy bench lands.

To Everett's right rose a mesa with many names. Near the town of Escalante it was called the Escalante Rim, while farther south, where the sheer cliffs rose almost 2000 feet, it was called the Straight Cliffs. The mesa itself was called Fifty-Mile Mountain by the residents, but mapmakers titled it Kaiparowits Plateau. In this land of jumbled red rocks and deep narrow canyons, Kaiparowits Plateau was one of the dominant features that could be seen scores of miles away. Another prominent point visible from a distance was Navajo Mountain, rising over 10,000 feet out of a slickrock desert less than twenty-five miles southeast of Kaiparowits.

Generally, Everett's road followed near the base of Kaiparowits Plateau where it headed toward the deep side canyons of the Escalante River, which cut through the rocky land six to twelve miles to the east.

The side canyons did not necessarily contain much water. Even though the main canyon was that of a river, the Escalante almost never flowed more than knee deep. In more watered lands such a small flow would be termed a *creek* or a *brook*. Tributaries to the Escalante, in side canyons such as Coyote, Willow, Soda, and Davis, were either dry or ran with barely a shoe-top trickle. On benchlands between the canyons lay bare sandstone, broken rock, and thin, dry soil supporting sparse desert vegetation.

That afternoon Everett, camped beside the road near town, penned long letters to his parents and brother. Mentioned in those letters were plans for his future: first, he wished to redecorate his room in Los Angeles, upon his return; second, and somewhat contradictory, he did not desire to "visit civilization"; third, he planned to slowly proceed on south, to cross the Colorado River into the Navajo country, or alternately, he might choose to go north first through Boulder, Utah; fourth, he did not expect to be close to a post office "for a couple of months." Nothing in his letters would have alarmed his family in any way; his words indicated only a continuation of the vagabond-wanderer type of life that Everett had followed off and on for five years.

Norm Christensen and another boy met Everett for a last evening together around the campfire. Then in the morning Christensen watched him ride slowly away, seated on one burro while leading another.

At the end of the dead-end road that Everett traveled, and just beyond the south end of Kaiparowits Plateau, lay historic Hole-in-the-Rock, where Mormon pioneers, "called" by their prophet to emigrate to southeast Utah, spent six weeks in 1879 and 1880 making an incredible wagon road down through a narrow cleft in the cliff to reach and cross the Colorado River. Everett cared little for history, but he could see that the country became more wildly dramatic, more teeming with color and contrast, as he approached Hole-in-the-Rock.

On Monday, 19 November, when he was about fifty miles from town, Everett came upon two sheepherders, Clayton Porter and Addlin Lay, who were camped near the head of Soda Gulch. Accepting their invitation to join them, Everett stayed not one, but two nights, plying Porter and Lay with questions about the nearby topography. Particularly he wanted to know about the canyons, the trails, the Indian ruins, and scenic points of interest. According to Lay, Everett did not seem curious about either how to cross the Colorado River or about the Navajo country on the other side. When Ruess was ready to leave, the two men

Descending the only horse trail into Davis Gulch, September 1982. Photo by W.L. Rusho.

offered him a quarter of a mutton, but Everett declined. He said he had a full load of groceries and could not add so much weight.[25]

As the two men watched, the young artist prodded his burros southward, supposedly on his way to paint and make sketches at Hole-in-the-Rock.

We have no record that Everett was ever seen again. So the veil of mystery falls; real knowledge ends and speculation begins.

Everett had written his parents that he would be out of touch for as much as two months, but when almost three months had elapsed, Christopher and Stella Ruess received Everett's uncalled-for mail from the postmaster at Marble Canyon, Arizona, the post office nearest Lee's Ferry, where Everett said he would be heading. Alarmed by the returned mail, they wrote a letter of inquiry, dated 7 February 1935, to Postmistress Mildred Allen at Escalante. Mrs. Allen, who had met Everett when he came to the post office to mail letters, turned the letter over to her husband, H. Jennings Allen, a Garfield County Commissioner, who was immediately curious.

Taking a personal interest, Jennings Allen wrote to the Ruesses that he would make inquiries in the local area. The entire population of Escalante was alerted to the disappearance. Even though the Allens could find no clues, it was a mystery that galvanized the community, especially those who had known Everett personally.

185

A network of canyons forms along the lower Escalante River. The Colorado River, in Glen Canyon, flows from right to left. Davis Gulch is the third Escalante River tributary, counting from the mouth, on the left side. Photo September 1962 by W.L. Rusho.

Indian pictographs in Davis Gulch. Everett inscribed a tiny NEMO 1934 to the right of and below these pictographs.

Photo by Ken Sleight.

Jennings Allen organized a search party which left town on horseback about 1 March to start looking at the sheep camp of Clayton Porter and Addlin Lay, where Everett had last been seen. When Porter and Lay told the searchers that Everett seemed interested in the nearby canyons, the men turned east, then successively investigated the deep gulches named Willow, Soda, and Davis.

In Willow and Soda they found nothing, but upon descending the rocky trail into Davis Gulch they very quickly spotted Everett's two burros, which were contained in the upper part of the canyon by a brush fence. Some have maintained that the burros were in starving condition, having eaten nearly all of the grass in the "corral." Jennings Allen, however, as well as others, reported that the burros had a long section of canyon floor to wander in, that there was plenty of grass and water, and that the burros were "fat and healthy."

Searchers from Escalante, Utah bring Everett's burros out of Davis Gulch in March 1935.

Everett carved the words NEMO 1934 on the rock, shown in this photo slightly below center.

Photo by Ken Sleight.

On the fence were a bridle, a halter, and a rope, which Gail Bailey, one of the searchers, picked up. While most of the men rode on down Davis Gulch, Bailey forced the burros up the steep slickrock trail and on out of the canyon. Allen said that since Davis Gulch was used each spring as a place to keep cows and their newborn calves, the burros were removed because they were consuming too much good grass.[26] Bailey led the burros on to Escalante where they were kept in a corral and ridden occasionally by the village children. He later took them into the high country, to another sheep camp.[27] No one seems to have seen them again.

Everett's burros were located just upstream from the point where the trail winds down the cliff on the north side of Davis Gulch. Southwest of the trail, the narrow canyon extends upstream for a few

187

miles, ending abruptly in a jump-up, impassable to horses or burros, but scaleable to an agile human being. Downstream from the trail, the sinuous canyon descends between towering sandstone cliffs about three miles to its junction with the Escalante River. Throughout its length flows a delightful stream of clear water, fringed occasionally with stately cottonwood trees, and almost constantly lined with flowers and grass. Deep within several of the sheltered alcoves in the cliffs are ruins of ancient Anasazi dwellings or granaries. Centuries-old petroglyphs and pictographs on shaded rock walls are picturesque, unusual, and undecipherable. Two magnificent arches, now called Bement and LaGorce, curve outward and downward from the north wall. It is a place where a person can wade happily through the gentle streamflow aware only of beauty and mystery. It is no wonder that Everett's long searching finally brought him into this marvelous canyon.

While Gail Bailey was removing the burros, the remainder of the search group rode slowly downstream, pausing to investigate alcoves containing ruins or pictographs. Passing LaGorce Arch (called by the cowboys Moqui Window), they climbed to a high, small ruin and suddenly stopped in surprise. There on the base of the doorway were carved the words *NEMO 1934*. A mystery indeed! Nearby were four Anasazi pottery jugs lined up on a flat rock.

As news of the search party reached Escalante, Jennings Allen passed it on to Christopher and Stella. On 3 March Allen telegraphed news of the discovery of the burros. Then on 8 March he wrote: ". . . searchers went into Davis Gulch where burros were and there they located Everett's tracks where [he] had been the last of November. There they found up and down the canyon his tracks where he had been traveling back and forth. Also where he had been in several Moqui houses and caves. Also where he had been examining Indian drawings and writings on the ledges and also where he had written *NEMO* on the ledge and also carved the date *Nov 1934* but did not put the day of the month . . . from where the bridle and rope were located they tracked him out of the canyon; he had followed an old Indian trail."

Allen also reported that after studying Everett's tracks the searchers had determined that he had apparently scaled "many dangerous cliffs," but there was no evidence of an accident. In a sheltered alcove near the bottom of the trail into the canyon they found numerous tracks, empty condensed milk cans, candy wrappers, and marks in the dirt where Everett had laid his bedroll and then rolled it up. Obviously this had been his camp.

The Indian ruin where the searchers found NEMO carved on a rock and on the dwelling. Photos by Ken Sleight.

One peculiarity—and one that was to influence all theories about Everett's disappearance—was the absence of his bedroll, his cook kit, his food, his paintings and paint kit, his journal, and his money. How could Everett have carried his outfit out of the deep canyon without the aid of his burros? Gail Bailey, who trailed the burros out of the canyon, denied that he or anyone else could have removed the outfit before the main group of searchers found the camp site.

Jennings Allen also reported that Everett's footprints were spotted "from where the burros were found to the foot of the Fifty-Mile Mountain." Allen conjectured that Everett might have taken his camp outfit to the top of Fifty-Mile (Kaiparowits), where "he could see and paint the country for miles around." He might then have returned his burros to Davis Gulch and climbed back to his camp. Then, while high on the mountain, he might have been cut off and isolated by heavy snowfall. Pursuing this theory, Allen and the search party waited for the warm sun to melt the snow. He said they would climb to the top and, hopefully, find Everett.

On 15 March, however, apparently after a thorough search of Kaiparowits, Allen reported in a discouraging letter: "We have searched the country good on this side of the Colorado River and haven't been able to find any fresh sign of Everett."

Implicit in all the correspondence between Allen and the Ruesses and in all newspaper accounts of the search was the notion that Everett may simply have fallen from some high precipice and that in this greatly bisected rock country the searchers could not find the body. Almost anyone who knows the character of the country would suggest falling as the probable solution. Everett himself, in his letters, mentioned the danger. In June 1934 he wrote from Monument Valley: "Hundreds of times I have trusted my life to crumbling sandstone and nearly vertical angles in the search for water or cliff dwellings." A month earlier he wrote: "Yesterday I did some miraculous climbing on a nearly vertical cliff, and escaped unscathed. . . . One way and another, I have been flirting pretty heavily with Death, the old clown."

Clay Lockett, the archaeologist who spent a week with Everett in a lofty cliff dwelling in July 1934, said that he was appalled by the seemingly reckless manner in which Everett moved around the dangerous cliffs.[28]

Still, there isn't a hint of hard evidence that he did actually fall to his death. Places in Davis Gulch and in nearby areas where a person might be tempted to climb are not numerous; an attraction—a ruin, an arch, a spring, an unusual viewpoint—has to be combined with an apparently possible climbing route. Such combinations were readily spotted by the searchers and were closely inspected. Everett's body could not be found. Given the topography, the suggestion that his body could have been covered by drifting sand in the short space of three months is very unlikely. Searchers who are still living believe the accidental falling theory has little validity. Norman Christensen, who saw much of Everett in Escalante, says that Everett was careful and "able to take care of himself."[29]

The theory that Everett fell also requires an explanation for the missing camp outfit. It might have been removed from Everett's camp by one of the searchers, who, having discovered the beautiful Navajo blankets, the paintings, and the money while alone, hid the outfit, then returned, perhaps weeks later, to retrieve it. To pull off such a theft, the man would have to have uncanny skill or luck, as well as the unusual ability to keep his mouth shut for many years. Several accusations along these lines have been made in private, but never has one piece of evidence been produced; Everett's outfit remains missing today, nearly fifty years later.

A thief, perhaps a wandering cowboy, could have found the outfit *before* Everett was known to be missing and could have taken it away. But if this did happen, the thief would have had to know that Everett was dead, or he would have had to callously violate one of the basic unwritten laws of the wilderness: to steal a man's essential camp outfit was akin to murder.

By the middle of March 1935, the first search party had returned to Escalante. Gail Bailey had brought in the burros, which

The search party from Escalante near Davis Gulch, March 1935.

were identified by people who had seen them with Everett in November. Jennings Allen, although discouraged, wrote to Christopher and Stella Ruess that he was organizing a second search party for the express purpose of examining the south rim of Davis Gulch, which had not yet been thoroughly covered. Allen himself headed the group, spending about two weeks in late March and early April on a fruitless search. He wrote to the Ruesses that "Everett must [have] left this section and gone to the Navajo reservation; he can't be anywhere on this side of the Colorado River alive because every inch has been searched."

As to the word NEMO found carved on the cliff dwelling in Davis Gulch, an inquiry telegraphed in June 1935 to the Ruesses produced this reply:

> Everett read in desert Greek poem *Odyssey*, translated by Lawrence of Arabian desert. Here Odysseus Greek word for nobody, "Nemo" being Latin word for nobody. Odysseus trapped by man-eating giant in cave, saves life by trick of calling himself Nemo. Everett dislikes writing own name in public places.
> Mrs. Christopher G. Ruess

A few months later, at the suggestion of a friend, Christopher decided that NEMO was an echo of Jules Verne's *Twenty Thousand Leagues Under The Sea*, in which Captain Nemo, like Everett, was trying to escape from civilization.

The possibility arose that Everett had disappeared intentionally, an idea discussed more in detail in the final chapter of this book.

Allen, although discouraged, was not yet ready to quit until he had exhausted all of his resources. He drove to Salt Lake City hoping to see the governor, but was frustrated to find that Governor Henry Blood was out of town. Allen also paid calls at the *Deseret News* office in Salt Lake City, only to be told by the editor that the story had insufficient interest for them to sponsor another search. He therefore turned to the Associated Civic Clubs of Southern Utah, a loose organization made up of representatives of fifteen counties and headquartered in Richfield. In Frank G. Martines, President of the Associated Civic Clubs, Allen at last found full cooperation.

Martines at first contacted the office of Governor Blood, where he found no interest in conducting an official state search. Martines then called upon his fellow members to contribute funds that the Associated Civic Clubs could use to sponsor its own search. Appealing to their pride that "*no one* gets lost in southern Utah," Martines quickly obtained necessary contributions. A search team from the town of Escalante, organized under the direction of P.M. Shurtz, left town on 1 June 1935.[30]

On 14 June 1935, Ray E. Carr, Secretary of the Associated Civic Clubs, wrote to Christopher and Stella that the search party had been out eleven days without success. The searchers, however, did find additional evidence of Everett's activity in lower Davis Gulch—size nine boot prints leading to an Indian pictograph panel, an old Anasazi pot nearby, and on the panel the inscription *NEMO 1934*. This, of course, was similar to what had been found farther up Davis Gulch in March, and did not add any really new clues.

One different item reported by Ray Carr was that the team located a man who had been camped at Hole-in-the-Rock from early December until April. The man, whose name was not given, said that he was confident he would have seen anyone riding through that area to cross the Colorado River. From his statement the searchers concluded that Everett probably did not cross the river.

At that time the search was temporarily halted so that the men could harvest their hay and take cattle to the high country. Carr said the search would resume later with five men to cover the Escalante River Canyon and the rough country to the southeast. No record exists, however, that the extended search was ever made.

During the search for Everett, no one mentioned in writing the possibility of foul play. Yet stories began to circulate that he could have been killed by rustlers. The theory slowly gained credence as one of the few explanations that could fit with known facts. Most of the residents of Escalante suspected that cattle rustlers might be involved, but as they lacked (and still lack), definite proof, they kept their suspi-

Hole-in-the-Rock, as seen from the air, looking south across the Colorado River and Glen Canyon. In January 1880, Mormon pioneers drove 83 wagons down through this steep notch on their way to settle Bluff, Utah. Searchers found Everett's bootprints on the rim of Hole-in-the-Rock in March 1935. Photo taken May 1962 by W.L. Rusho.

cions to themselves—at least for a few years. Furthermore, the rustlers, whatever their degree of guilt, lived as neighbors in Escalante.

Rustling cattle brings forth stereotyped images from many Hollywood-produced Westerns, movies that depict the villainous criminals making off with scores of cattle in clouds of dust. In actuality, it didn't often happen like that. Big-time rustlers were extremely rare in the West, but small-scale cattle thievery continues to operate up to the present day. So it was also operating in 1934.

Cattle rustling was a known, if not always reported, fact along the Escalante River and its tributary canyons in the mid-1930s. The crime took three forms: on occasion a thief would shoot another man's steer far out on the range and would butcher it for his own use; a more common form of rustling was to find a cow with an unbranded calf that was old enough to be weaned, in which case the thief would simply kill the cow (often driving it off a cliff), dispose of the carcass, and brand the calf as his own; the third form, more rare, was for the rustlers to herd a few head of cattle across one of the roughest trails in the canyon country. The trail descended into Clear Creek Canyon, a tributary just south of Davis Gulch. Then it crossed the Escalante, ascended a steep slickrock trail to a point near the confluence of the Escalante and Colorado Rivers, then tortuously wound its way over the Circle Cliffs into the Halls Creek drainage, where it ended at the Baker Ranch. There the cattle could be rebranded with a "running" iron and trucked off to market.[31]

Rustling in the Escalante Desert had one common characteristic— no outsiders were, or could be, involved. The residents knew each other, knew what was happening in the area, and knew when a stranger entered their valley. A stranger attempting to rustle cattle might not only have been suspect; he would probably have been quickly caught and prosecuted. A cowboy, however, who was employed in the area, could secretly make off with one or two head of cattle. Though he might be suspect, proof was usually lacking. An accused thief could simply claim that cattle were missing because of depredation of coyotes, fierce storms, or because the cattle had found an obscure hiding place.

Just before Everett's arrival in Escalante, rustlers had apparently overextended themselves, bringing down the wrath of the local cattle owners. To try to scare the hooligan-type rustlers, the owners decided to spread a false story to the effect that they were hiring an undercover agent to infiltrate the range and to obtain incriminating evidence. They were not explicit about who they would hire, or when, preferring to keep the thieves guessing. At any rate, the rustlers were expecting a mysterious stranger to show up.

It was into this atmosphere of deceit and suspicion that Everett innocently rode his burros south from Escalante. Of course, Everett must have looked about as dangerous as a puppy dog, but who can account for the possible reaction to him in the mind of a worried petty thief? Naturally, the cattle owners were not going to hire an investigator who *looked* like an investigator. And Everett certainly acted and talked like an outsider.

We know that Everett did visit two nights with sheepherders Clayton Porter and Addlin Lay, but did he encounter someone else? Perhaps a cowboy rustler ambushed him as he passed by a slickrock outcrop. Or more probably Everett, while out looking for scenes to paint, accidentally witnessed a crime, either the killing of a cow so as to claim her calf, or the illegal killing of a cow or steer for meat. One of the men who searched for Everett said that while he was in the Escalante River Canyon, a bloody cow limped by, shot but not yet down. No calf was anywhere near. The men looked for the rustler, but he had vanished.[32]

It is known for sure that three men were herding cattle or sheep near Davis Gulch about the time Everett camped there. One was said to act suspiciously during the search, but he has never been a really strong suspect. The other two had been rustler suspects for some time, but no one had enough proof to file a complaint in court—at least not until 1936. Both of these men were indicted for cattle theft at the Garfield County Court in Panguitch, Utah, in 1936. Although the official court record lacks a written judgment, witnesses report that one of the two men was convicted and sent to the Utah State Prison while the other was acquitted.

Some Escalante people feel that one of these men was "certainly mean enough to commit murder," and that he was the instigator of most of the rustling that occurred. One witness even reported that the man had on more than one drunken occasion bragged that he had shot the "goddamned artist kid" and dumped his body in the Colorado River.

Another Escalante resident reports that he was told by one of the local cattlemen that, while riding on the range, he rounded a hill and discovered the same rustler butchering another man's steer. The rustler became so enraged that he vowed to kill the intruder and ran for his rifle. The cattleman then rode his horse away at full gallop, dodging a hail of bullets. The cattleman, who was not wounded, decided not to file charges.

All of this evidence is, of course, weak, second-hand, and inadmissible in court. It is also contradicted by some people in Escalante who deny that the petty thief could have killed anyone.

During the latter part of 1982 I interviewed at his home the man who had bragged of killing Everett, but found his memory was suffering from old age. He did remember that a young artist had disappeared near Davis Gulch, yet he said that he knew absolutely nothing about the incident. When asked about cattle thieves, he denied that any rustlers *ever* operated in the vicinity of Escalante.

Those who searched for Everett along the Escalante River in Utah were sincere, compassionate men, who willingly donated time and energy to the effort. Most people would not have understood Everett's intangible objective of "following his dream." Most hadn't even met him. But when a man is lost in the wilderness, it matters little why he went there in the first place. Although some aspects of the search might seem, in hindsight, to have been poorly conducted, it was performed with as much dispatch and efficiency as one could expect in a season of adverse weather and in unbelievably tortuous terrain. The possibility of foul play, however, was apparently never seriously

The confluence of the San Juan (lower left) and the Colorado Rivers looking west, or downstream. At right center is Cottonwood Canyon, where mysterious, old camping equipment was found in 1957. Photo March 1963 by W.L. Rusho.

investigated, in spite of a pronouncement from the Utah Attorney General that, ". . .the state will go to the bottom of this case, and if a crime has been committed swift prosecution will follow."[33]

In the summer of 1957, an archaeologist working on the Glen Canyon Archaeological Survey (prior to the filling of Lake Powell) came across the remains of camping equipment—possibly Everett's—in a canyon tributary of the Colorado River southwest of Hole-in-the-Rock. Dr. Robert Lister, employed by the University of Utah, Edson B. Alvey, and Lloyd Gates, both of Escalante, Utah, were surveying Indian ruins in Cottonwood Canyon when they found the camp remains, including rusty cup, spoon, fork, kettles and pans, and a large canteen. Most interesting was a box of razor blades from the Owl Drug Company of Los Angeles. All three men believed immediately that it was the remains of an Everett Ruess camp.

Cottonwood Canyon is only about eight to ten miles southwest of Davis Gulch. Whereas Davis Gulch flows northeast into the Escalante River, Cottonwood Canyon runs south, directly into the Colorado River between Kaiparowits Plateau and Navajo Mountain. During the searches of 1935 and later, no one ever mentioned Cottonwood Canyon. Edson Alvey says he is sure the area was never considered when the Ruess searches were underway.[34]

Cottonwood Canyon has since been renamed Reflection Canyon, and its lower portion is filled with Lake Powell. Lake water also covers the campsite in question.

Immediately after the items were found, they were turned over to the County Sheriff at Panguitch, who sent them on to Stella Ruess for possible identification. She could not be sure, but she doubted that they belonged to Everett.

Still, one wonders why important camp items, such as a canteen and kettles, would be abandoned in the desert canyon. If it actually was a campsite, why would the camper depart, without his valuable equipment, in a remote site almost eighty miles from the nearest village? Could the items have been the remains of Everett's missing camp outfit? If so, how did he transport the heavy items to Cottonwood? Did Everett abandon everything there? Or did some thief who took the outfit from Everett's camp in Davis Gulch simply dispose of it in Cottonwood? Could outlaw Navajos have killed Everett, returned to the Reservation by way of Cottonwood Canyon, and on the way disposed of the unwanted portion of Everett's pack? Or could the camp items constitute an enigmatic bit of possible evidence in the maze of theories about Everett's disappearance?

By late summer, 1935, efforts to locate Everett on the Utah side of the Colorado River were about exhausted in futility and frustration. What had started with the early promising discovery of the burros, Everett's bootprints, and the NEMO inscriptions was stopped cold, in spite of the many man-hours spent on searches. By then, most people in Escalante were convinced that Everett could not possibly still be in Utah, but that he had most certainly gone on south, into the mysterious and esoteric land of the Navajos.

EVERETT RUESS IS MISSING
◈ 8 ◈

SPECULATIONS IN
NAVAJOLAND

In this incredible complex of slickrock canyons, Rainbow Bridge lies hidden just to the left of center. At lower right is the Colorado River. Photo taken November 1959 by W.L. Rusho.

22 January 1938

Dear Mr. and Mrs. Ruess:

Your remembrance reached me in Santa Fe. I don't forget Everett—it was kind of you to include me as one of his friends. The way of his going, I feel, is the way I would like to depart—close to the soil. But he was so young.

Kind regards from
Edward Weston

If the complex pattern of mesas and deep canyons on the north side of the Colorado River was a difficult place to look for a man, the south side, especially around Navajo Mountain, was considerably worse. Fed by the snow and rains that strike the forest-topped, ten-thousand-foot-high dome, the small streams have carved a jumble of deep, winding gorges through the sandstone, separated from each other only by slickrock mounds and ridges. Everett, gazing in wonder on this scene from high on Navajo Mountain in late June 1934, wrote, ". . .the country is as rough and impenetrable a territory as I have ever seen. Thousands of domes and towers of sandstone lift their rounded pink tops from blue and purple shadows." Northeast of the mountain lay the confluence of the Colorado and San Juan rivers, sunk deep into the rock jumble. A few miles farther northeast were Hole-in-the-Rock and the mouth of the Escalante River.

In the triangle between the Colorado and San Juan Rivers was another rock maze, inoffensively named Wilson Mesa. It was in this triangle that the Hole-in-the-Rock pioneers of 1880, doggedly pursuing their "call," built dugways, blasted rocks, and pushed their battered wagons towards the eventual settling place—Bluff, Utah. Their's was a terrible journey through a land that contained no natural roadways.

Everett may have crossed the river into this slickrock wilderness, possibly in company with the Navajos who had been trading at Escalante. He had told friends in Escalante, and had written to relatives, of his intention to cross the river. He could speak enough Navajo to survive. He not only liked the Indians but felt a kinship with them in their relationship to the earth and what he saw as their natural artistry.

Navajos had been in Escalante just before Everett left for the canyons in November 1934. Furthermore, Everett had been seen visiting with them, conversing in Navajo, and eating with them.[35] Before the formation of Lake Powell in 1963, it was fairly common for Navajos to travel north across the rough trails to Escalante where they sold blankets and jewelry in the towns. In warmer months, part of a Navajo group might climb Kaiparowits Plateau, make camp in the forest, and spend several days poaching deer. They would de-bone the meat to make it more easily transportable. Upon descending to the Hole-in-the-Rock road, they would meet the remainder of their group returning from Escalante and other towns. Having completed their hunting and trading endeavors, they would cross the Colorado and return to the reservation.[36]

To support the theory that Everett joined the Navajos, search-er Ches Lay reported that he found size nine boot prints in three places: (1) near the head of Davis Gulch at a point where he could have climbed out, (2) around a group of high, rounded sandstone knolls, mixed with moccasin footprints of Navajos, and (3) at the top of the Hole-in-the-Rock, on the canyon rim above the Colorado River, also mixed with Navajo footprints. Lay explained that the sandstone knolls area was a common place for Indians to camp while waiting for their tribesmen to return from trading in Escalante. At these knolls, Lay also saw camp-fire circles and many of the sharpened sticks commonly used to roast meat.

The plausibility of footprints remaining from late November until early March may be questioned, but several people familiar with the country state that damp or frozen sand could retain such marks for months—at least until obliterated by heat and wind. An area sheltered from the wind and rain could hold footprints indefinitely.

Even Jennings Allen suggested that Everett might have joined a group of Navajos on the canyon rim, transferred his outfit to one of their horses, returned his burros to the grassy floor of Davis Gulch, climbed the cliff (not the trail) to rejoin the group on the rim, then traveled with them to the Navajo Reservation across the Colorado and San Juan rivers. Whether he intended to ever return to Davis Gulch is an open question.

Searches for Everett on the Navajo Reservation were con-ducted, if haphazardly, by a neurotic man who suffered delusions of grandeur, yet whose unstable personality was masked by his solemn appearance of rational conversation, letter writing, and behavior. Neal Johnson, who listed his address as Escalante or Hanksville, worked most of his time as a miner in other areas. Few Escalante residents even knew him. His background was obscure, although he alluded to having once served as a pilot in the Mexican Air Force. He signed his name, and asked others to call him, Captain Neal Johnson.

Johnson, concluding that Everett had probably continued on south across the Colorado River and into the reservation, telegraphed Stella Ruess from Phoenix on 22 February 1935:

Regarding Everett Ruess leaving Escalante November eleventh I am placer mining Colorado River same district. Will conduct search your request. Know Indian scouts. Know region well. No water except snow. If lost can be found. Snow melt soon: No water, will perish. Search must start immediately. Have not reached Marble Canyon. I am here on business. Return mine

Red Rock Canyon. *Blockprint by Everett Ruess.*

twenty fourth. Will conduct search for expenses for Indian scouts only. Wire here immediately by Western Union.

Cap. Neal Johnson

Christopher Ruess cautiously wired the Chief of Police in Phoenix to inquire about Johnson's reliability, but apparently no police record was found. About two weeks later Johnson suddenly showed up in Los Angeles, called on Christopher and Stella, and stated that he was in town on business. During this visit Christopher, although dubious, gave Johnson enough money to send the Indian trackers out into the canyons. But the day after Johnson left, Christopher had second thoughts and wired Johnson. "Please let Allen conduct search instead. Return balance our money." Christopher's telegram, however, was sent to Hanksville, Utah, and Johnson did not receive the forwarded communication until May. In the meantime he continued to spend the money, supposedly for the "scouts' expenses."

From March to August 1935, Johnson wrote to the Ruesses at least seventeen times, many of the letters postmarked with a succession of small town names, in order: Cortez, Colorado; Holbrook, Arizona; Moab and Blanding, Utah; Dove Creek, Colorado; Richfield, Marysvale, Hanksville, and Strawberry Lake, Utah. In all of them he expressed continued optimism and hints of clues that might lead to Everett. On 14 March, for instance, he stated that he had stopped at many Indian trading posts on the Four Corners to make inquiries.

"There is several that know of Everett," he wrote. "One Chief told me today. Picture man heap savy wild mountains O.K."

Later, Johnson reported that most of the Indians knew of the "paint man," and that Navajos called him "Yabitoch," meaning "fun, or good humor." He also passed on a report from his supposed Indian trackers that two Indians and a lone white man had entered the area between the Colorado and San Juan Rivers. On 22 March he wrote that he was sure that Everett was on the reservation and with friendly Navajos. Money, of course, was always a problem to Johnson, who telegraphed on 2 April that he was "out fifty-four dollars," and that he needed forty-five dollars more to go searching himself with the two Indians. Always hopeful, Christopher Ruess sent him forty dollars in two installments.

Johnson also came up with the idea of making an aerial search, not an unusual suggestion. But because the country was too rough to fly low enough to spot any evidence, he suggested that Christopher Ruess should ". . . have some small bills made about four inches square say about 1,000 if you can afford it. Every time we hit places where I know there is watering holes we will turn loose a hand full. Which the propeller will scatter well. They will settle to the Earth and Everett is bound to pick one of them up." Johnson's wacky suggestion was not mentioned again.[37]

In late April he wrote that his Navajo tracker, Cidney, had found two Indians who had accompanied the mysterious white man into the northern part of the reservation. Alas, Cidney (assuming there really was such a person) could learn only that the unnamed white man "did not wish to be bothered."

Johnson later sent an artist's paint brush and a shirt button that he said had been picked up by his Indian trackers from a rock near the confluence of the Colorado and San Juan Rivers. Stella Ruess examined the brush and proclaimed that it was not sable, as all Everett's brushes were, but was merely a cheap one that a serious watercolorist like Everett would not have in his paint kit.

Jennings Allen, in the meantime, was writing Christopher and Stella to warn them about Neal Johnson:
"I hope that Neal Johnson isn't misleading you, but don't take too much stock in what he says. Johnson may be O.K. but has a bad record thru this section. When he left this section he run away from the law and has a shady record."

Allen later wrote to the Ruesses that Everett was probably not in the Navajo country, that he had trouble believing Johnson's Navajo stories, and that "if I had of had any such leads as he claims he has I could have found Everett in a week." He further complained that Johnson's optimistic stories had served to delay the search on the northern side of the river.

In July 1935, the Ruesses received a letter from Neal Johnson saying that he had encountered three Navajos whose statement "more than ever convinces me that Everett is still alive." He would not reveal what was said, declaring that he wanted to check it out first. Then, on 12 August he wrote that ". . . there is a boy living with a bunch of Navajos in the vicinity of Navajo Mountain. He has had a tribal wedding. I am most sure this is Everett." His biggest news, however, was that he had talked the editor of the *Salt Lake Tribune* into conducting and financing a new search in the Navajo Mountain area. Ace reporter John Upton Terrell was assigned to write daily stories from the search area. The only discouraging note in Johnson's letter is that, as usual, he needed money for expenses. Obligingly, Christopher sent him twenty-five dollars.

With Johnson as instigator and guide, the Terrell-Johnson trip naturally concentrated on the Navajo country, to which Johnson seemed virtually certain Everett had gone. Starting at Blanding, Utah, the party crossed the San Juan River at Mexican Hat, drove through Monument Valley to Kayenta, where they interviewed John Wetherill, then to Betatakin Ruin, to Shonto, and on to Navajo Mountain Trading Post, on the southeast side of the mountain.

At the trading post they met Dougeye, "a famous Navajo trailer," who stated that he was one of the three Navajos who had been seen talking to Everett in Escalante. Dougeye and his associates, Hosteen Nath Godi and Azoli Begay, had left Escalante, he reported, but on their return, while they were crossing one of the rivers, they met and passed three other Navajos heading toward Escalante to trade. Terrell implied in his *Tribune* article that one of these unnamed Indians might have murdered Everett and stolen his outfit.

Dougeye's statement was significant, for it tended to confirm that Everett did not join the Navajos, who had been trading in Escalante, on their return to the reservation. Dougeye further stated that *no* white man had crossed the river in that area during the past year and the only known people to cross were the two parties of three Navajos each, who passed each other in November 1934. In other words, according to Dougeye, Everett did not enter the Navajo Reservation from the north. Had he done so, stated the Indian tracker, his footprints would still have been visible in a few sheltered parts of the trail.

Furthermore, Everett's need for food would have forced him to contact a trader, or at least an Indian or two, thus making his presence known. Terrell concluded his first *Tribune* article by stating that, unless everyone on the reservation was an accomplice and they were all lying in unison, Everett was not in Navajoland.

Terrell and Johnson then followed Dougeye by horseback around Navajo Mountain, down Trail Canyon to the San Juan River, where they crossed, rode up Wilson Creek Canyon over Wilson Mesa, then down Cottonwood Gulch to the Colorado River, which they crossed near Hole-in-the-Rock. North of the Colorado they examined Davis Gulch, which yielded no evidence beyond what Allen and the searchers from Escalante had already discovered.

Terrell and Dougeye returned to Navajo Mountain Trading Post, but Johnson left to search "other areas" on his own. They agreed to meet several days later at Marble Canyon Lodge. At the isolated village of Kaibeto, Terrell talked with a well-known Navajo named Geishi Betah, who assured him that "news travels swiftly over the barren wastes and high ranges of the Navajo country" and that no stranger could have entered the reservation without almost all Navajos in the vicinity knowing about it.

Terrell ended his four-day series of articles on 28 August 1935, with the conclusion: "Everett Ruess was murdered in the vicinity of Davis Canyon. His valuable outfit was stolen. He never reached the Colorado River."

What then was the outcome of all of Neal Johnson's glowing optimism? Did a white man recently marry a Navajo girl near Navajo Mountain? Did a white man accompany two Navajos and state that he did not wish to be disturbed? Johnson wrote to Christopher Ruess that, "I have found several things they [the Indians] told me were lies. . ." Were they lies, or were they Johnson's fantasies?

Although no trace of Everett was found, John Upton Terrell and the *Salt Lake Tribune* had performed the apparently valuable service of narrowing the probabilities. Terrell and Johnson did not conduct a search, as such, but their talks with local Navajos had almost the same result, since the Indians reported that through their keen powers of observation and their fast communications network, no stranger had come into their midst. Of course, it all rested on Dougeye's veracity, which could not be known one way or the other. Christopher and Stella Ruess steadfastly refused to accept either Dougeye's statement or Terrell's conclusion that Everett had never crossed the rivers, for to have done so would have eliminated the only possibility that their son was still alive.

In September 1941, seven years after Everett disappeared, Christopher Ruess heard that an outlaw Navajo, then being held in the tribal jail, was a suspect in Everett's death. Upon receiving Christopher's letter of inquiry, Superintendent E.R. Fryer of the Indian Service replied:

"We believe that you have received information prematurely. Jack Crank is being held for an attack on federal officers while in the performance of their duties. We cannot at this time, with any justice, accuse him of any responsibility in connection with the loss of your son. Our present meager evidence leads us only to be suspicious. Therefore, we can go no farther than say at this time that Crank is a suspect."

Six weeks later, Fryer wrote again to state that Navajos John Chief and Jack Crank had admitted complicity in the murder of a white man in Monument Valley. He added, however, that the body had been found and that it was that of an elderly man who had just before his death stopped at Oljato Trading Post. Fryer added the teaser: "There are rumors about the involvement of these two men in the disappearance of Everett. However, these are merely unfounded rumors and must be treated as such."

Apparently, that was the last letter Fryer wrote to the Ruesses. A few weeks later, however, a Gallup, New Mexico, businessman named Curtis G. Ring learned that two Navajos, who believed that Jack Crank had implicated them in the Monument Valley crime, informed the police that years earlier, Crank had murdered a lone white man in the "country above Rainbow Bridge." Crank's motives were that he needed the scalp of a "blood enemy" for ceremonial use, and that he simply hated white men. After the murder, Crank buried the body and the pack outfit, then took the burros to a point "some distance" away, where they were placed in a corral, and where they were later found. Or so Ring wrote to Christopher Ruess.

Superintendent Fryer also reported on the phone to Ring that "Jack Crank, now in Phoenix penitentiary awaiting trial on another count. . .has himself bragged in detail of murdering Everett Ruess. No confession has yet been signed but the evidence at hand and many peculiarities relative to this case make it look as though the case is genuine."[38]

Christopher and Stella certainly believed the theory that Jack Crank killed Everett. On 7 August 1952 Christopher wrote to Randolph Jenks (who had known Everett in 1931):

". . . a trial came up on an entirely different ground and the information (unverified by any evidence good in a court) that this man had probably murdered Everett years prior to this trial in 1942. No doubt the information influenced the court and the jury (tho not proved). The man was given 10 years rather than a very short term. It was expected that he would die before the years were out. But he was released in 1951 or 1952 and is free again. He was a sort of outlaw among his people even. He was probably drunk when he did the deed. . . . For us, this seems to solve the riddle."

Dougeye, the Navajo tracker, never told John Upton Terrell the names of the three Navajos who were headed toward Escalante in November 1934, and who passed him on the trail. Could these three have been Jack Crank and his two nefarious companions? And could Everett have innocently invited them into his camp in Davis Gulch, where they killed him, buried his body and took his pack when they left? Admittedly, the theory is a long-shot, yet it would account for all of the known facts—or lack of facts—about Everett's disappearance. Against this theory is the fact that no searcher reported seeing any footprints other than Everett's in Davis Gulch.

In an effort to better understand the people involved, as well as to meet them in person, Stella and Christopher Ruess, in late June 1935, visited many of the localities in northern Arizona and southern Utah about which Everett had written. They also wished to see the country and to talk with the men and women who had helped in the search. On their trip they visited Grand Canyon, Cameron, Tuba City, Marble Canyon, and Kayenta, Arizona; Zion National Park, Bryce Canyon National Park, Panguitch, Tropic, and Escalante, Utah. They met and talked with John and Louisa Wetherill, Ranger Maurice Cope, Frank Martines, Ray Carr, and Jennings Allen, as well as practically all members of the search team. Allen drove them as far toward Hole-in-the-Rock as the primitive road would allow. It was, for Stella and Christopher, a highly emotional experience to gaze at the colorful terrain that Everett had loved and so vividly described, and to meet and talk with many of the people he had known.

Although Christopher and Stella had concluded that Everett was not likely to return soon, they were not yet ready to declare him dead. They guarded the hope of his reappearance the rest of their lives. In fact, some have suggested that Everett could have carefully planned and orchestrated the whole disappearance, and that he might still be alive.

EVERETT RUESS IS MISSING

❾

WHEREVER HE MAY BE

Untitled blockprint by Everett Ruess.

21 March 1937

Your son was a most unusual spirit. I have never known a youth of like endowment and predilection. He is a most interesting character. If he should ever come out of his hiding he will bring a noble book in his knapsack!

Hamlin Garland

That Everett could have somehow departed from the Escalante River country, without his burros, and without anyone's knowledge, and have made a new life for himself elsewhere may sound to many like a fairy tale, mere wishful thinking. Yet conceivably, he could be alive in the Southwest, in Mexico, or most anywhere else in the world. Although it would have been difficult for him, he could have severed all contact with the family for which he seemed to care so much and abandon his few friends. He could plainly and simply have disappeared.

    Everett's personality—as we know it from letters, mostly to parents—would suggest that he was not the type to voluntarily withdraw from the world. He was not a recluse; he liked to converse with everyone he met, and seemed to enjoy writing to friends and relatives. His letters were as emotionally intense as he could write them. One can sense in these letters a sincere desire to fulfill his chosen role of artist, poet, and writer. Though he appeared to many to be an aimless vagabond, he was in fact driven, not only to find beauty, but to communicate an interpretation of that beauty to the world. In a real sense, he was not a free spirit. Furthermore, at age twenty, his quest had just begun. In spite of the overtones of depression in some of his letters written during and just after his winter in San Francisco, there is little evidence that he was seriously despondent or that he wanted to "escape."

Whatever his feelings upon leaving the cities, his letters indicate a gradual return of confidence and good humor as he roamed Monument Valley, Navajo Mountain, Rainbow Bridge, the Hopi Mesas, the Grand Canyon, and southern Utah in 1934. He wrote of his intention to return to Los Angeles. A Hopi at Chimopovi was reported to have said about Everett: "He was a good white boy. We liked him."[39] People who met him in Escalante also reported that he was cheerful and self-confident.

From his letters, it appears that he remained too close to his parents and to his brother, Waldo, to suddenly and deliberately cut all communication—forever. Even had he done so, his main obsession was to communicate to the world through words and visual art. Had he gone into hiding, in the nearly fifty years since he vanished, surely a few of his sketches, paintings, or writings would have surfaced. But nothing of this type has ever appeared.

And yet, assuming the cooperation of the Navajos to conduct him onto, or even through their reservation and to keep quiet about it, it is possible that Everett may actually have escaped into a new life with a new identity.

If we concede that such a voluntary disappearing act was possible, the question then is *why?* A possible reason is that he might have been seeking to join a Navajo sweetheart.

Many in Escalante have suggested that Everett probably had a Navajo sweetheart, but these stories could be pure speculation. One who knew him best at Escalante, Norm Christensen, said that Everett never talked about *any* girlfriends, whether Navajo or otherwise.[40]

The Navajo sweetheart theory would have Everett falling in love with an Indian girl during the summer of 1934. Later, the theory goes, he traveled south, from Escalante, crossed the Colorado River,

Everett entitled this photo "My Navajo Wife."

married his girl in a tribal ceremony, and is now living happily, protected by the secrecy of his adopted Navajo in-laws and friends.

When examined closely, the Navajo sweetheart theory grows weak. Though he could easily have loved such a girl, he would have found it hard to conceal at least a hint of such an emotional event in his letters. Furthermore, during the summer and fall of 1934, he kept traveling—alone—across the reservation and finally into Utah; he would have had little time for courtship. The theory would also require Everett to have disappeared, thus denying to himself both his art and his writing the rest of his life, which would have been unlikely. Finally, it would have required a massive, long-term conspiracy on the part of the Navajos and the white traders to keep his presence among them secret, undoubtedly the most far-fetched possibility.

We have to understand, however, that we have five decades of hindsight. We know that Everett has not been found alive or dead on the reservation, and that the chances that he is living there grow smaller every day. In 1935, however, the theory that he had crossed the river either to visit Navajos or to live with them indefinitely sounded believable. Jennings Allen was only one of many to conclude that because two exhaustive searches on the north side of the Colorado had been fruitless, Everett was almost certainly with the Navajos.

If he did not leave to join a Navajo sweetheart, could there have been another reason for doing so?

A nagging possibility exists that he may have believed that he was failing, as an artist, to live up to his parents', and his own, expectations. He did sell a few art works during his travels of 1934, but maybe it was not enough to maintain his confidence. Perhaps the parental pressure to excel was more than he could stand. His letters, although sensitive and imaginative, had little colloquial, chatty news. For the most part, they can be read as reports to his parents, his artistic mentors, on his progress in visually interpreting the landscape.

The questions are: How much was he pulled to the landscape— and how much was he pushed? Was he really as free as we would all like to think? Could he have been harboring, perhaps for years, a growing determination to strike out on his own, by cutting all ties to his parents? In later years, even Christopher Ruess acknowledged the many unanswered questions when he wrote in his diary: "The older person does not realize the soul-flights of the adolescent. I think we all poorly understood Everett."

In Davis Gulch, Everett twice inscribed the name NEMO on Indian ruins, possibly to be deliberately enigmatic, but possibly also as a hint that he thought himself to be a real life Captain Nemo. In Jules Verne's *Twenty Thousand Leagues Under the Sea*, Captain Nemo (whose Latin name meant *no one*), drove the submarine *Nautilus* on a cruise of the world, hell-bent to escape the disappointments and frustrations of civilization. Nemo's motto for the *Nautilus* was *Mobilis in Mobile*, or "mobile in a mobile element," freely translated as "free in a free world." Nemo was solitary, arrogant, sensitive, even a little romantic, but above all free. Perhaps most important to Everett was that Nemo had broken every tie upon earth.

Responding to reader demand to know more about Nemo, Jules Verne included a chapter in a subsequent book, *Mysterious Island*, that related how Nemo had once been a wealthy, well-educated, Brahmin from India named Prince Dakkar. Forsaking all worldly pleasures, Dakkar sought only the betterment of his people. He joined, then led a revolt against the ruling British, only to be utterly devastated by defeat and the senseless killing of his family. Branded a fugitive outlaw, Dakkar swore vengeance, then escaped to study and construct the *Nautilus*. He then changed his name to Captain Nemo.

It is quite possible that Everett, like Nemo, felt that he had suffered too many defeats. He could have felt depressed and withdrawn, notwithstanding cheerful posturing in his letters. Such a defeat could have been a rejection in a hoped-for love affair, perhaps in San Francisco. Or it could have been a criticism of his basic ability to become a fine painter. Maybe his defeat was simply his reaction to the chaotic state of the world in 1934. Whatever the cause, his withdrawal from organized society, his disdain for worldly pleasures, and his signatures as *NEMO* in Davis Gulch, all strongly suggest that he closely identified with the Jules Verne character.

According to his parents, Everett had read *Twenty Thousand Leagues Under the Sea* several times. He was, at age twenty, still impressionable, still able to project himself into idealistic, if unrealistic, roles. Could Everett have consciously determined that he would disappear, that he would "break every tie upon earth," so as to turn into Nemo himself?

Everett's letters occasionally foreshadow his death or disappearance, almost as if he were making plans for one, or perhaps both, of these eventualities. As far back as May 1931, he wrote:

"I intend to do everything possible to broaden my experiences and allow myself to reach the fullest development. Then, and before physical deterioration obtrudes, I shall go on some last wilderness trip, to a place I have known and loved. I shall not return."

During the summer of the next year, 1932, he wrote, "And when the time comes to die, I'll find the wildest, loneliest, most desolate spot there is." A touch of foreboding may be read into his June 1934, statement: "When I go, I leave no trace." His intention to remain in the wilderness is clear in his last letters, sent from Escalante, when he wrote, "As to when I shall visit civilization, it will not be soon, I think" and "I have known too much of the depths of life already, and I would prefer anything to an anticlimax. That is one reason why I do not wish to return to the cities."

A retired librarian named Alec W. Anderson reported that Everett spent considerable time at his Covina, California, home in early 1934, listening to recordings and writing poetry. When Everett left for Arizona, he said goodbye to Anderson, then added, as an afterthought, "And I don't think you will ever see me again, for I intend to disappear."

If Everett vanished voluntarily, the plan could have evolved around the campfire near Davis Gulch, when he met Dougeye and his Navajo associates. It would have to have included the following: to succeed in vanishing from the canyon country without anyone ever learning of it, Everett would require the cooperation of the three Navajos, who would furnish him with horses and would whisk him through the Navajo Reservation. Everett would have to have their complete silence, so that not even local medicine men would know that he had traveled through their land. (Such silence was not infeasible for someone considered to be a good friend.) He would also require his camp outfit, which of course, *did* utterly vanish from Davis Gulch and Everett's footprints were discovered among moccasined Navajo footprints both at the site of the Navajo camp and near Hole-in-the-Rock, the crossing point of the Colorado River.

In March of 1983, river runner Ken Slight reported that years earlier he had seen "NEMO" inscribed into the chinking of an Anasazi ruin in lower Grand Gulch, a southward flowing tributary of the San Juan River about forty miles due east of Davis Gulch. Sleight could not be certain that Everett made the inscription, but he thought it possible. Everett, perhaps just exploring, perhaps on his way to "disappear," could have crossed the Colorado at Hole-in-the-Rock, then followed the tortuous trail of the 1880 pioneers on foot, carrying his supplies in his backpack. After passing through Clay Hills Divide, Everett could have left the Hole-in-the-Rock trail by descending Collins Spring Canyon into Grand Gulch. Upon reaching the San Juan River he would have been only about twenty miles north of Monument Valley, and in country familiar to him from his travels there in 1931 and earlier in 1934.

If Everett was in fact heading for Monument Valley—perhaps to join someone there—a swing through Grand Gulch would have required a side trip of only a few miles, since the more direct route would have been south from Clay Hills Divide to Clay Hills Crossing on the San Juan River.

Everett did enjoy visiting Indian ruins and rock art panels, both of which Grand Gulch has in abundance. Besides, he would probably have been in no hurry. A side trip of perhaps three days through Grand Gulch would seem perfectly reasonable.

Monument Valley would be a logical destination for Everett, since he had spent so much time there, as recently as six months earlier. The theory that he may have taken a Navajo bride, discounted earlier in reference to Navajos around Navajo Mountain, would seem to have greater validity in Monument Valley, where he was probably well-acquainted with several Indian families. Even if he were just passing through, perhaps intending to disappear with a new identity, his entrance into Monument Valley from the north might not necessarily have become known to Navajos in the Navajo Mountain area who gave only negative responses to reporter Terrell of the *Tribune*.

In the months that followed the search for Everett, reports were received that he had been seen elsewhere. A man and his wife, who had vacationed near Moab, Utah, wrote that they had seen a young man who strongly resembled Everett on the eastern Utah desert in the late 1930s, but that the man avoided conversation, as if he were trying to avoid detection. Another woman wrote that she had most certainly seen and talked with Everett near Monterrey, Mexico, in 1937. The man told her that he had once lived with American Indians, that he had studied art in Chicago, and that he made his living doing watercolor paintings. Furthermore, she positively identified Everett's photograph as that of the man she met.[41]

Captain Neal Johnson reported to Christopher Ruess that while in Phoenix, he saw a young man who looked familiar, then realized that it must be Everett Ruess (whom he had never met). Johnson crossed the street, asked the man if he was Everett, whereupon the man excused himself and departed, saying that he would be right back. But the young man never returned. Christopher Ruess simply put this story down as another of Johnson's fantasies.

It is tempting to suggest that Everett simply moved on, then escaped to a new identity in an unknown land. Perhaps he did head for Mexico, although there is no hint that Mexico held any fascination for him. The chances of this having actually happened are small to the point of being remote, but the possibility does still exist.

Throughout the years other reports surfaced that Everett Ruess had been seen. Yet, when examined closely, all traces and clues disintegrated like wisps of cloud vapor in the sunlit Grand Canyon.

Our own assumptions about Everett, however, may lead us astray. Everett was totally unlike young men of his age and time. To conclude, for instance, that as he matured he would lose his playful notions of emulating Captain Nemo and that he would return to his parents' home may be an unjustified assumption.

EVERETT RUESS IS MISSING

TO THE END OF
THE HORIZON

In the family album, this photo was captioned "Everett trudged on—forgetting to return."

The story of Everett Ruess is still alive. It is one of romance, idealism, sensitivity, beauty, independence, youth, freedom, and mystery, set against some of the West's most dramatic landscapes. It is a truly American story, combining elements of art history, Indian culture,and the settlement and development of the wilderness.

One who came to appreciate the fascinating aspects of Everett's story was his mother, Stella, who received much reflected fame and interest, particularly after initial publication of a selection of Everett's writings in 1940. Throughout the rest of her life she continued to receive letters and callers making inquiries about her son. Even in his absence, Everett and his story were a major part of her own life.

It is probable that Stella—and perhaps Christopher, also—came to know Everett better after his disappearance, by rereading his letters, through letters from others, and as a result of conversations with friends. In her missing son, she seemed to find a focus for her artistic energy. The Ruesses used some insurance money to found The Everett Ruess

Poetry Awards at Los Angeles High School, with Stella serving as judge.[42] She sent off collections of Everett's writings to publishers seeking publication and maintained files of clippings and correspondence.

In a letter Everett once asked his father, "Can one make great sacrifices without submerging oneself?" Christopher replied, "Yes, wives of many great men, mothers of great sons, teachers of leaders, have found their lives by losing their lives. A seed fulfills itself by losing itself in the ground. So did the men at Thermopylae." So also did Stella find fulfillment through the lyrical life and writings of her son.

In 1948, at the invitation of professional river guide Harry Aleson, Stella and a woman friend made a difficult trip to southern Utah, particularly to see Davis Gulch. After a night in a range cabin near the Hole-in-the-Rock road, they hiked the very long, rocky, and obscure trail leading to the deep gorge. Assisted by Aleson, Stella climbed to the high alcove and saw where Everett had carved the words "NEMO 1934" on the door sill of an Anasazi ruin. Under a canopy of trees on the canyon floor, they spent the night, then set off in the morning light for the long hike back.

Stella paused at the rim of Davis Gulch and reached into her bag for a small bundle of flowers she had been gathering. With a few words of remembrance for Everett, she lofted the bouquet of flowers into the canyon. It was a dramatic, fitting gesture—and it was typically Stella Ruess.

Christopher Ruess died in 1954 and Stella in 1964. Both were active until the ends of their lives, Stella in art and poetry organizations and Christopher in helping senior citizens feel constructive and worthwhile. Waldo, Everett's older brother, married his Andalusian wife, Conchita, in 1957, then moved in 1960 to Santa Barbara, California, where they live with their four children.

Neal Johnson, who tried in some manner to conduct searches in the Navajo Mountain area, was murdered. There are many vague stories of Johnson becoming an outlaw and a fugitive, hiding out in a cave along the Colorado River. In the 1940s his body was found hanging in a mine "on the Arizona side of the river," probably near Navajo Mountain.[43] Who committed the murder, as well as the reason, remain a mystery.

Considering that a half-century has elapsed since Everett roamed the canyon country, and that the world is a different place than it was in 1934, what relevance does Everett's life hold for us in the 1980s? At age twenty, still wavering on the edge of maturity, still needing much more visual art training, Everett could nevertheless write in astonishingly

215

lyrical, descriptive passages. Important also was his *spirit*, the life force of an active, intelligent imagination that refused to idle away his youth in dull conformity. Most of us only wish our lives could be different, daring, and uncomfortable for a time. But Everett actually *did* it.

The drama of Everett's disappearance, with its abundance of clues and theories, would be interesting anywhere. What makes it especially fascinating is the cast of characters involved—Mormons, cowboys, rustlers, a neurotic miner, Navajos, medicine men, and traders. And the complex, colorful canyon country provided a perfect backdrop. To relate Everett's story is to describe the landscape itself.

We are left without a final answer, only riddles within riddles. With the passing of nearly fifty years, Everett's fate has been discussed many times among the people of the canyon country. Those who met Everett have either reached advanced age—or have passed beyond earthly bounds. Time has marched on, changing even the remote land where Everett and his burros passed the early days of the 1930s. The Sierras, Grand Canyon, and Mesa Verde are now in danger of being loved to destruction, overpopulated, even rationed to meet the demand. Monument Valley now includes paved highways and a Navajo Tribal Park. Canyon de Chelly is a National Monument, and the Colorado and San Juan Rivers are now flooded by a manmade reservoir, which backs even under Rainbow Bridge. This body of water, Lake Powell, has even invaded Davis Gulch, where it has covered the ruin Everett inscribed with *NEMO*, and has backed almost up to his 1934 campsite. The arch which was called Ruess Arch because of the nearby "NEMO 1934" inscription has been renamed.

As great as are these changes, the West of Everett Ruess remains much as it was then, not a place so much as an experience, where the least artistic of us all can occasionally feel a touch of inspiration. Though we may not find Everett himself, we can share with him, over the years, enthusiasm for the color, magnitude, even the emotional impact of a Western landscape.

His love of wilderness, his sense of kinship with the living earth, his acute sensitivity to every facet of nature's displays—all of these, because of their intensity in one young man, gave Everett rare qualities. What made him unique were his reactions to the striking and dramatic landscapes of the American West.

If Everett could return to the canyon country today, he would find ignorance and insensitivity, but he would also discover far more understanding of his goals, more appreciation for his talent, than he ever knew in the early 1930s. It can be hoped that his spirit, at least

The Colorado River sparkles as morning light streams into Glen Canyon, June 1962. Photo by W.L. Rusho.

in a universal sense, resides within us all. Perhaps somewhere, across a distant horizon, silhouetted against a golden sky, Everett may yet ride his faithful burro toward his mystic dream. . .*Mobilis in Mobile.*

EDWARD ABBEY

Everett Ruess. Photo by Dorothea Lange.

A Sonnet for Everett Ruess

You walked into the radiance of death
through passageways of stillness, stone, and light,
gold coin of cottonwoods, the spangled shade,
cascading song of canyon wrens, the flight
of scarlet dragonflies at pools, the stain
of water on a curve of sand, the art
of roots that crack the monolith of time.

You knew the crazy lust to probe the heart
of that which has no heart that we could know,
toward the source, deep in the core, the maze,
the secret center where there are no bounds.

Hunter, brother, companion of our days:
that blessing which you hunted, hunted too,
what you were seeking, this is what found you.

Edward Abbey
Oracle, Arizona
1983

Chapter 1

1. Interview with Randolph Jenks, Alamos, Sonora, Mexico, 1 December 1982.

Chapter 2

2. Edward Weston is widely recognized as one of this century's great photographers. In the 1930s he was living in Carmel, having moved there after his lengthy sojourn in Mexico and a brief stay in San Francisco. It was in Carmel in the 1930s, when he himself was in his forties, that Weston fully united within himself the creative energies that allowed him to make some of the world's most remarkable photographs. Weston made explicit in his mode of living the philosophy that allowed him to create.

He achieved a remarkable harmony between simplicity of living, which to a large extent freed him from the demands of the material world, and good taste, which enabled him to enjoy life on a high level. He had but a few material possessions. He immersed himself in classical music, partook of a modest, mostly vegetarian diet, reveled in the conversation and company of friends, and, above all, achieved a daily routine that allowed him to submerge himself in the beauty of nature.

Weston's successful lifestyle, centered about artistic freedom, was seen as an ideal model for Everett Ruess, who was discovering similar ideas on his own.

3. Harry was the son of Harry Leon Wilson, novelist, author of *Ruggles of Red Gap* and *Merton of the Movies*, and close friend of Edward Weston. In 1937, Weston married the elder Wilson's daughter, Charis.

Chapter 3

4. *Lan Rameau* was Everett's newly assumed name, adopted as he had promised his brother Waldo in an earlier letter, when he told of his plan to name his burro *Everett*.

5. At the time, John Wetherill, age sixty-five, had been an Indian trader for twenty-six years. Headquartered at Kayenta, Arizona, just south of Monument Valley, he thoroughly explored the canyons and plateaus to the north, and was noted as the best guide and most knowledgeable regional expert on both the terrain and its Indian inhabitants. In 1909, as part of the Byron Cummings Expedition, he may have been the first white man to walk under Rainbow Bridge. Although John did not discover Mesa Verde, his older brother, Richard, did discover some of the major ruins, such as Cliff Palace, in 1888, while the Wetherill family was living at nearby Mancos, Colorado. John, together with his brothers, Richard, Al, and Clayton, explored and collected relics from many of the ruins. John's wife, Louisa Wade Wetherill, became noted for her sympathetic understanding of Navajo culture. John Wetherill died in November of 1944.

6. Just before graduation from high school, Everett entered a poster contest for National Trade Week, sponsored by the Los Angeles Chamber of Commerce. He was notified by his parents that he had won the $25 prize.

7. Interviews with Tad Nichols, Tucson, Arizona, 29 November 1982, and Randolph Jenks, Alamos, Sonora, Mexico, 1 December 1982.

8. Through scenic Blue Canyon flows Moenkopi Wash, heading west. It is located about thirty-five miles east of Moenkopi village.

9. Three Salado Indian villages, built in natural caves high above the Salt River, are preserved at Tonto National Monument. The little which is known about the Salado people is known mainly because of the Tonto ruins.

10. Four Peaks, north of the Superstition Mountains and about fifty miles northeast of Phoenix, is rich in the history of Apache Indian-U.S. Army warfare in the 1860s and 1870s.

Chapter 4

11. Louisa Wade Wetherill, wife of John, and resident of Kayenta, coauthored, with Frances Gilmore, the book *Trader to the Navajos*, which, though copyrighted in 1934, was not published until 1953, nine years after Louisa's death.

Chapter 5

12. Everett here refers to *Gargantua and Pantagruel*, a satirical work by Francois Rabelais, originally published in five parts from 1532 to 1564.

13. Paul Elder Bookstore in San Francisco was a significant cultural institution in the Bay Area. Along with books, Elder exhibited paintings, sold Rockwood pottery and Tiffany glass, and sponsored lectures of cultural interest to the community. The bookstore was designed by famed architect Bernard Maybeck. It was a significant achievement for the young Ruess to have placed his woodblock prints there.

14. Dixon's paintings can be found in many major museums. His murals may be seen on the walls of the Interior Department Building in Washington, D.C., as well as in several public buildings throughout the West. In his later life he moved to Mount Carmel, Utah, and commuted seasonally to Tucson, Arizona, where he died in November 1946.

15. Other photographers on the staff of the Farm Security Administration were Walker Evans, Russell Lee, Carl Mydans, Arthur Rothstein, Ben Shahn, and John Vachon. Lange also took striking photographs of the Japanese-Americans interned in relocation camps during World War II. She divorced Maynard Dixon in 1935 and married Paul Schuster Taylor. In later years she owned a studio in San Francisco. She died 11 October 1965.

16. "Uncle Emerson" was Emerson Knight, brother of Everett's mother, Stella. Knight was a noted landscape architect in San Francisco and throughout northern California. Two of his best-known projects are the series of trails around Point Lobos and the amphitheater on Mount Tamalpais. He continued working on landscape projects until his death in 1960.

17. Practically all readers will be familiar with the work of Ansel Adams, the dean of American landscape photographers. By this time, he was already well-known. Adams had opened a studio gallery in downtown San Francisco at 166 Geary Street in the summer of 1933. His goal was to "bring things to San Francisco that should have

come years ago," with sales of his own work hopefully paying the rent and expenses. But in January 1934, Adams withdrew from the pressures and commercial concerns of operating the gallery to "the simple photographic life." Ruess was fortunate to have entered San Francisco just during the few months Adams was manning his gallery, and it was during this period at the gallery that he became acquainted with Adams.

Chapter 6

18. See letter of 23 March 1933.
19. Walter Hampden, whose real name was Walter Hampden Dougherty, was a famous actor who often performed in Shakespearean plays and other well-known productions such as *Cyrano de Bergerac*, *Arsenic and Old Lace*, *Ethan Frome*, and others. He also appeared in various motion pictures. Hampden died in June 1955, at the age of seventy-six.
20. Interview with Clayborn Lockett, 29 November 1982.
21. Karl W. Luckert, *Navajo Mountain and Rainbow Bridge Religion*, (Flagstaff, Arizona: Museum of Northern Arizona, 1977), p. 5.
22. See Charles L. Bernheimer, *Rainbow Bridge* (New York: Doubleday, Page, and Co., 1924).
23. Two trails reach Rainbow Bridge from the south. From Navajo Mountain trading post around the east and north flanks of Navajo Mountain winds the fourteen-mile-long route first used by the Cummings and Douglass discovery expedition of 1909. In 1934, however, Everett hiked from Rainbow Lodge around the west side of Navajo Mountain on the rougher and steeper seven-mile-long trail that had been pioneered by the Bernheimer Expedition of 1922.

24. The expedition was entitled the Rainbow Bridge-Monument Valley Expedition, under the general direction of Ansel F. Hall.

Chapter 7

25. Interview with Addlin Lay, Salt Lake City, Utah, 27 December 1982.
26. Interview with Jennings Allen, 5 January 1983.
27. Interview with Gail Bailey, Escalante, Utah, 26 September 1982.
28. Interview with Clayborn Lockett, Tucson, Arizona, 29 November 1982.
29. Interview with Norman Christensen, Escalante, Utah, 27 December 1982.
30. Allen later gave the names of men on the search party as: P.M. Shurtz, George Davis, Gail Bailey, Chester Lay, Alton Twitchell, Ronald Schow, Jack Woolsey, Prudencio Gabala, Walt Allen, Frank Barney, Earl Woolsey, Claude Haws, Alden Moyes, and Loran Blood.
31. C. Gregory Crampton, "Historical Sites in Glen Canyon, Mouth of Hansen Creek to Mouth of San Juan River," *Anthropological Papers*, No. 61 (Salt Lake City: University of Utah, December 1962), p. 28.
32. Interview with Chester Lay, Escalante, Utah, 26 November 1982.
33. *Salt Lake Tribune*, no date, probably August 1935. The same *Tribune* article quoted Attorney General Joseph Chez as saying, "The best men available will handle this case, and we will not stop until we have determined beyond a reasonable doubt that Ruess was slain or met an accidental death, after which his outfit was stolen." Chez also stated that he

would confer with Governor Henry H. Blood on the matter. A January 1983 search through the Utah State Archives, however, uncovered no file on Everett Ruess in either the Attorney General or Governor sections. Archivist Val Wilson stated that it is not unusual for such archives to be incomplete.

34. Letter from Edson Alvey to Randall Henderson of *Desert Magazine*, dated 3 July 1958, copy in possession of Waldo Ruess.

Chapter 8

35. Interview with Chester Lay, Escalante, Utah, 26 September 1982; and interview with Norman Christensen, Escalante, Utah, 27 December 1982.

36. Ibid. Chester Lay Interview.

37. The Army Air Corps was also called upon to help, the appeal based on a hope that someone in an airplane could spot, and even identify, a young white man walking or riding through the rough canyon country. As it was at least a faint hope, Christopher Ruess persuaded his former boss, Judge Ben Lindsey of the Superior Court of Los Angeles, to write to the Secretary of War, George H. Dern (a former Utah Governor), who then ordered the Commanding General at March Field, California, to conduct searches for Everett whenever training flights were made over the area. But nothing was ever heard from the Army Air Corps.

38. Letter of Waldo Ruess to Warden, Penitentiary, Phoenix, 23 January 1960.

Chapter 9

39. Letter of 26 September 1942 to Christopher Ruess from Harry C. James, Altadena, California.

40. Interview with Norman Christensen, Escalante, Utah, 27 December 1982.

41. Hugh Lacy, ed., *On Desert Trails With Everett Ruess* (Palm Desert, California: Desert Magazine, 1940).

Chapter 10

42. Each semester two students from Los Angeles High School whose original poems were judged the best of the entries were given a "kit of tools" consisting of a selection of books of value to a beginning writer. The list included Roget's *Thesaurus*, a rhyming dictionary, and collections of British and American poetry. The judges were the principal of the school, Stella Ruess, and a third person chosen by the other two. A brochure announcing the contest says, "As long as either of his parents live, each year or so boys and girls of the Southwestern states that Everett traversed will be invited to excel in one or another of the arts that Everett loved. So in his silence he will live on creatively. His parents hope that more fathers and mothers will establish similar living memorials to sons and daughters whose life songs break off after a stanza."

43. Interview with Addlin Lay, Salt Lake City, Utah, 27 December 1982.

28 March 1914

Everett was born in Oakland, California

1914 to 1926

Lived with parents as they moved to Fresno then Los Angeles, California; Brookline, Massachusetts; Brooklyn, New York; Palisades Park, New Jersey; Valparaiso, Indiana

1926

Commuted from Valparaiso to Chicago Art Institute every Saturday for several months for art classes.

1928-1931

Moved to Los Angeles. Attended Los Angeles and Hollywood High Schools, graduating in January, 1931.

1930

While in high school, also attended Otis Art School for six months.

July-August 1930

Solo trip to Carmel, Big Sur, and Yosemite, California. It was on this trip that he met photographer Edward Weston.

February-May 1931

Monument Valley, Arizona-Utah. Stayed with John Wetherill family.

May-June, 1931

Canyon de Chelly and San Francisco Peaks, Arizona

July, 1931

Grand Canyon, Arizona

August, 1931

Zion National Park, Utah

September-October, 1931

Grand Canyon National Park, Arizona

October-December, 1931

Salt River Valley and Superior, Arizona

December, 1931-March, 1932

Los Angeles

March-June, 1932

Salt River Valley and Roosevelt, Arizona

June-July, 1932

Ganado and Canyon de Chelly, Arizona

August, 1932

Mesa Verde National Park, Colorado

September, 1932

Grand Canyon National Park, Arizona

September, 1932-February, 1933

Attended University of California at Los Angeles (UCLA)

December, 1932

Christmas vacation at Carmel, California

February-June, 1933

Los Angeles

June-October, 1933

Sierra Nevada Mountains, Sequoia and Yosemite National Parks, California

October, 1933-March, 1934

San Francisco, with a side trip to Crescent City, California. Met painter Maynard Dixon and photographers Dorothea Lange and Ansel Adams.

April-June, 1934

Monument Valley, Arizona-Utah

June-July, 1934

Navajo Mountain and Rainbow Bridge, Utah

July, 1934

Worked with Rainbow Bridge-Monument Valley Expedition, Tsegi Canyon, Arizona

August-September, 1934

Gallup, New Mexico, Hopi villages, Grand Canyon, Flagstaff, Oak Creek Canyon, and return to Grand Canyon, Arizona

October-November, 1934

Bryce Canyon National Park, Tropic, and Escalante, Utah

November, 1934

Left Escalante, camped in Davis Gulch, then mysteriously disappeared.

INDEX

INDEX

1572081

Made in the USA